IMAGES
of America

TOWNSHIP OF HAMILTON ATLANTIC COUNTY

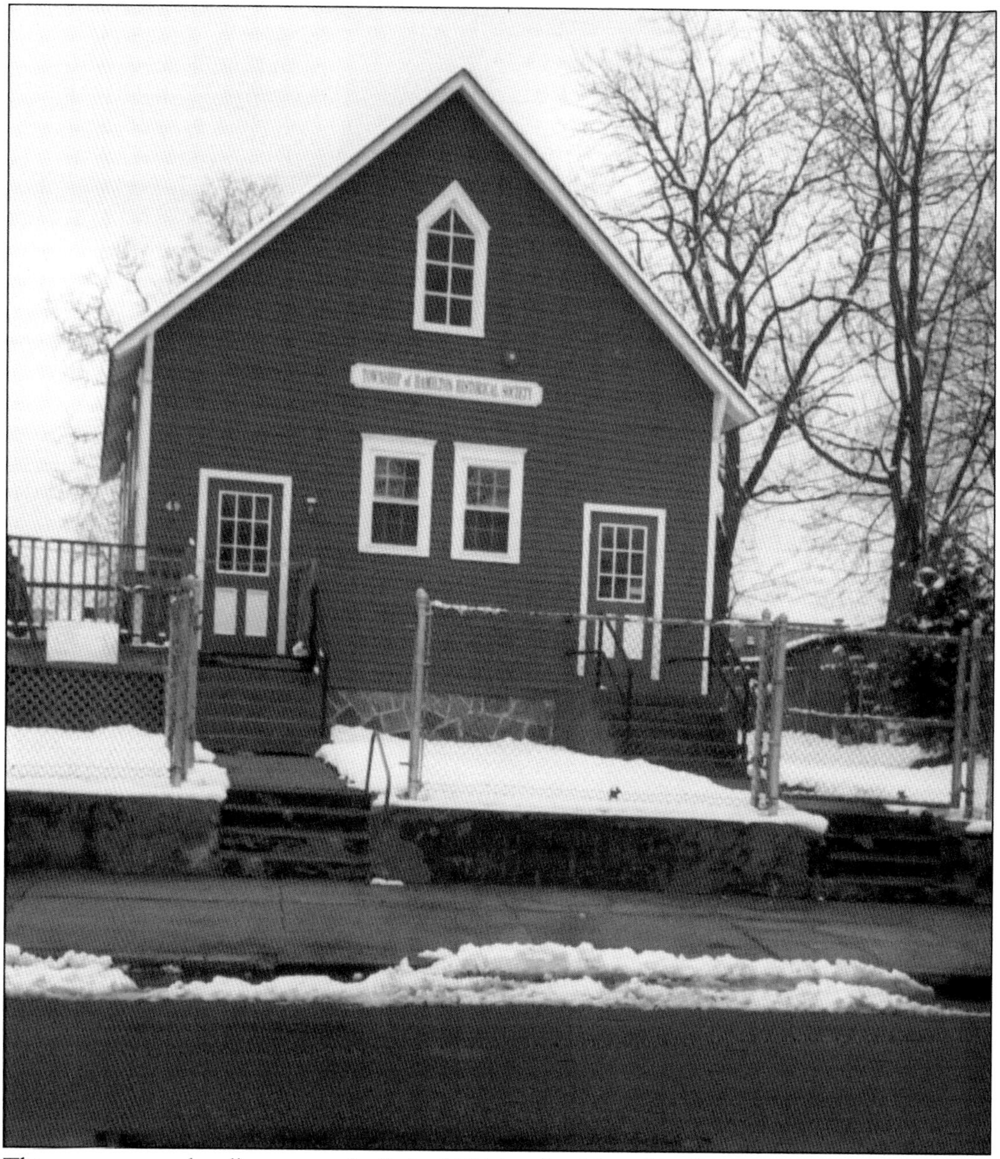

This one-room schoolhouse was built in 1904 by the Mays Landing Water Power Company for children of its factory workers. It is currently the site of the Township of Hamilton Historical Society.

IMAGES
of America

TOWNSHIP OF HAMILTON ATLANTIC COUNTY

Township of Hamilton Historical Society

ARCADIA
PUBLISHING

ISBN 978-0-7385-0942-6

Published by Arcadia Publishing
Charleston, South Carolina

Printed in the United States of America

Library of Congress Catalog Card Number: applied for.

For all general information contact Arcadia Publishing at:
Telephone 843-853-2070
Fax 843-853-0044
E-Mail sales@arcadiapublishing.com
For customer service and orders:
Toll-Free 1-888-313-2665

Visit us on the Internet at www.arcadiapublishing.com

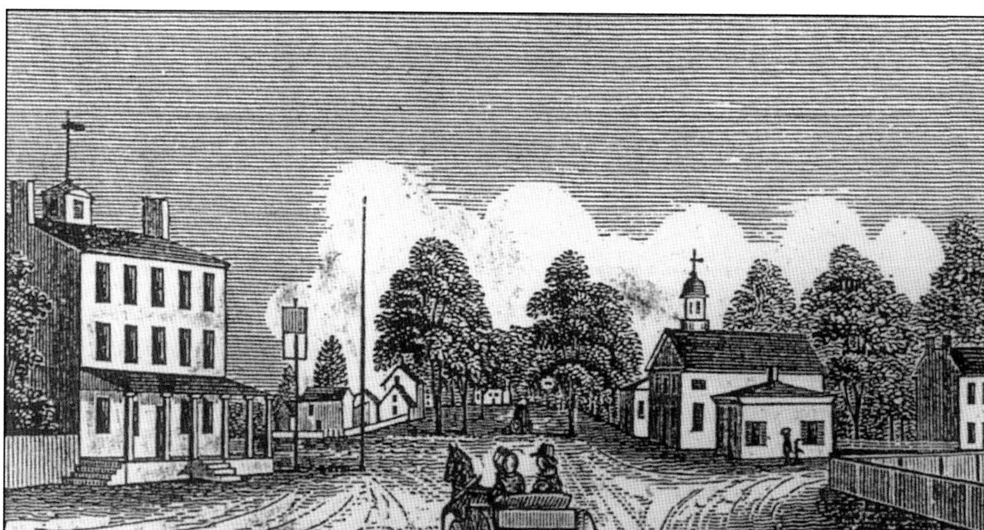

This drawing, published c. 1840, is the first image of Mays Landing to appear in print. The American Hotel is on the left, and the courthouse is on the right.

Contents

ACKNOWLEDGMENTS

Many of the photographs and sketches in this publication are from the collection of the Township of Hamilton Historical Society. The society thanks all members and friends for their contributions, with special appreciation to Joan Cradock, Dottie Kinsey, Kathleen Logan, Miriam Patterson, and Suzanne Willetts Smith for their work on the production of this book.

The Township of Hamilton regrets the lack of available photographs of some parts of the township.

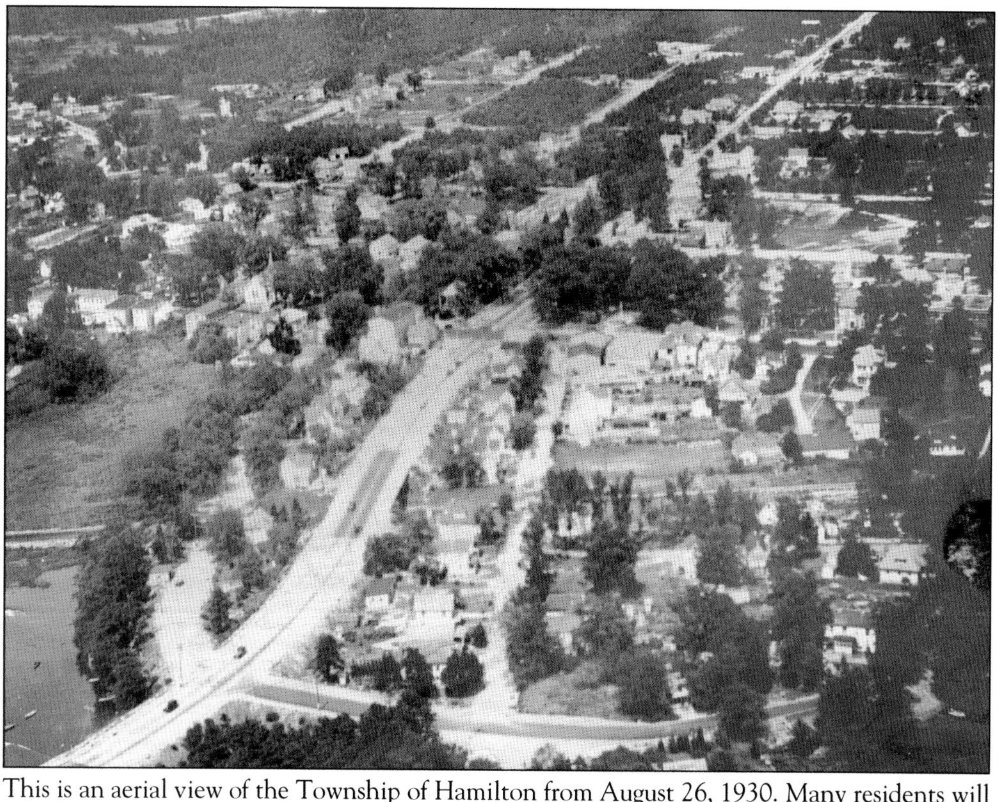

This is an aerial view of the Township of Hamilton from August 26, 1930. Many residents will recognize their homes or places of business. The main highway is the new state cutoff. In the foreground is the road around Pennington Point.

INTRODUCTION

In 1813, the Township of Hamilton was formed from parts of Egg Harbor and Weymouth Townships but remained a part of Gloucester County. Peter Steelman was the first settler in the Gravelly Run area in 1710, followed in 1735 by Edmund Iliff, who began a settlement at Babcock Creek near the Great Egg Harbor River. This area was called Iliff Town. In 1749, George May bought Iliff's property at a sheriff's sale.

The first recorded tavern on the land, an indication of permanent settlement, was that of Samuel Snell in 1765. It was located at Hamilton Bridge, which was the upper section of Mays Landing. (The tavern later became known as Baker's Hotel.) The lower section of the landing, divided by the Great Egg Harbor River, was called simply the Landing. In 1880, the two were combined to form the town of Mays Landing.

The Great Egg Harbor River, formerly called the Basse River, was at one time navigable for four-masted ships and for ships weighing up to 1,000 tons. During the Revolutionary War, military supplies and cargo from captured British ships were unloaded at local shipyards. Sugar Hill, it is said, received its name from the large quantities of molasses and sugar unloaded there. The Coal Landing, likewise, got its name from the cargo unloaded there. With the shipping industry thriving, shipyards were built along the river by men with names such as Pennington, Rape, Taylor, Wheaton, Clark, Gaskill, and Vaughn. It was a usual sight to see a ship docked at a local yard taking on a load of wood and charcoal from the local forests, cranberries from the Makepeace Bogs, or iron pipe made at the Weymouth Forge from local bog iron. Much of the iron pipe was shipped to Philadelphia.

In 1837, Atlantic County was formed, and the economic and industrial center of the region, Mays Landing, was named the county seat. Samuel Richards donated land on Main Street in Mays Landing to build the county court. (The site is still that of the county buildings.) With the coming of the courts (and therefore many lawyers, reporters, spectators, and families), Mays Landing's need for suitable lodging increased. Hotels and inns were constructed to answer this need.

With the onset of the Industrial Revolution, a railroad line was established from Mays Landing to Egg Harbor City along the present Farragut Avenue. The West Jersey and Seashore Line ran from Atlantic City to Newfield, stopping at various points in the Township of Hamilton. The line carried goods and travelers. By 1850, the outlying areas of the township began to be settled. The Liepe family came to Cologne. The Carmen families settled in Laureldale and McKee City. Weymouth Forge and Foundry attracted many workers, as did Walker's Forge in the Bears Head area. The Da Costa section and Mizpah also expanded.

With the introduction of the rail line, businesses began to open—glass and shoe factories, grocery and clothing stores, sawmills, barbershops, and the brickyard. The Mays Landing Water Power Company, makers of toweling from raw cotton, had its own company store, where its employees could purchase anything they needed for daily living.

Of course, with the people and industry came schools, churches, homes, and shops. After so much construction, the Hope Fire Company was founded in 1895. Like other companies of the time, it had a bucket brigade and several hand pumps, and firemen were summoned by the striking of a 300-pound bell. Utilities, such as the waterworks in 1907, also followed.

Socially, there was no lack of entertainment or recreational activities. One could choose from plays at Veal's Opera House, Leiling's Park, band concerts, ice-skating on Lake Lenape in the winter, boating in the summer, or fishing in the lake or river. Baseball and other sports teams were organized. Fraternal and veterans organizations, as well as social and service clubs, were formed. During every war, the Township of Hamilton's men and women responded to support their country, and veterans clubs were set up on their return home. Clearly, the Township of Hamilton is a special place, which is why so many descendants of original settlers still reside here.

The largest township in New Jersey is unique in that it has kept its small-town image. Naturally, however, there have been changes through the years. These pages tell part of the story of the Township of Hamilton.

One

From the Beginning

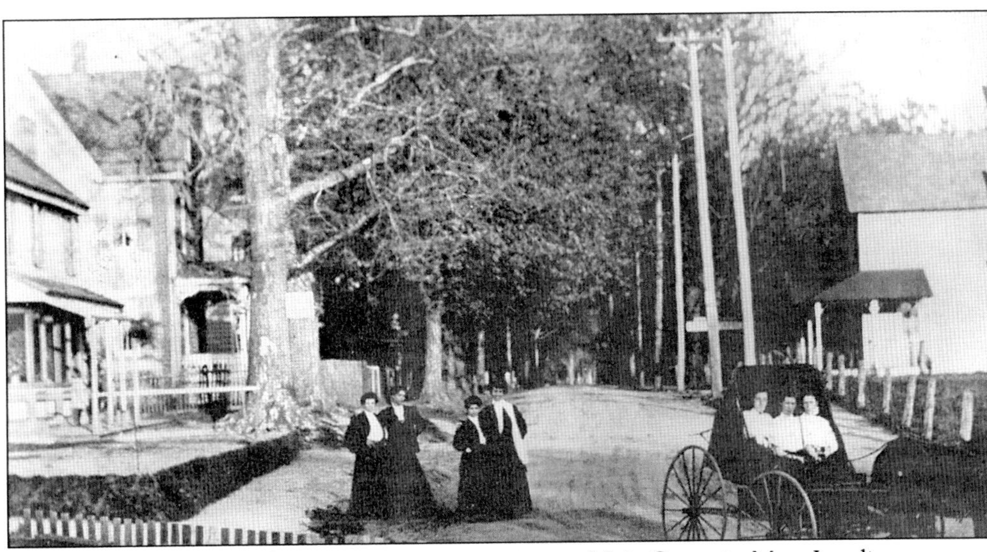

Turn-of-the-century residents enjoy a sunny outing on Main Street in Mays Landing.

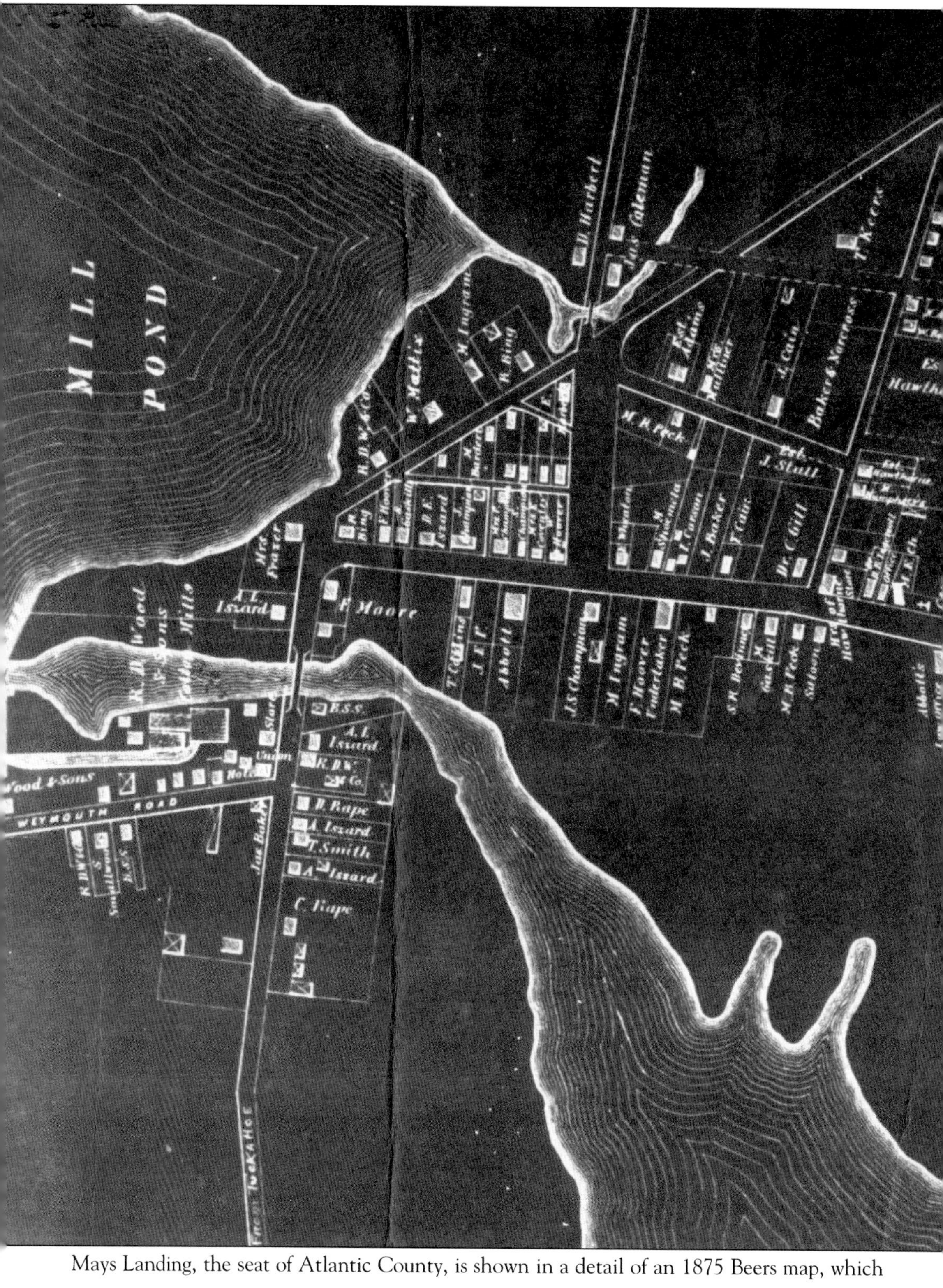

Mays Landing, the seat of Atlantic County, is shown in a detail of an 1875 Beers map, which

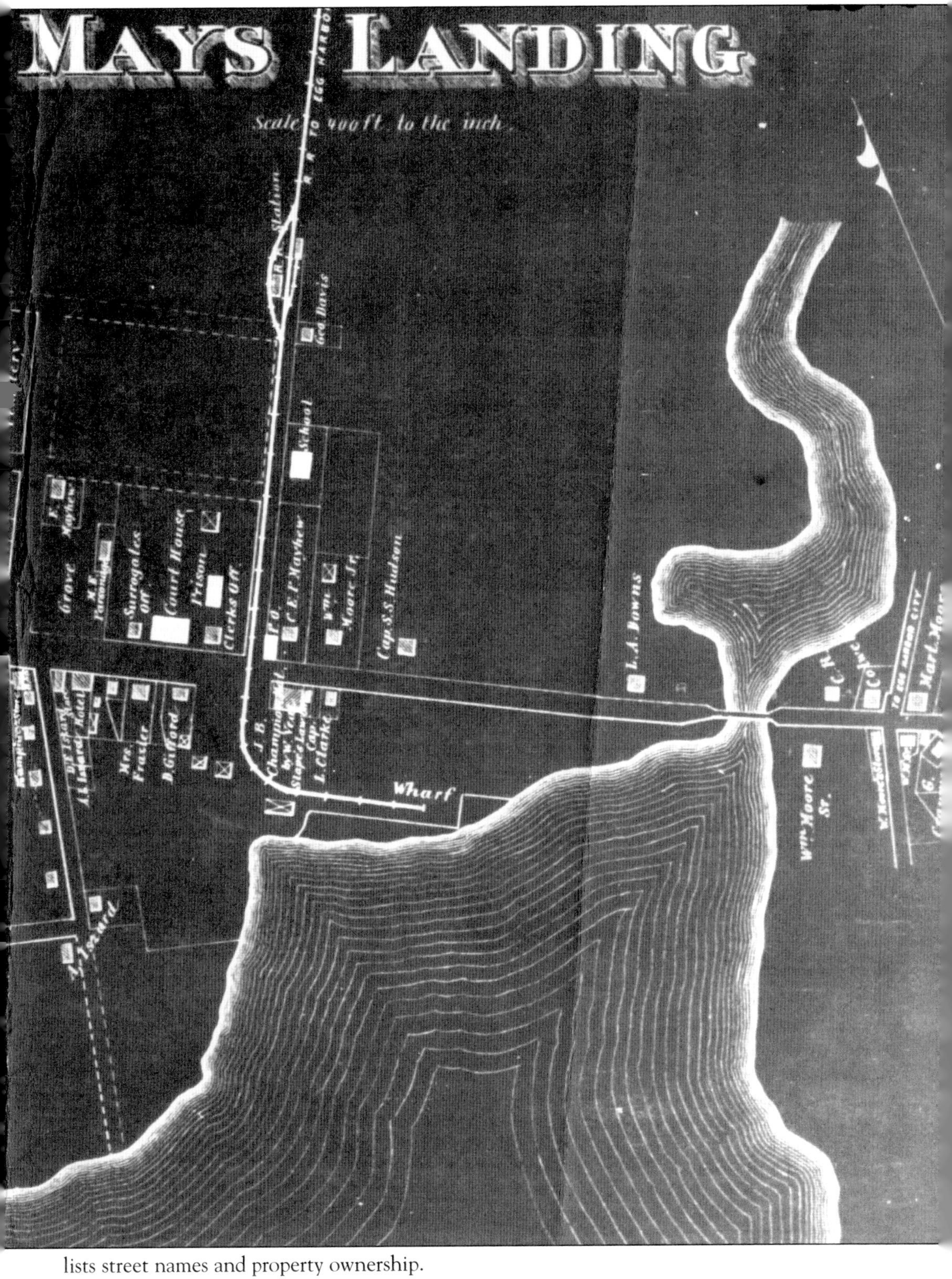

lists street names and property ownership.

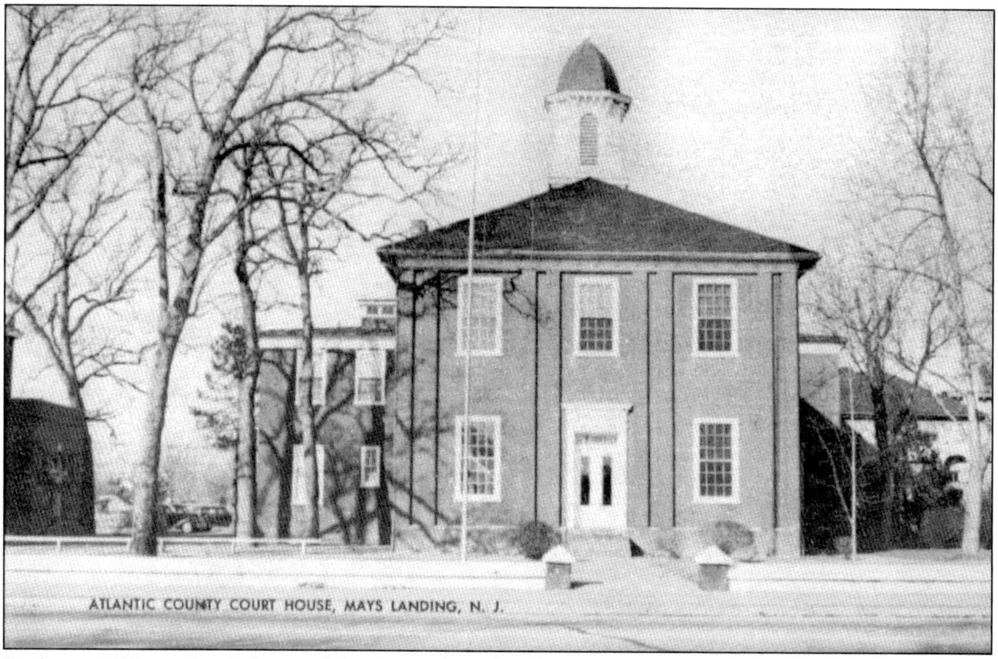

Built in 1839 on land donated by Samuel Richards, the Atlantic County Courthouse is still located on Main Street in Mays Landing.

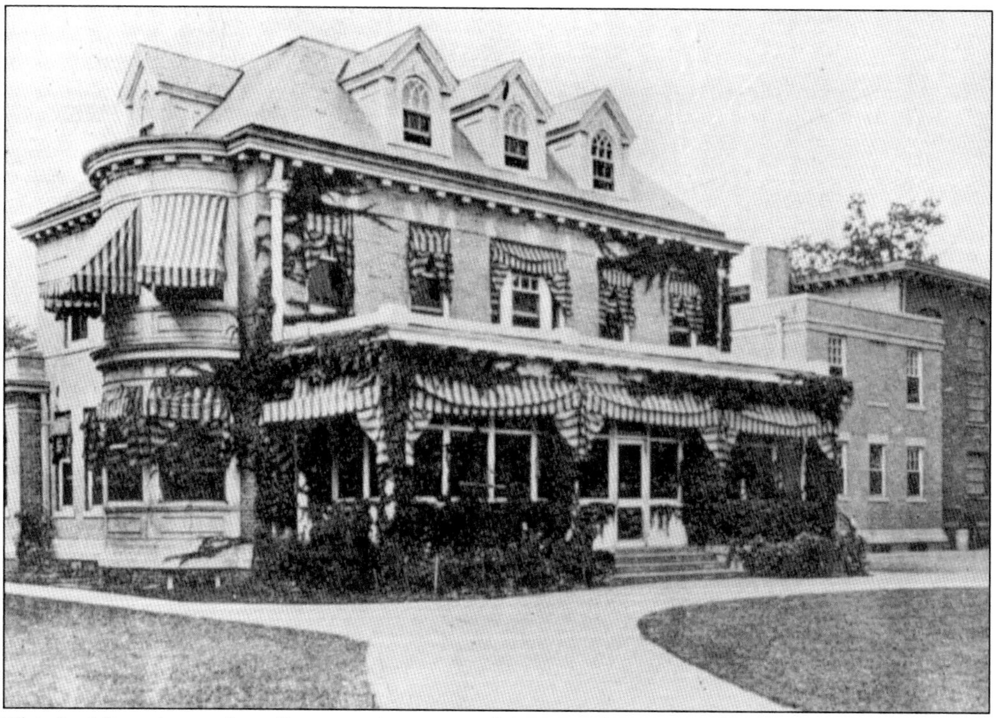

This building, located on Farragut Avenue in Mays Landing, served as the sheriff's residence and is shown *c.* 1900. It was designed by Thomas U. Walter, architect of the Capitol dome in Washington, D.C., and Girard College in Philadelphia, Pennsylvania. Records show that Walter was paid $15 on May 18, 1835, to design a courthouse and a prison.

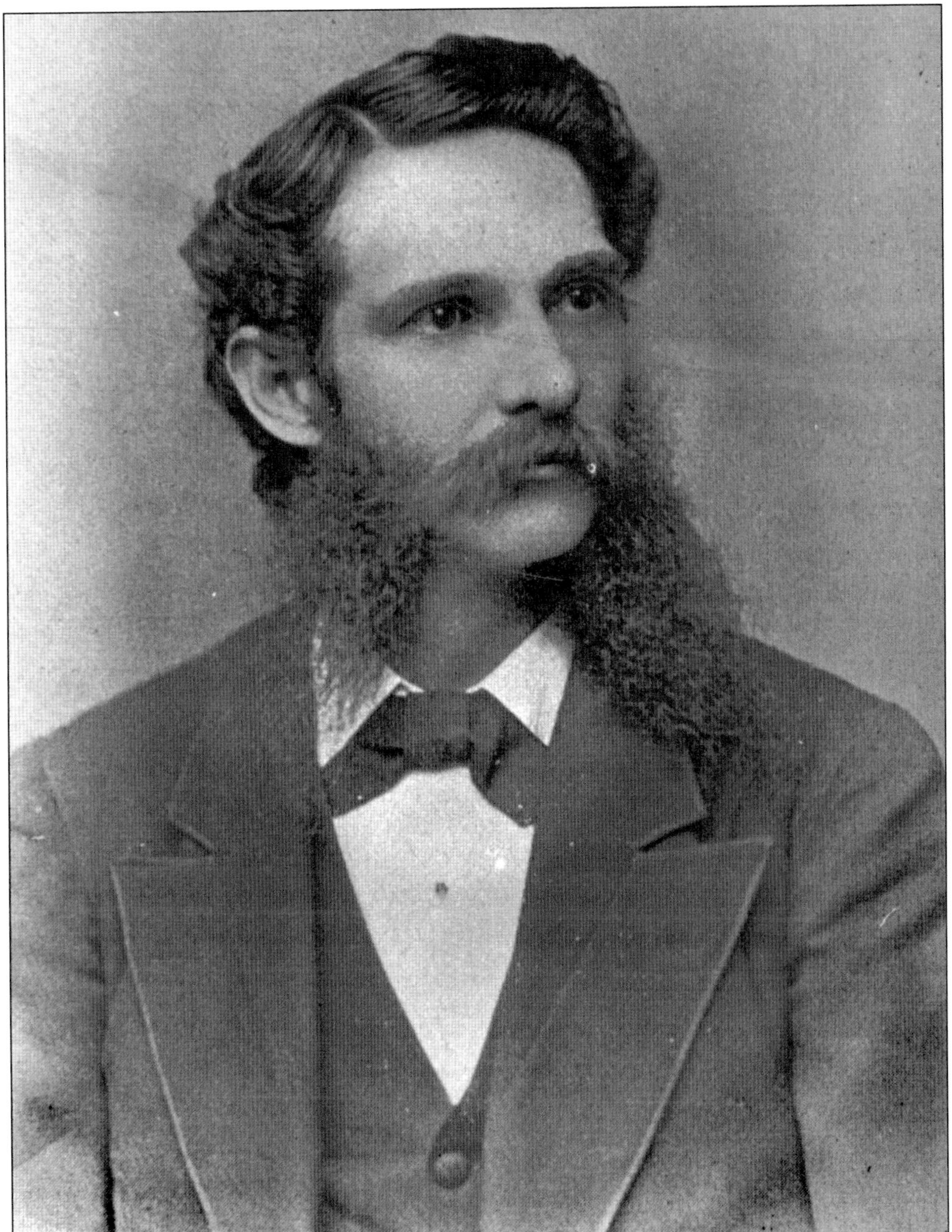

Joseph E. Potts Abbott, son of John C. and Ann G. (Treen) Abbott, was born in Mays Landing in August 1840, the third of eight children. He was educated in the pay schools of Atlantic County and was a teacher for three years before entering the law office of the Honorable George S. Woodhull of Camden. He was admitted to practice law in November 1865 and took over a practice in Mays Landing that December. His practice covered many areas, including real estate and corporation cases. He was appointed prosecutor of the pleas for Atlantic County and was known as the father of the Atlantic County Bar. He married Adeline H. Gibson of Doylestown, Pennsylvania.

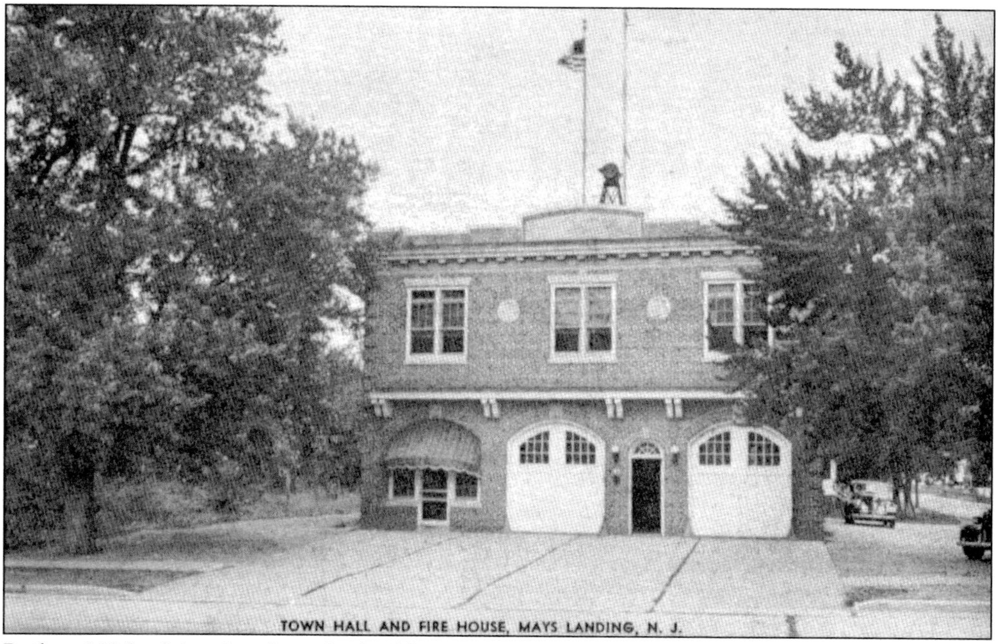

Built in 1925 in Mays Landing, this building once served as the town hall and firehouse. Although gutted by fire in 1988, it was restored in 1996 by Collective Bank, now Summit Bank.

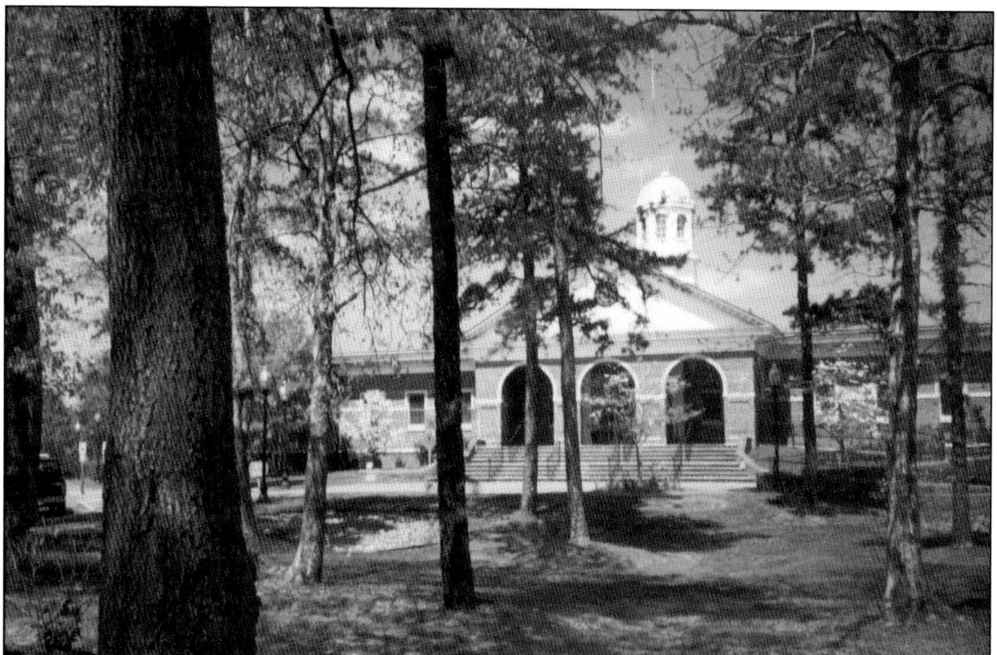

This handsome building serves as the town hall and police station for the Township of Hamilton. It was dedicated in 1992.

John Sacchinelli is currently the mayor of the Township of Hamilton, Atlantic County.

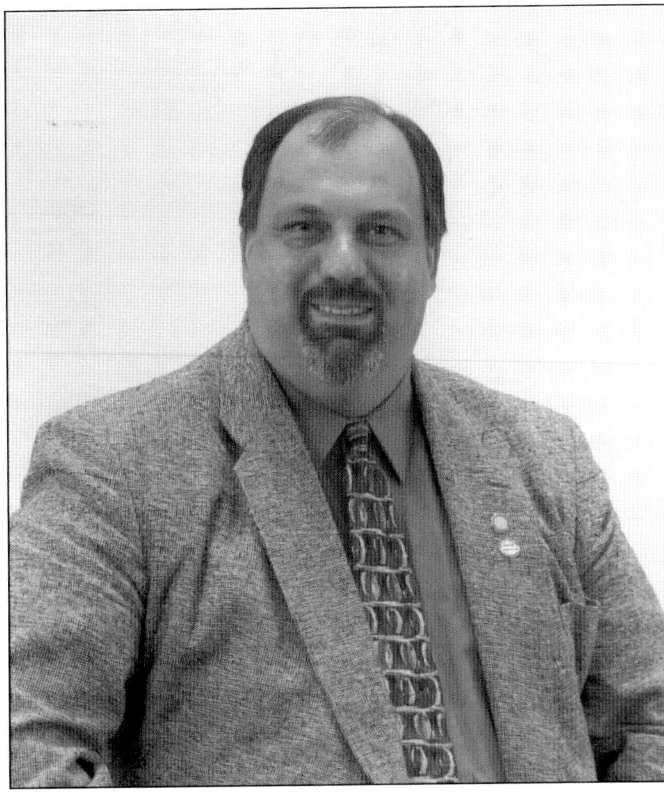

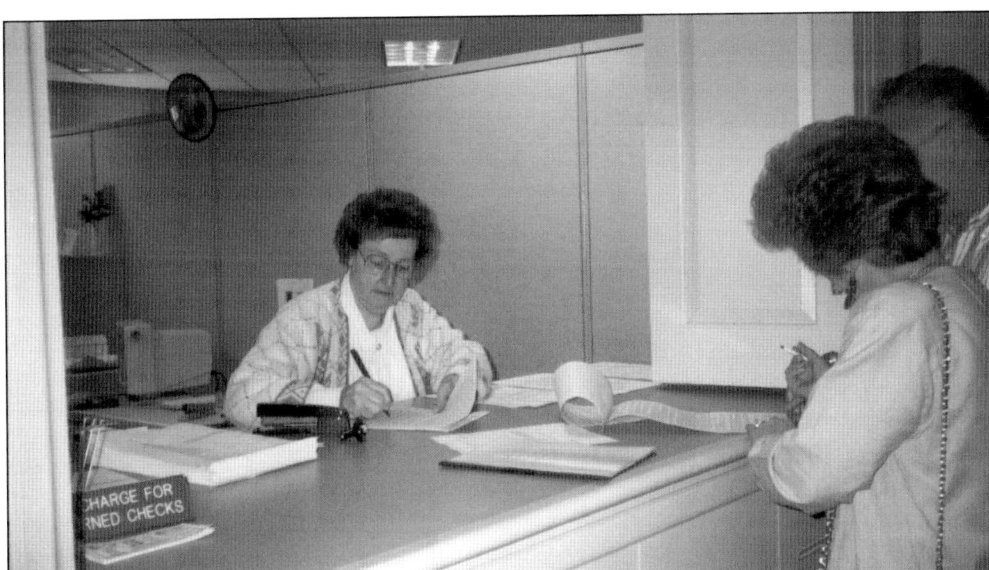

Joan Anderson, clerk of the Township of Hamilton, assists historical society members Cheryl Fetty and Marshall Cradock in filling out forms.

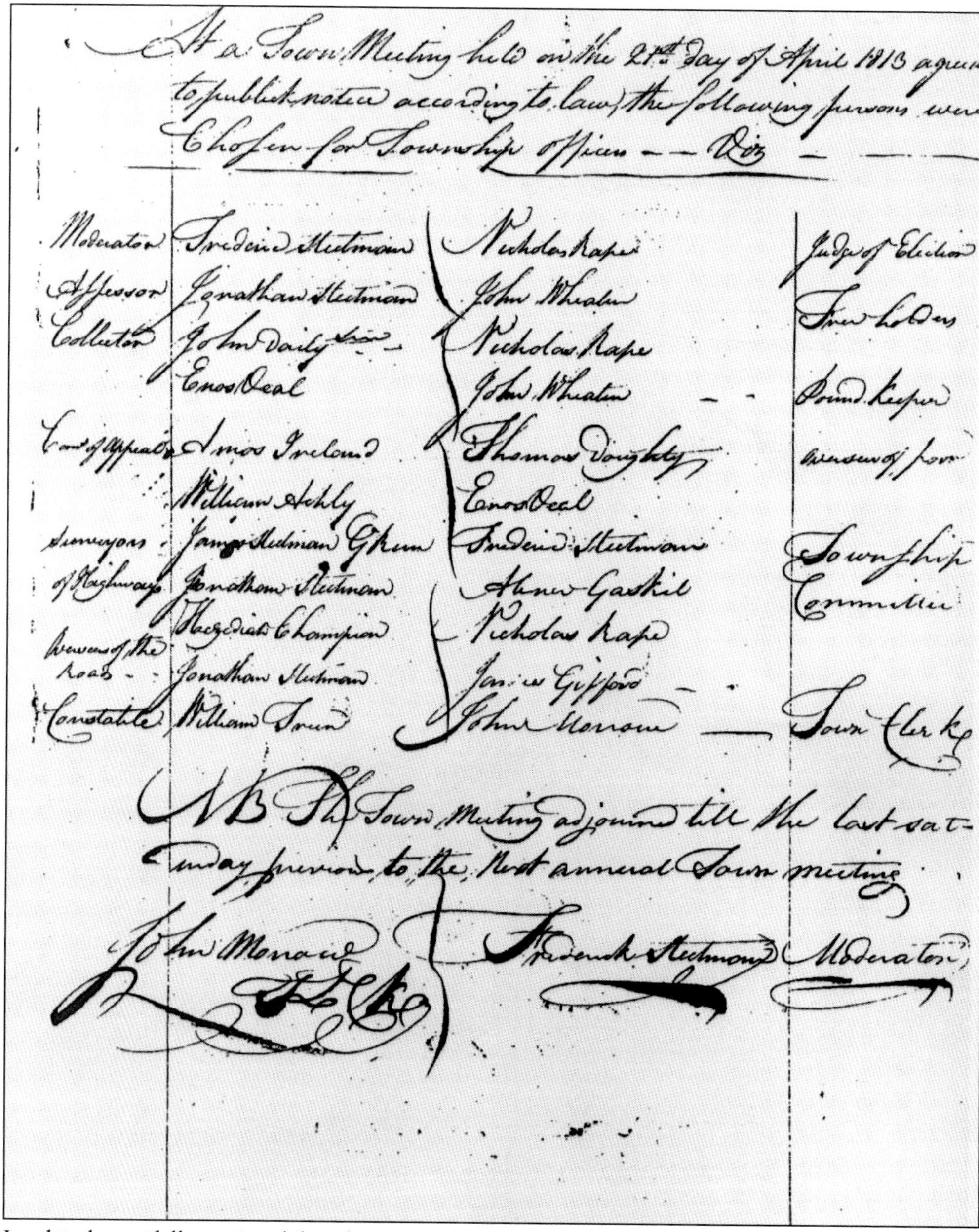

At a Town Meeting held on the 21st day of April 1813 agreeable to publick notice according to law the following persons were Chosen for Township officers — Viz

Moderator	Frederick Steelman	Nicholas Rape	Judge of Election
Assessor	Jonathan Steelman	John Wheaton	Free holders
Collector	John Daily Junr	Nicholas Rape	
	Enos Deal	John Wheaton	Pound Keeper
Com of Appeals	Amos Ireland	Thomas Doughty	Overseers of poor
	William Ashly	Enos Deal	
Surveyors of Highways	James Steelman	Frederick Steelman	Township Committee
	Jonathan Steelman	Abner Gaskil	
	Hezekiah Champion	Nicholas Rape	
Overseers of the Roads	Jonathan Steelman	James Gifford	
Constable	William Town	John Morrow	Town Clerk

NB The Town Meeting adjourned till the last saturday previous to the next annual Town meeting

John Monroe Clerk — Frederick Steelman Moderator

In this beautifully scripted handwriting, the names of elected officials attending the first township meeting on April 21, 1813, are set forth. Upon close examination, many current residents will recognize the names of their ancestors.

Two

Industry, Transportation, and Business

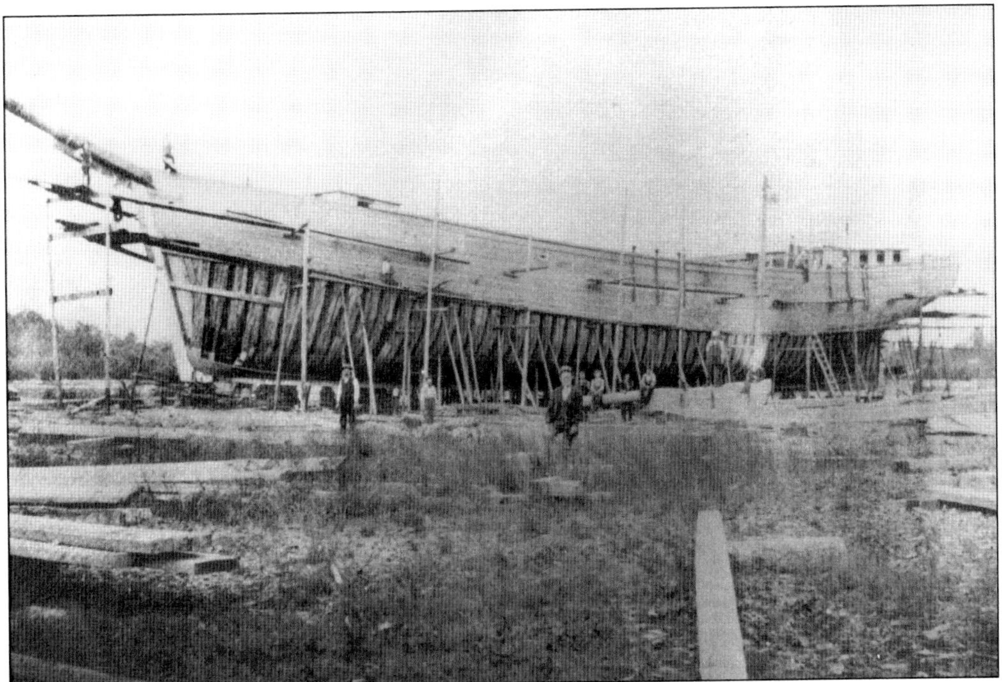

This three-masted schooner, the *Rebecca A. Taulane*, was built in 1882 by Samuel Gaskill at Pennington Point, Mays Landing.

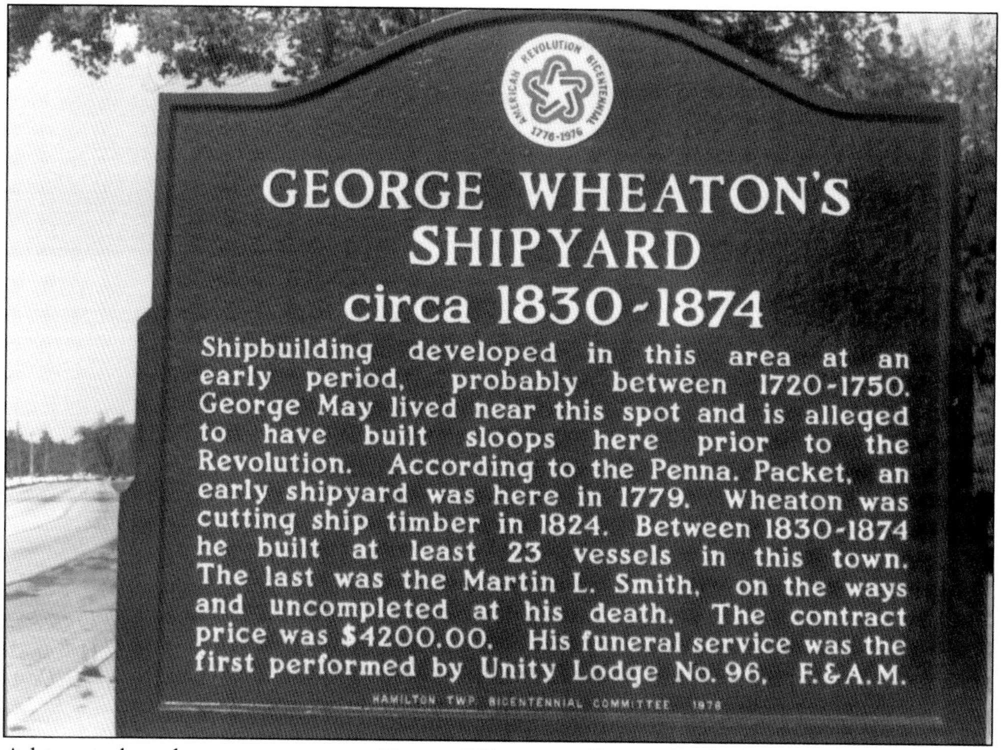

A historical marker commemorates George Wheaton's Shipyard, which was in operation from c. 1830 to 1874. During this period, he built at least 23 vessels at this location.

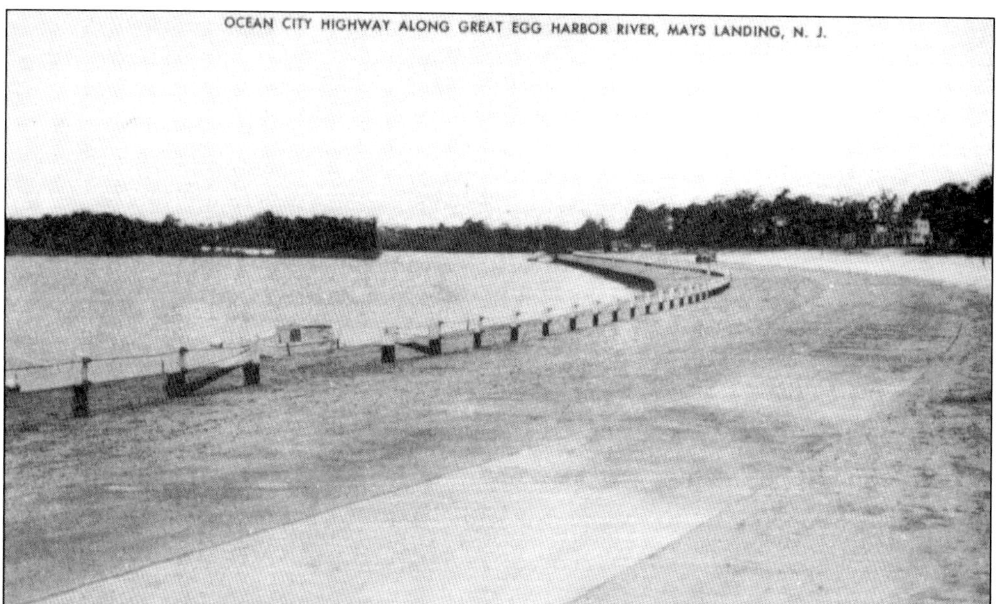

This scene shows River Drive along the Great Egg Harbor River in Mays Landing, a historical site of early shipbuilding commonly known as the Bulkhead. The county sponsored construction of this park, Gaskill Park, with fill dredged from the Great Egg Harbor River.

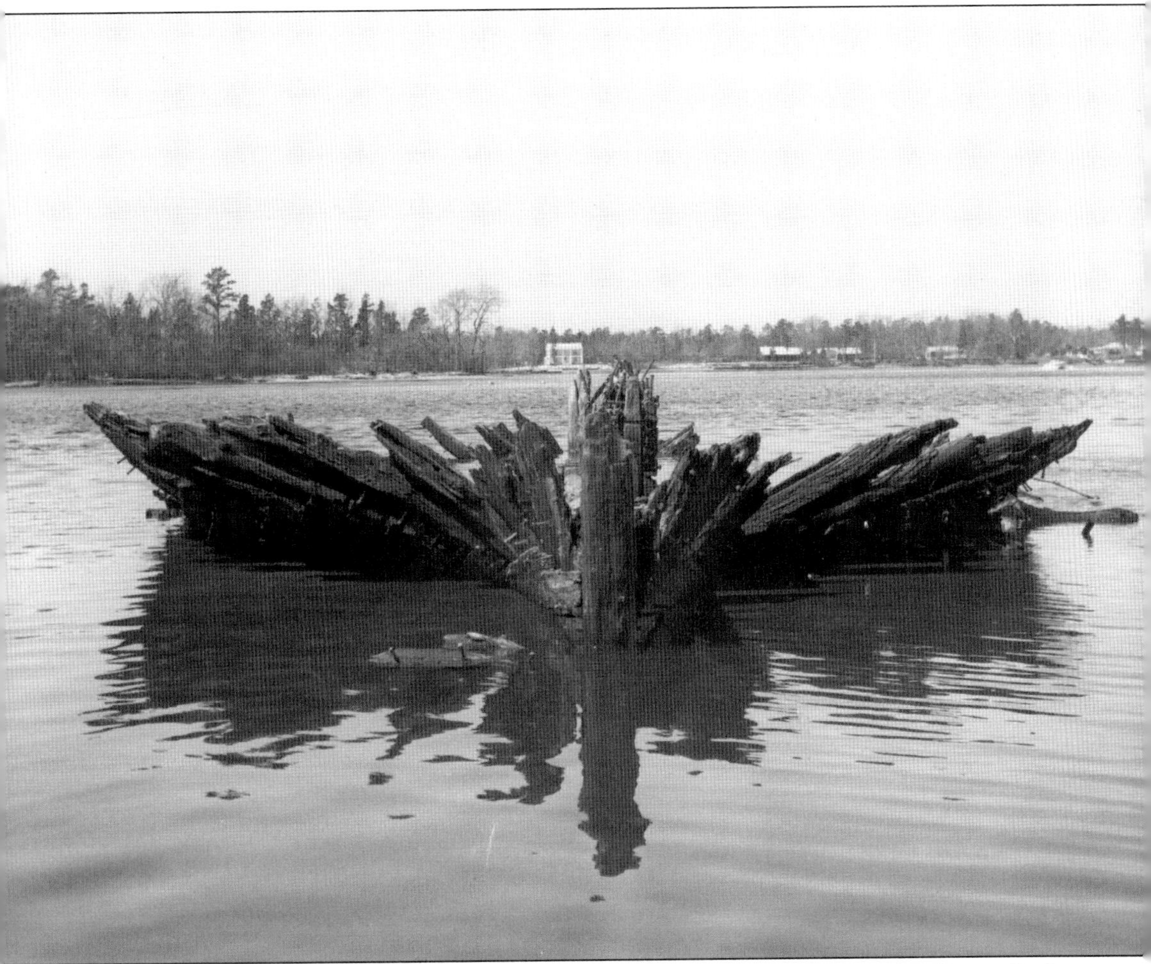

This is a view of the wreck of the schooner *Weymouth* in the Great Egg Harbor River. Built by Capt. Samuel Gaskill in Mays Landing in 1868, it was sailed by Capt. William Barrett and Capt. J.T. Coleman. Its route was often between Mays Landing and Philadelphia or New York. It was abandoned sometime after 1891.

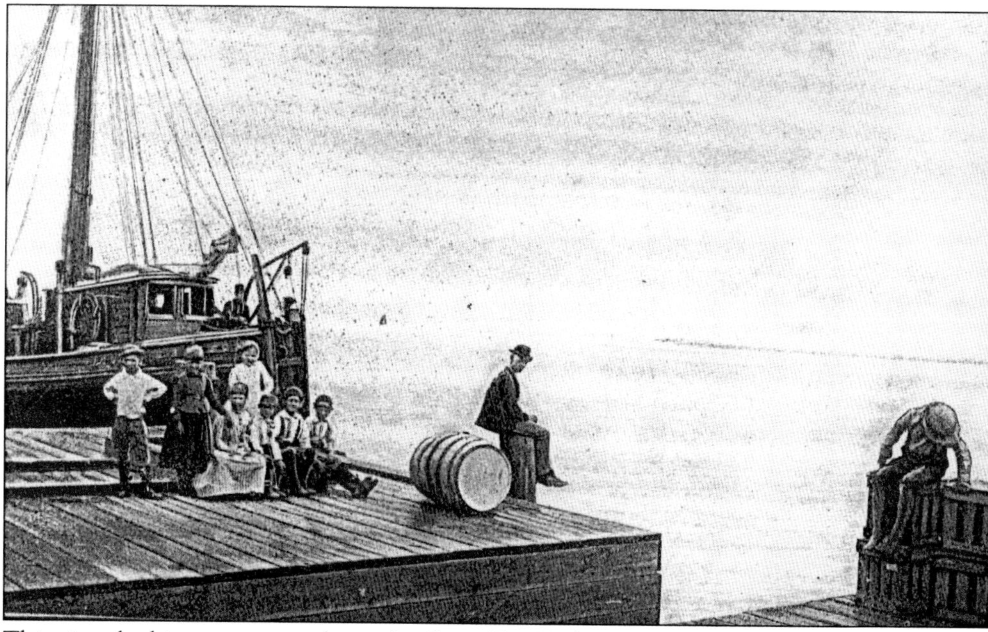

This view, looking out to sea, shows the Great Egg Harbor River. The river was formerly called the Basse River, named after the first English governor of New Jersey.

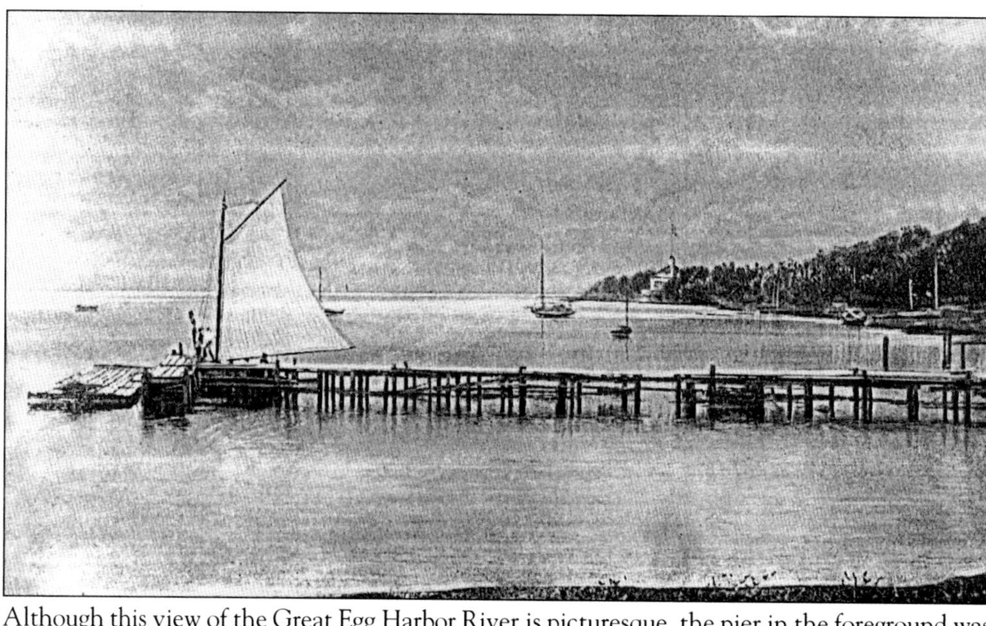

Although this view of the Great Egg Harbor River is picturesque, the pier in the foreground was commonly known as Junk House Wharf.

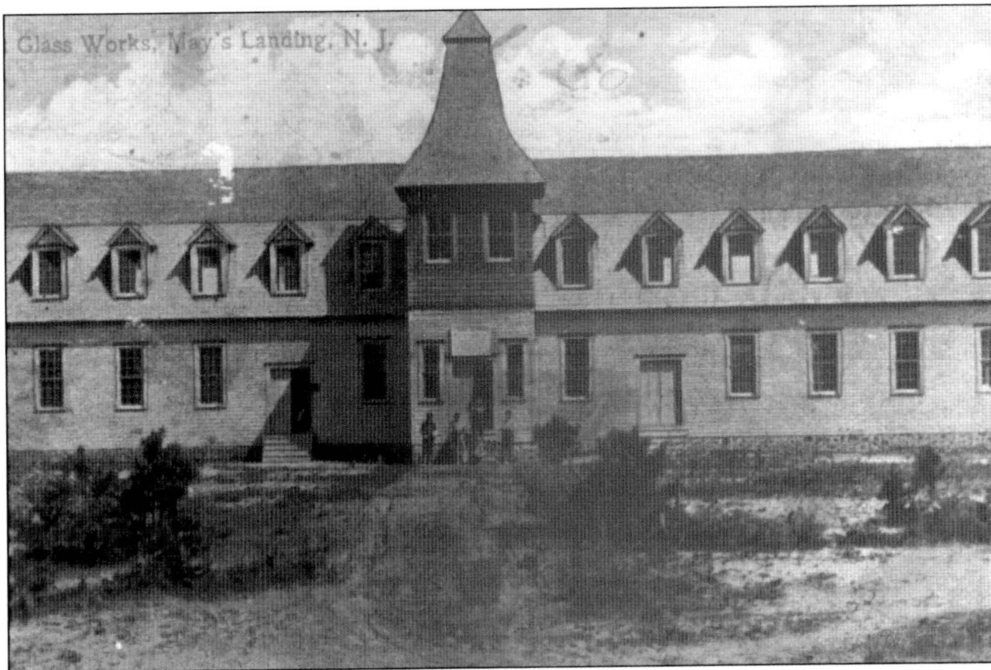

This building, located at Ninth Street and Farragut Avenue in Mays Landing, was once a cut-glass factory. It was operated by Joseph Thorpe and Sons in 1910. Before then, the building had housed a shoe-manufacturing plant.

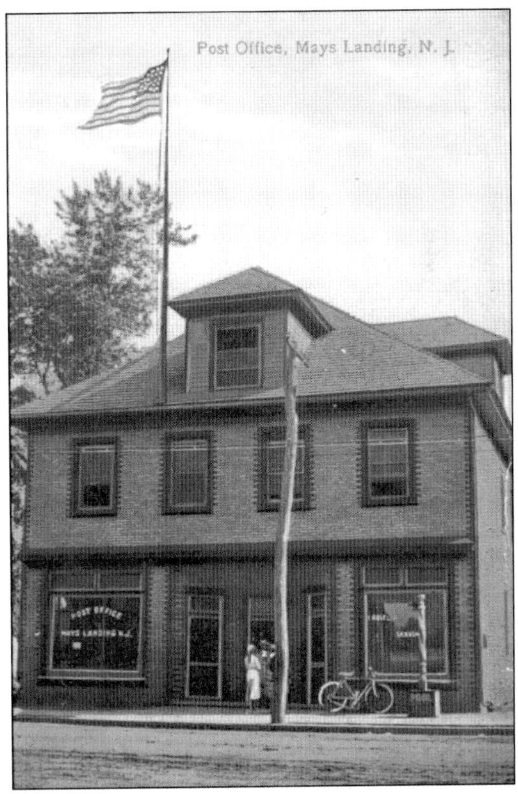

This building on Main Street in Mays Landing served a dual purpose—housing the post office (left) and Treidler's Court Pharmacy (right).

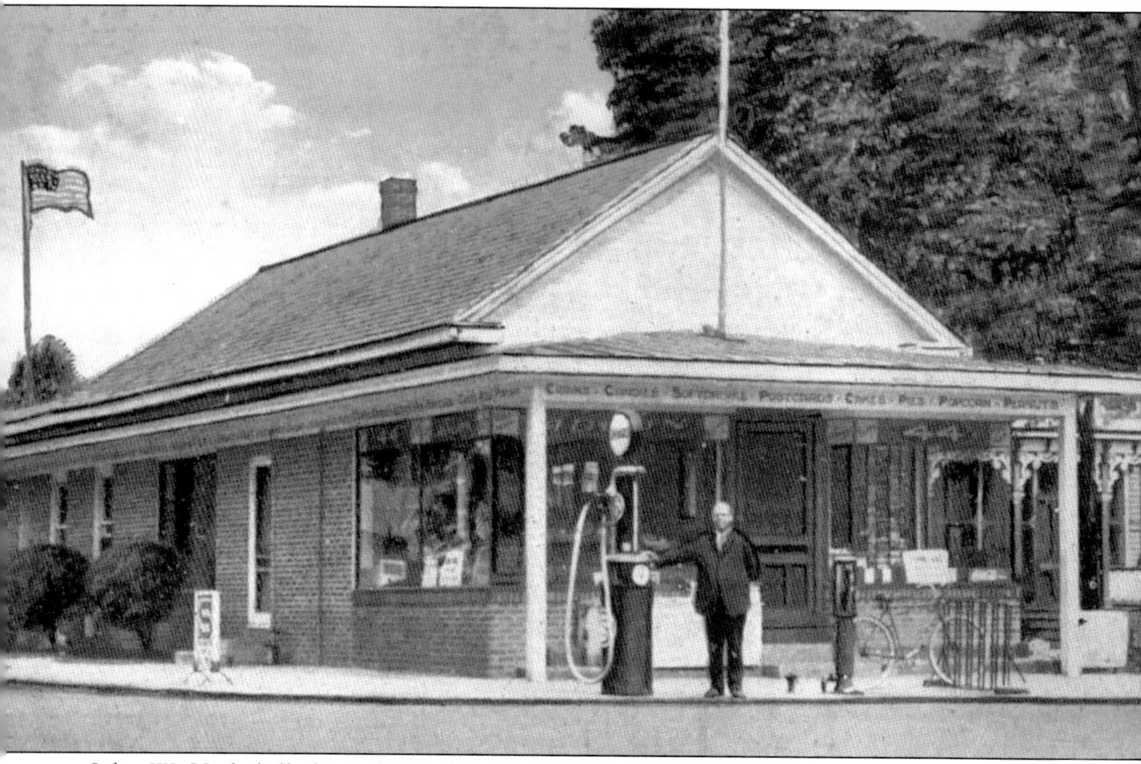

John W. Underhill chose this building at the corner of Farragut Avenue and Main Street in Mays Landing to serve as his store. Underhill arrived in town around the beginning of the 20th century and established his meager living quarters and curtained-off barbershop in an old shack. He later moved his barbershop and eventually developed a store, selling candy, cigars, and newspapers. He closed his business c. 1913. The building later housed Fiorey's Pool Room and Joe's Pool Room, where pictures of soldiers were proudly displayed on the walls during World War II. The site is currently the location of the St. Vincent De Paul School.

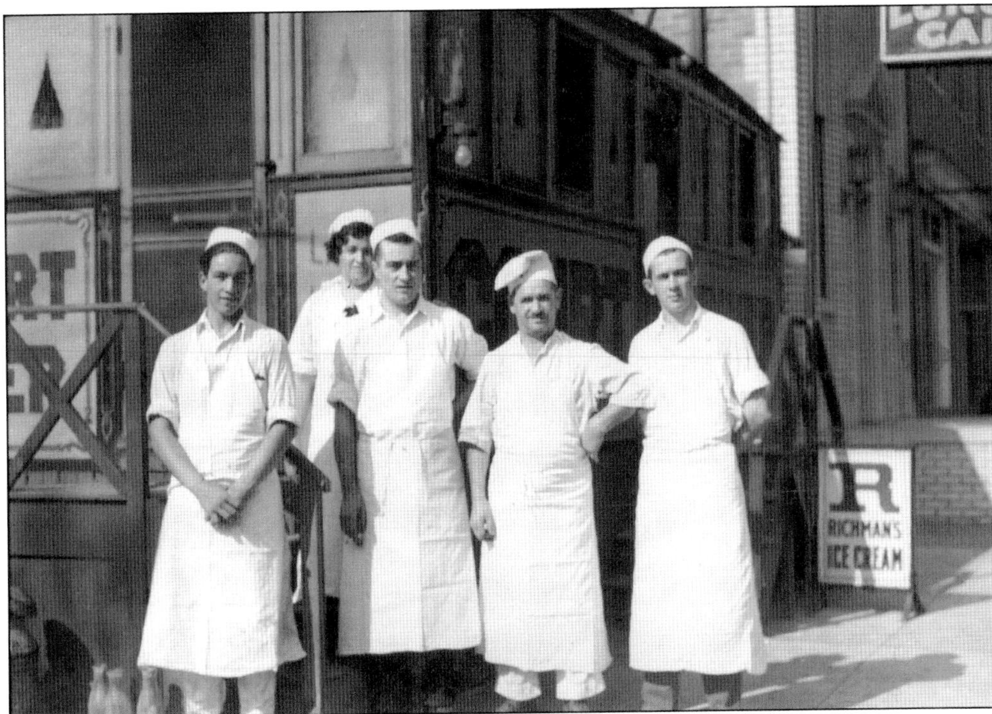

Staff members of the Court Diner in Mays Landing pose in front of the establishment in 1933. They are, from left to right, unidentified, Elizabeth Tessieri, John Tessieri (owner), Edmund Chiola, and Tommy Fiori. The diner was demolished in 1984.

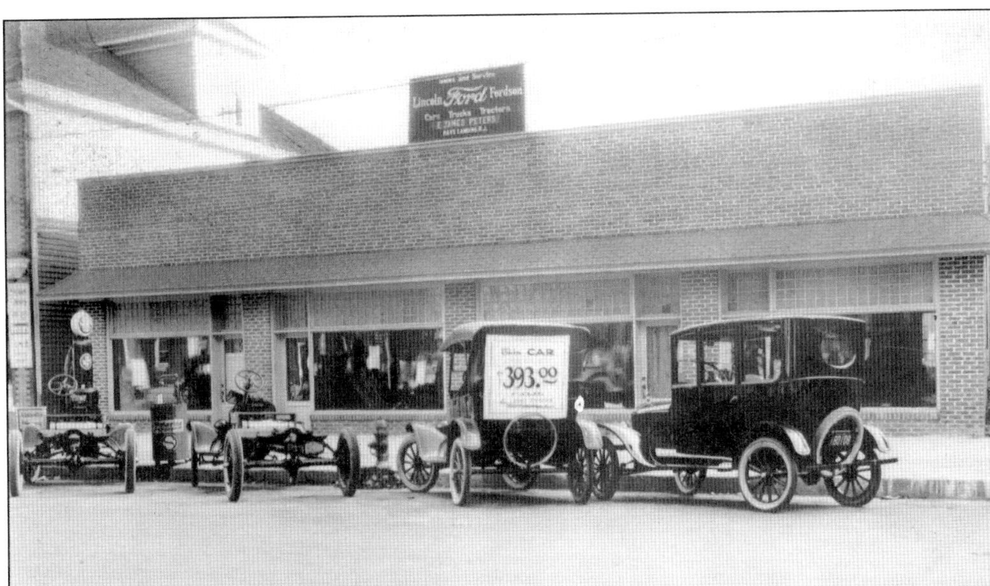

Automobiles are shown for sale c. 1924 in front of the E. James Peters Ford agency, on Main Street in Mays Landing. A large sign advertises a price of $393 for one of the vehicles. The building is now occupied by the Atlantic County Board of Elections.

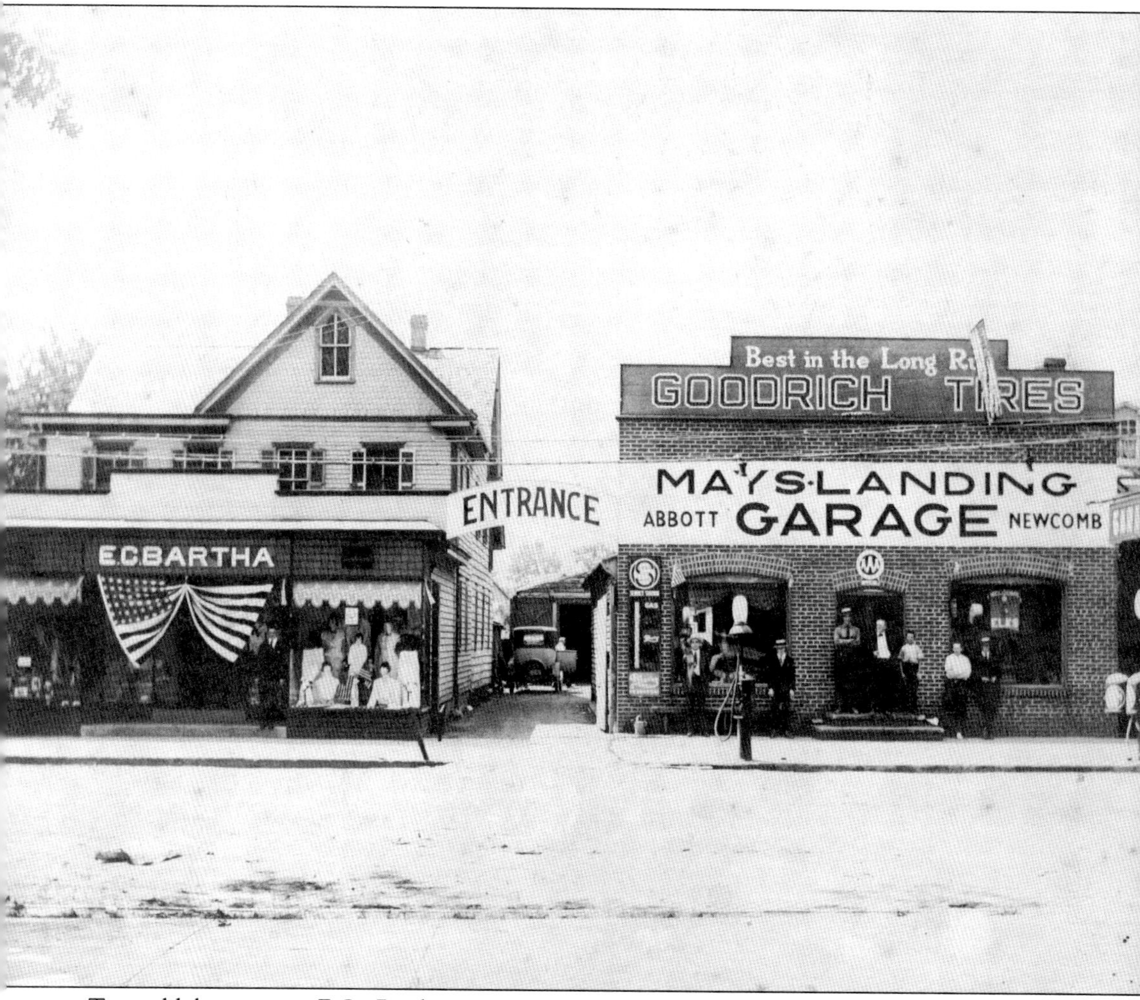

Two old businesses, E.C. Bartha's store and the Mays Landing Garage, are shown here. Bartha, an expert shoemaker, and his wife, Elizabeth, operated a haberdashery, which sold ready-to-wear women's clothing and accessories. Later, part of the building was rented to the U.S. Post Office. When Bartha's closed, Franklin Treidler's Court Pharmacy took over the entire store. It is now the site of the County Seat Florist. Mays Landing Garage, which was operated by John Newcomb, was moved to East Main Street to make way for the Cape May Avenue intersection in 1929.

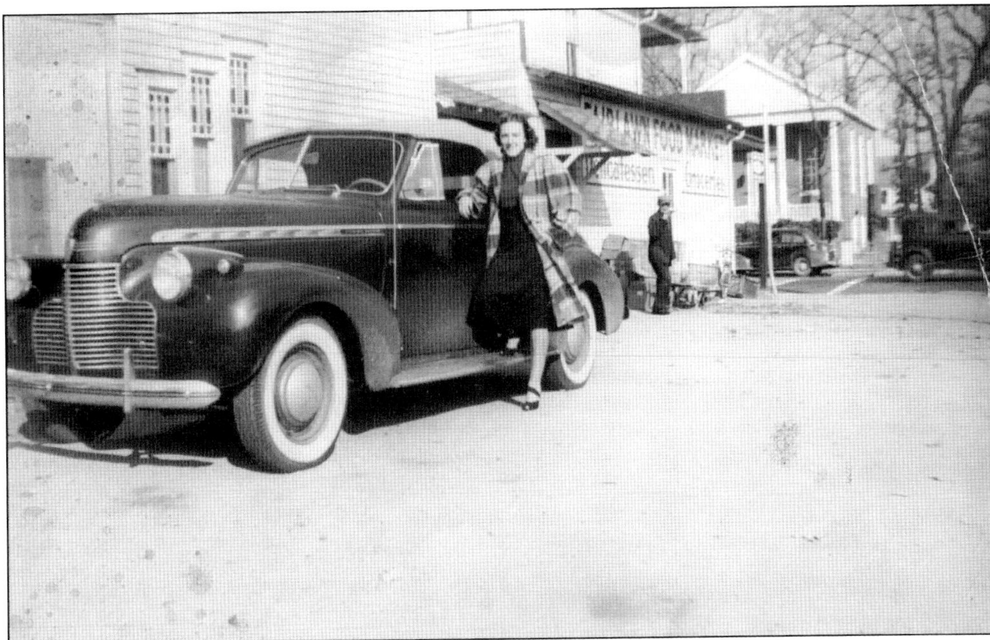

Elizabeth Haines McCallum is shown at the side of the Fairlawn Market, at the corner of Route 50 and Main Street in Mays Landing.

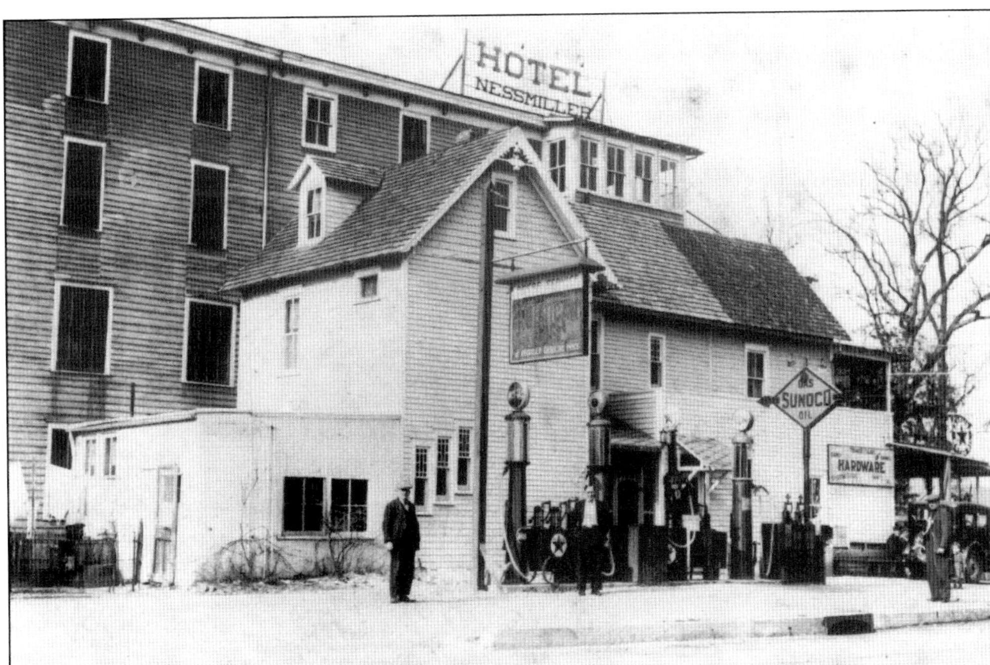

This is a side view of Beebe's Store, with the former opera house in the background, at the corner of Main Street and Cape May Avenue. Cappelluti's Restaurant is now located on this site. The three narrow windows in the lower center of the picture are still visible.

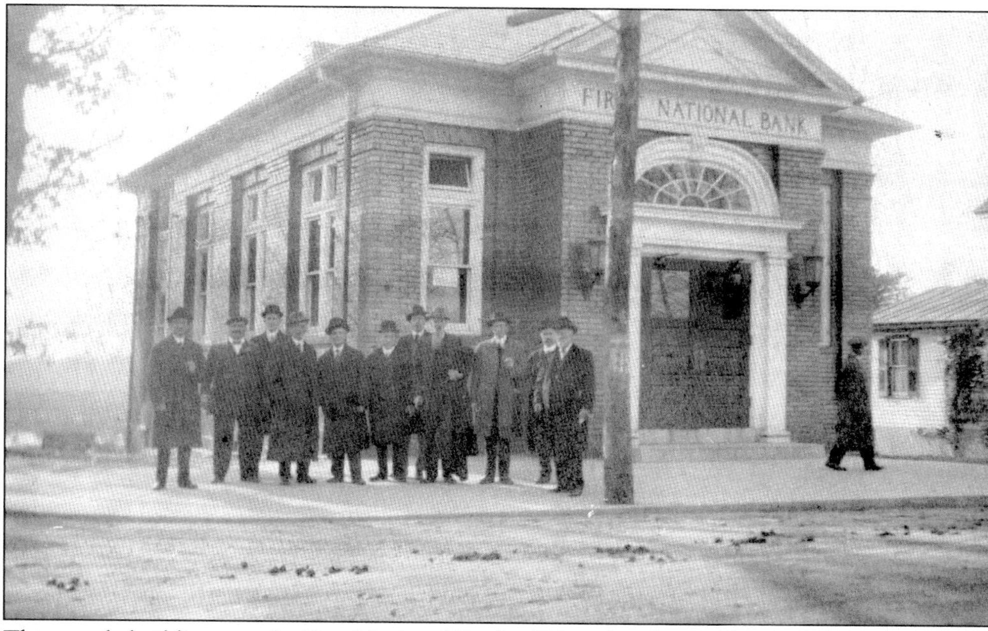

This stately building was the First National Bank of Mays Landing and is now the home of First Union Bank.

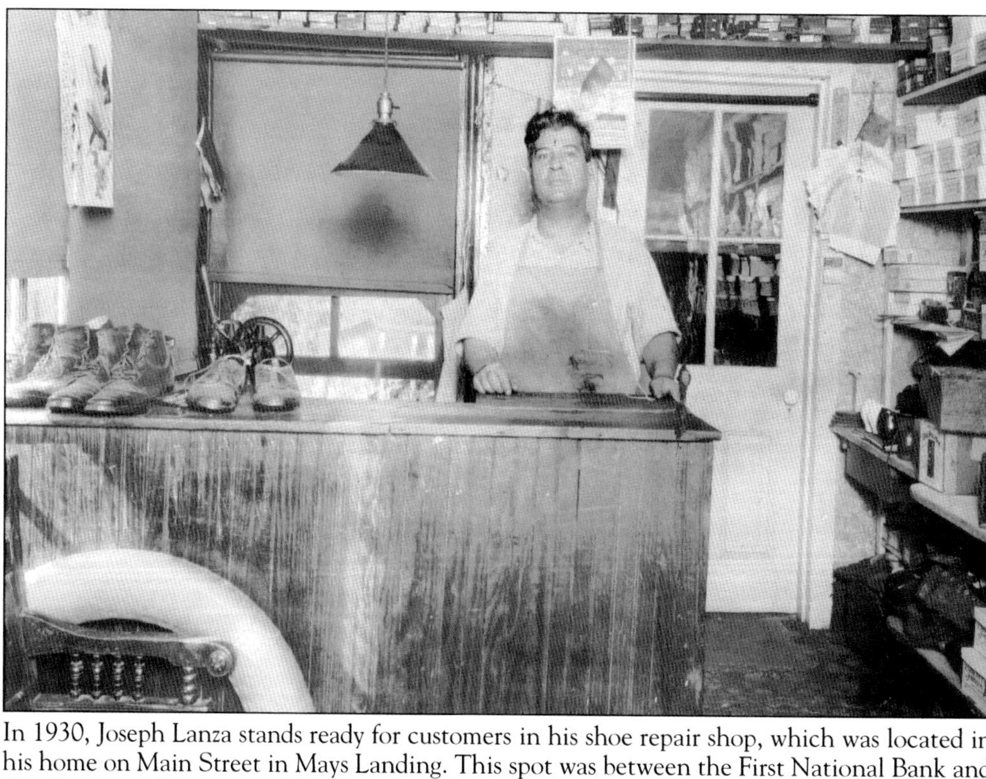

In 1930, Joseph Lanza stands ready for customers in his shoe repair shop, which was located in his home on Main Street in Mays Landing. This spot was between the First National Bank and the American Store.

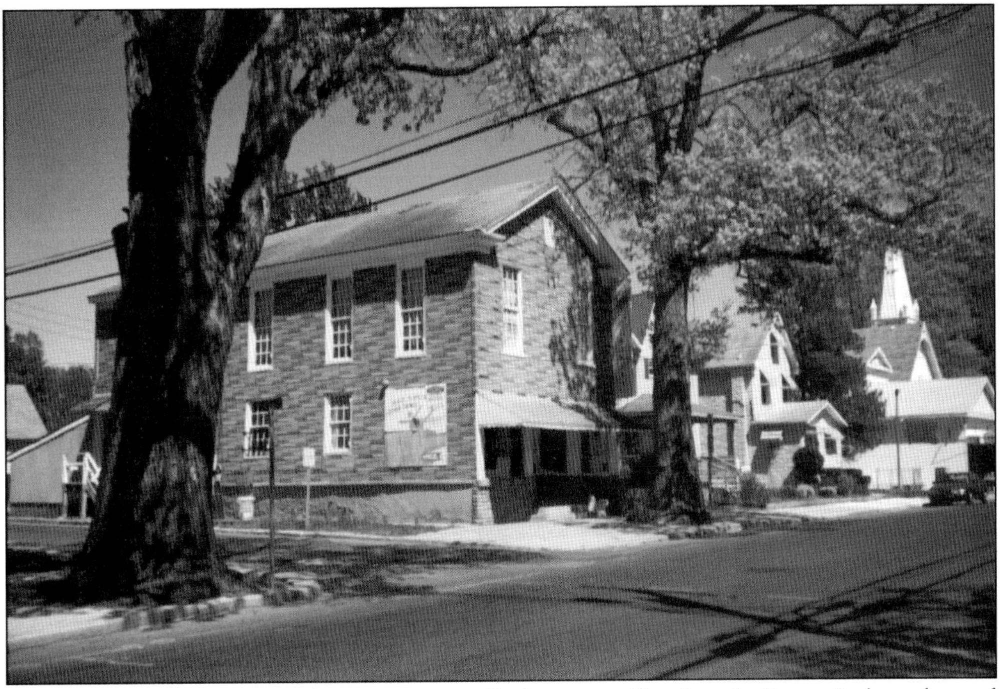

This building in Mays Landing was originally home to Hanthorn's Store. It later housed Abbott & Company and, still later, Main Street Bakery. The upper floor was once a Masonic meeting room.

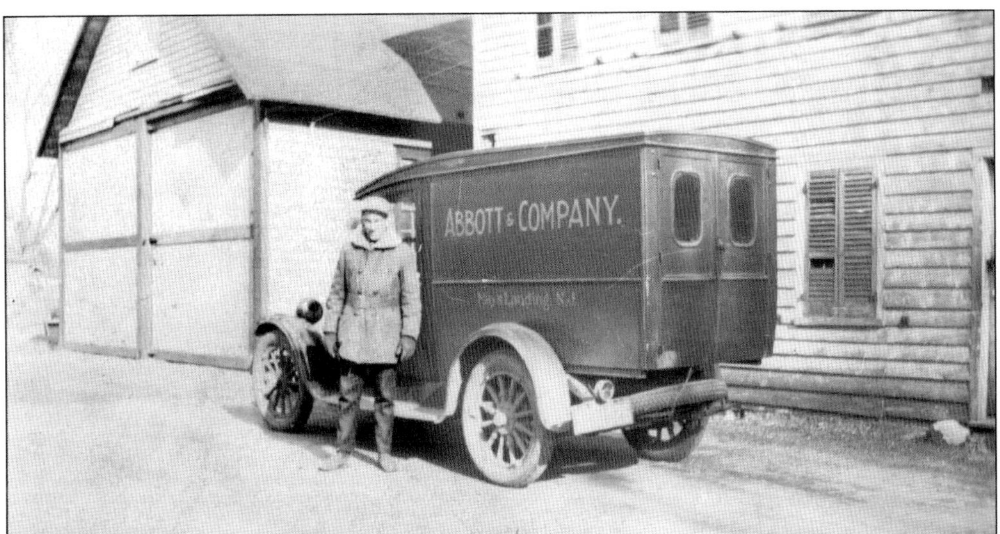

Myron Lashley is ready to deliver groceries *c.* 1929 for Abbott & Company in Mays Landing.

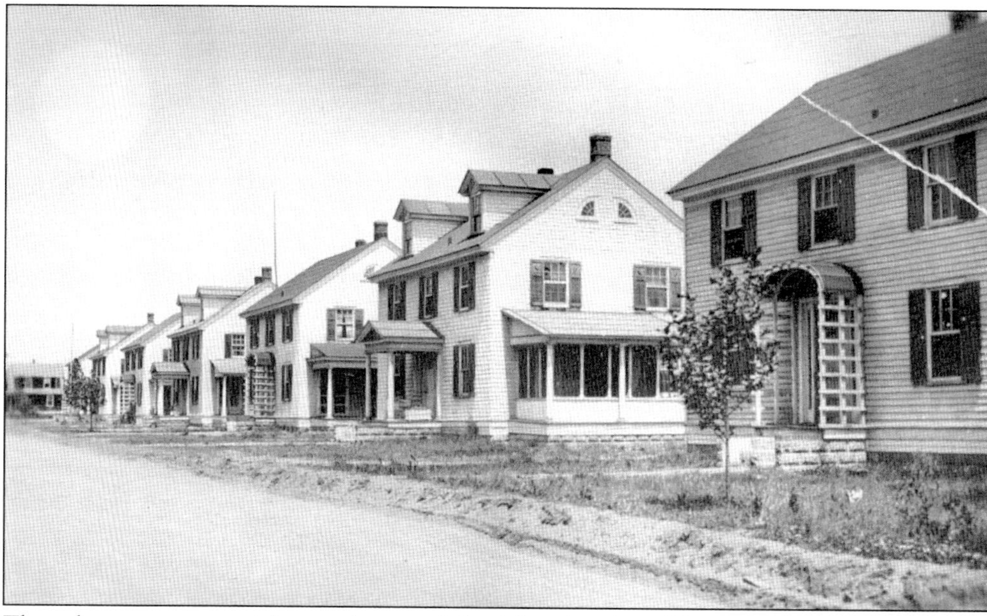

These houses were used for employees of the Mays Landing Water Power Company. Many of the homes were originally built in Belcoville by the Bethlehem Loading Company for its workers during World War I. The homes were advertised for sale in the 1930s and, once purchased, had to be moved to the buyer's property.

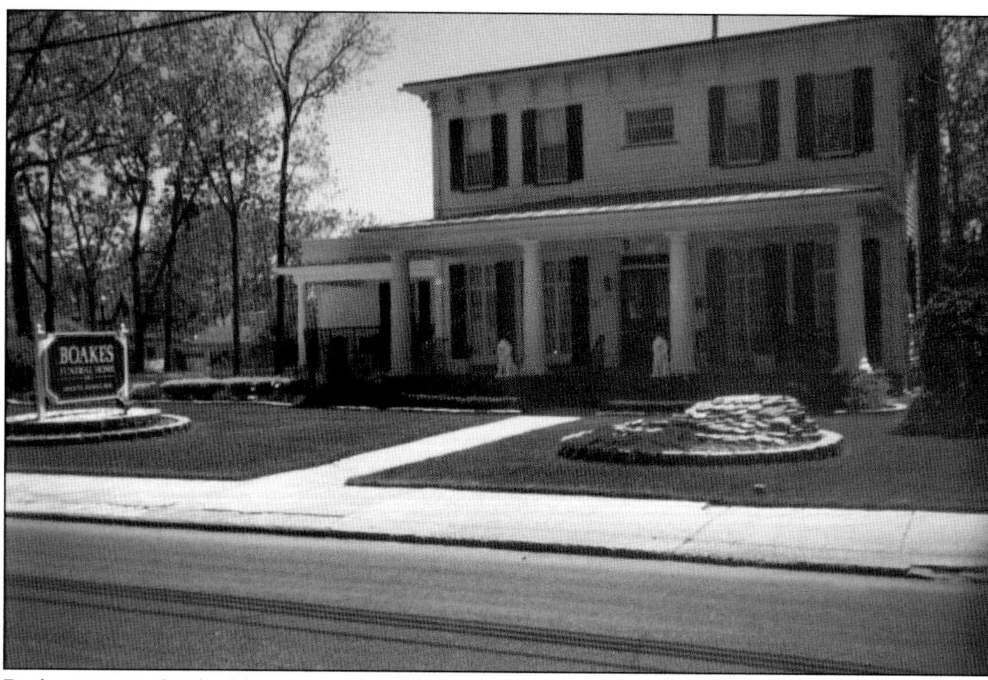

Built in 1860, this building in Mays Landing was known as the Champion House. It is now the site of Boakes Funeral Home.

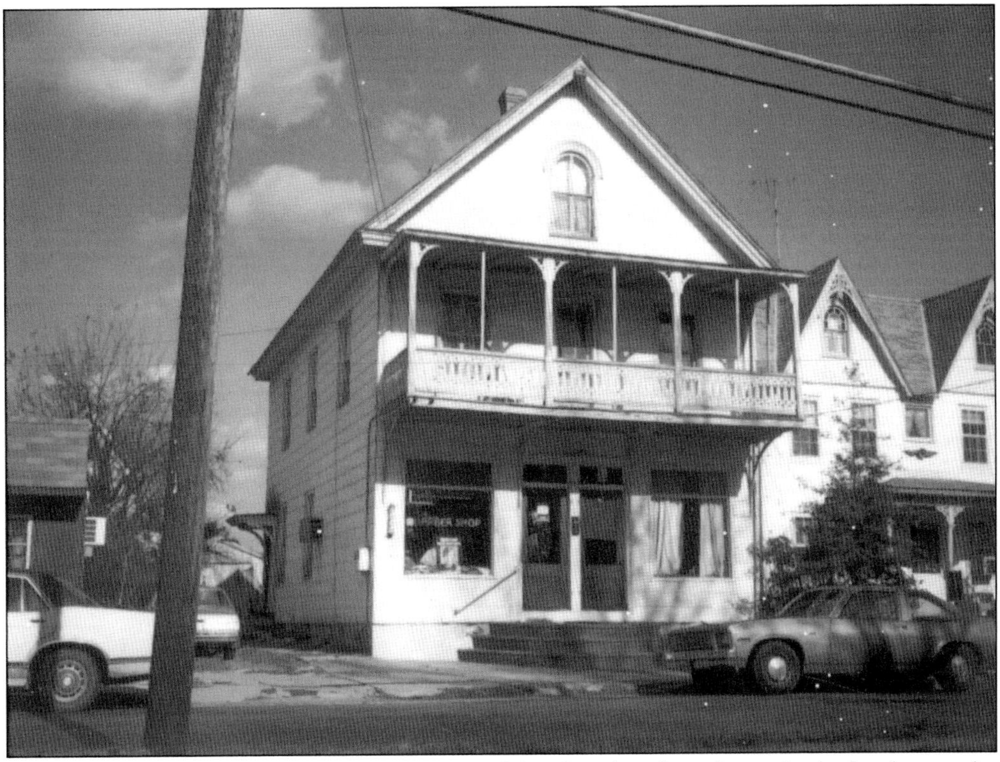

Built c. 1890, this building on Main Street in Mays Landing later housed a barbershop and a beauty parlor.

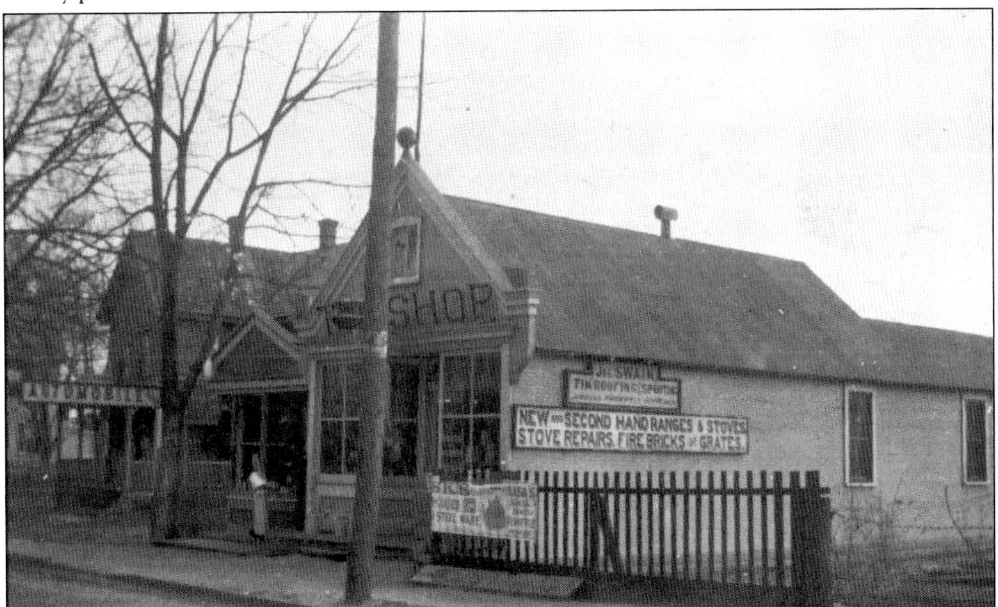

Originally the site of Austin's Photographer, this building on Main Street in Mays Landing later housed the Harry Collins Store. It was subsequently the home of Johnson Outboard Motors. Having returned to its roots, it is today the location of Doughty Studio.

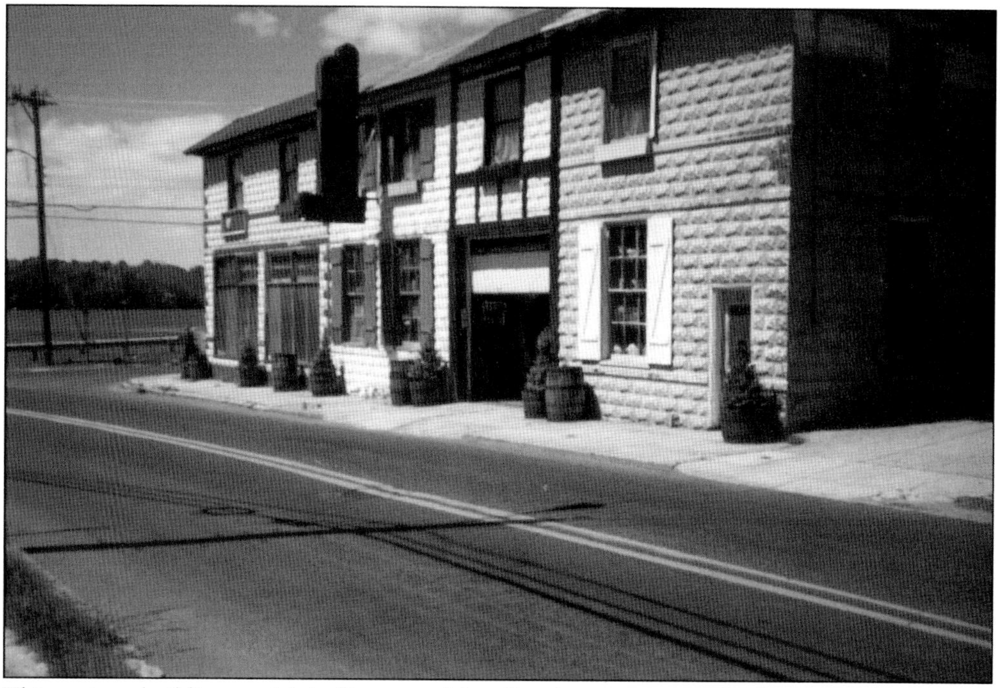

This unique building on Main Street in Mays Landing was once the location of the Beach Chevrolet car dealership. Today it is the site of Norman Gasko's Lenape Antique Shop.

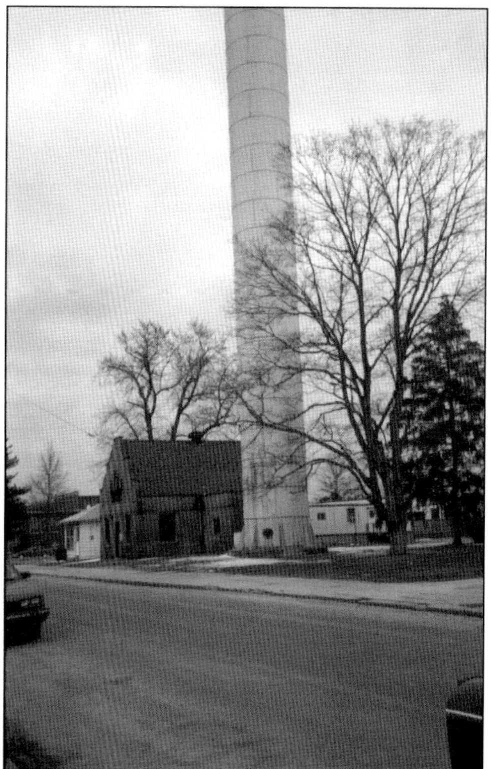

Built in 1907, the Mays Landing Water Works and its standpipe were located on Farragut Avenue.

These are the kilns of the Mays Landing Brick Yard, established in 1892. This was later the site of the West American Charcoal Company. Bricks manufactured here were used in the construction of the famous Traymore Hotel in Atlantic City.

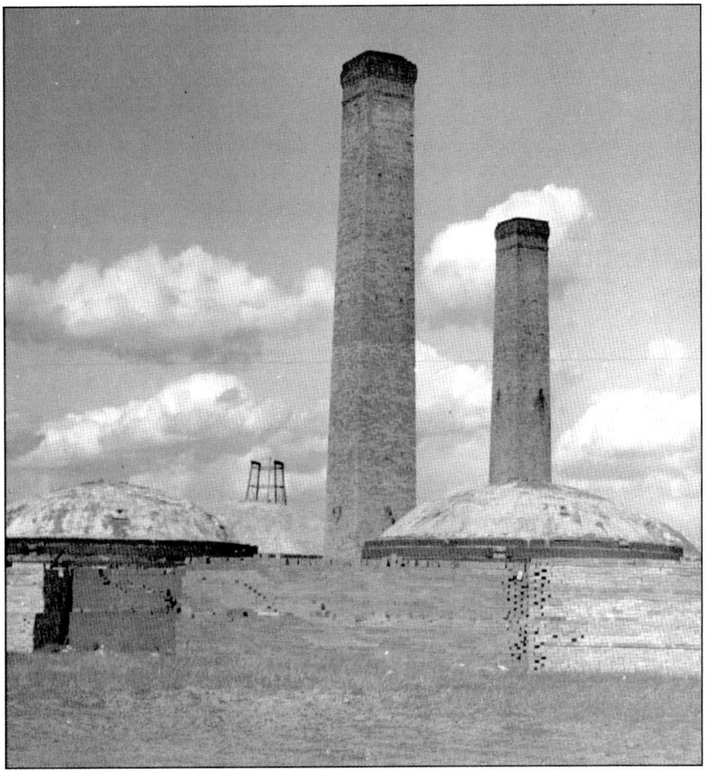

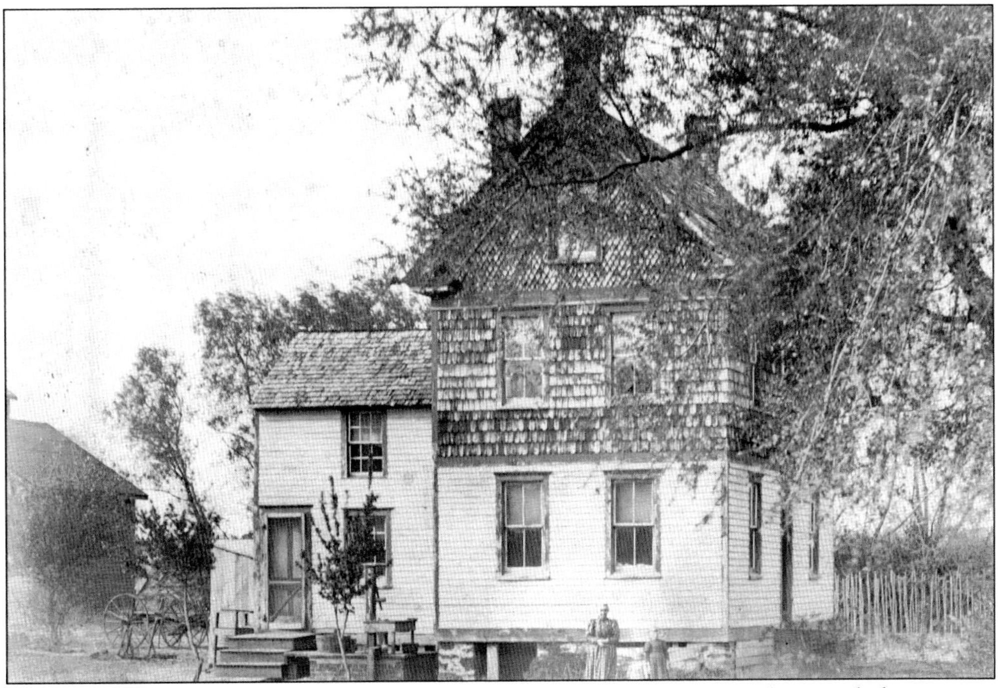

This is the Penn Taylor Home, located near Lenape Lake in Mays Landing, including a view of the icehouse in the side yard. Ice was collected every winter and shipped first by wagon and then by train to other towns in the county.

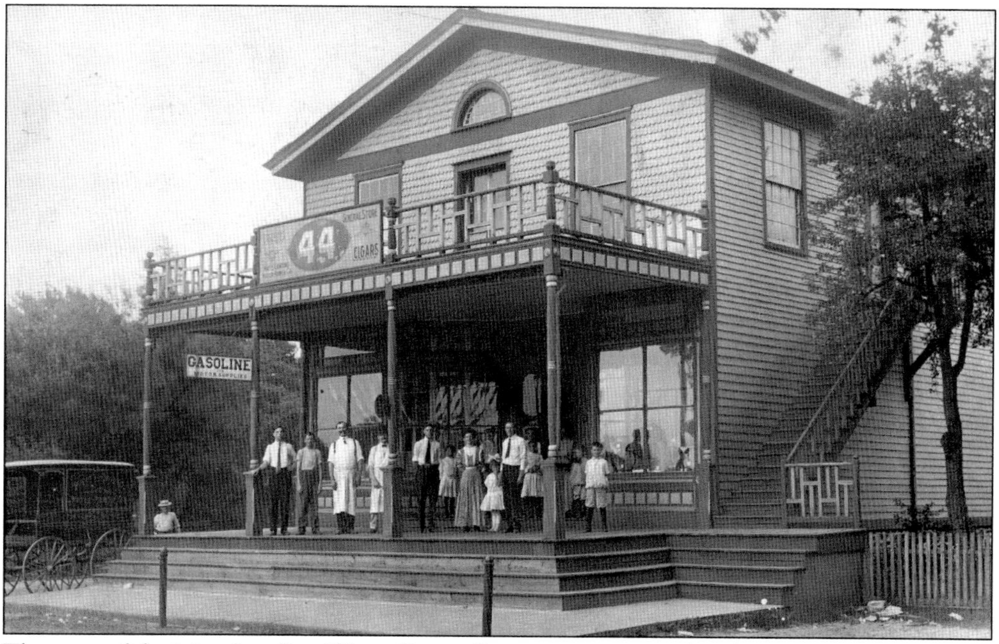

The store of the Mays Landing Water Power Company was owned and operated by R.D. Wood & Sons. You could purchase anything necessary for daily living—clothing, fabrics, groceries, meats, furniture, stoves, hay, coal, animal feed, tools, and more. The company's employees could buy on credit, with the payment coming out of their weekly wages. Today the building is the home of the Masonic Temple Unity Lodge No. 96.

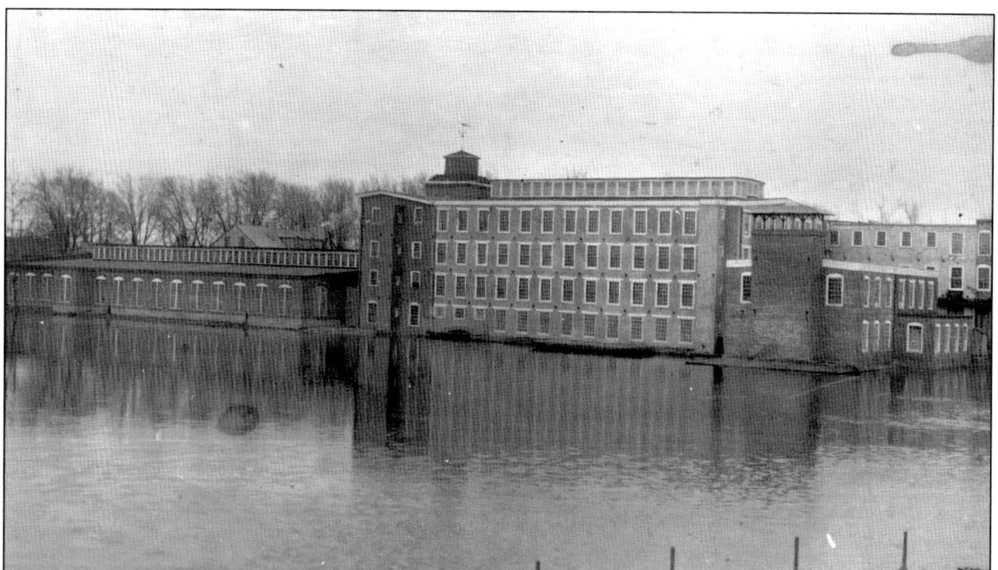

Incorporated in 1867 by George Wood & Sons, the Mays Landing Water Power Company manufactured toweling, sheeting, and other fabrics from raw cotton. The site is now the home of Wheatons Inc.

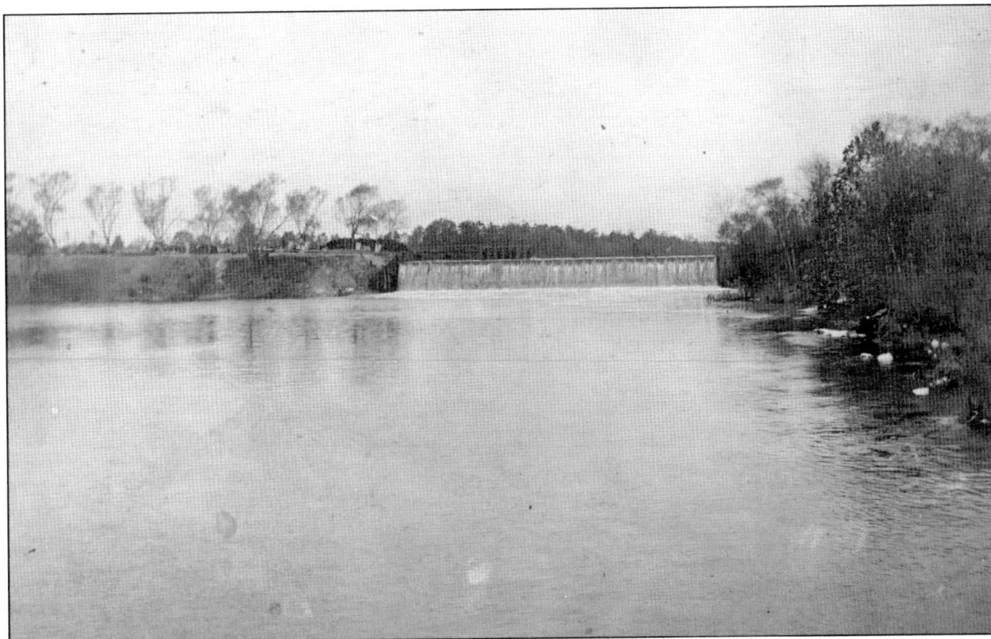

The Mays Landing Water Power Company dam is seen in this photograph taken from Mill Street. It was built in 1844 by Jeremiah Stull. In 1878, the dam broke and forever changed the shoreline of the Great Egg Harbor River.

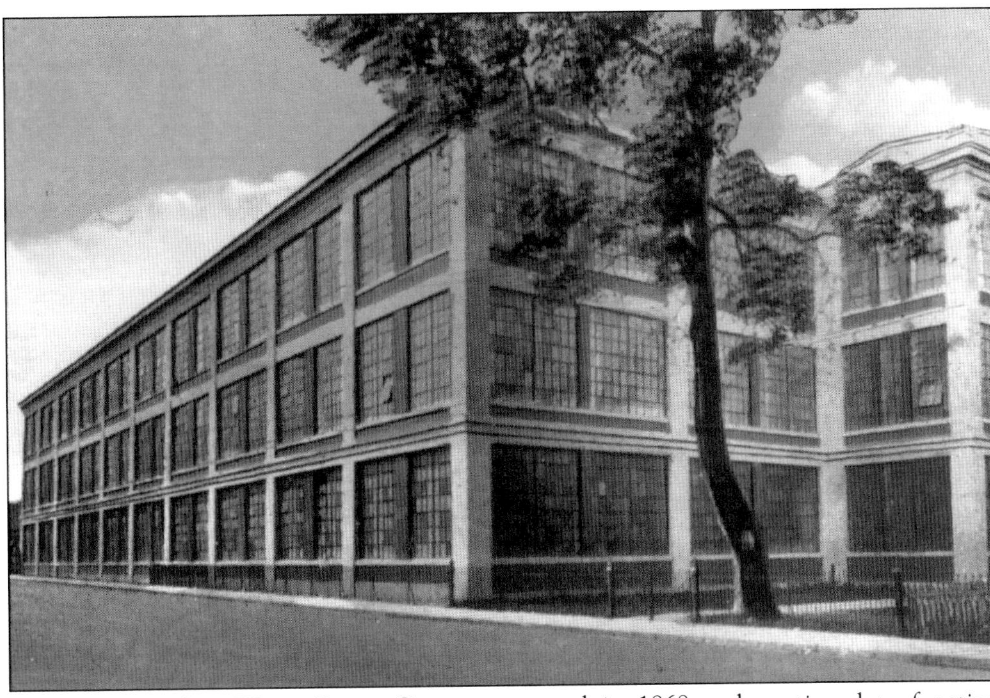

The Mays Landing Water Power Company opened in 1868 and continued to function until 1949, when workers went on strike for better benefits. The company closed its doors permanently during the strike, causing a large number of local residents to be out of work. In 1951, Wheatons opened its plastic-manufacturing company at this site.

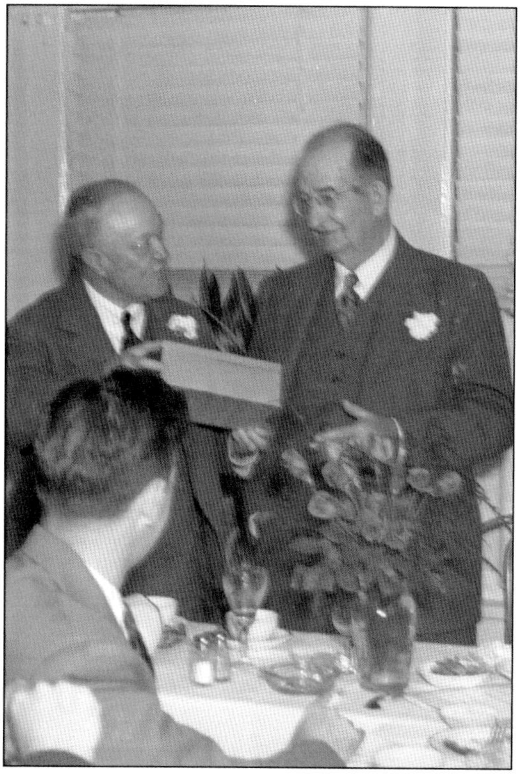

Pictured here is Richard D. Wood (left), president of the Mays Landing Water Power Company, making a presentation on May 3, 1947, to Robert H. Abbott for his 60 years of service.

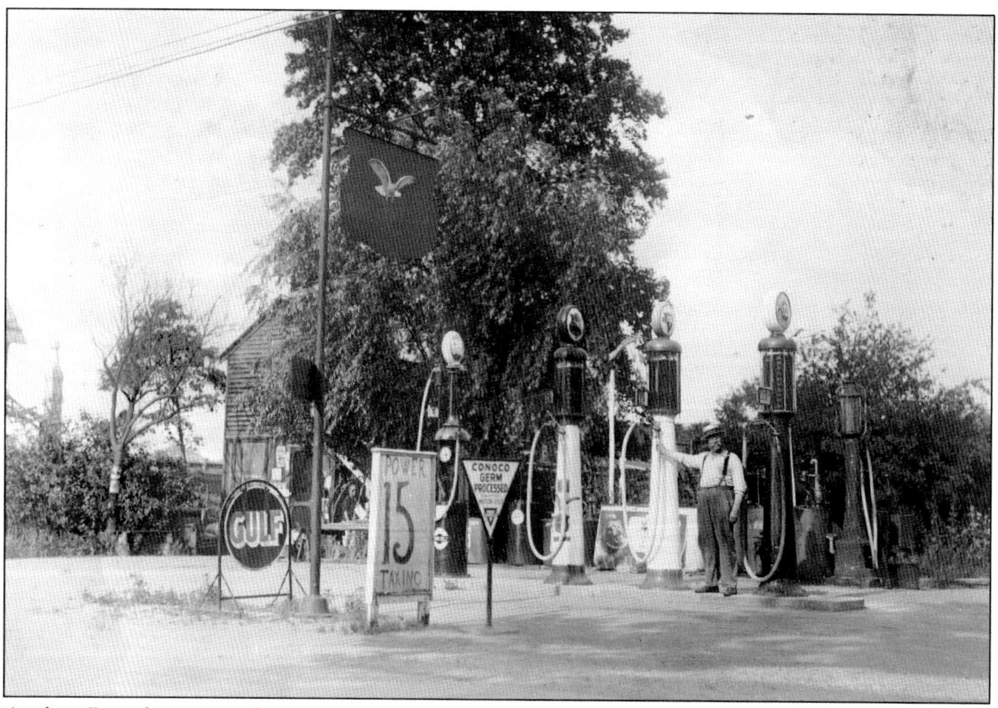

Andrea Bertolini awaits his next gasoline customer at his station on Mill Street in the Postville section of Mays Landing.

D. Repici's Barbershop was located on Main Street in Mays Landing and is shown in this calendar, which was given to customers. The building is now a private home.

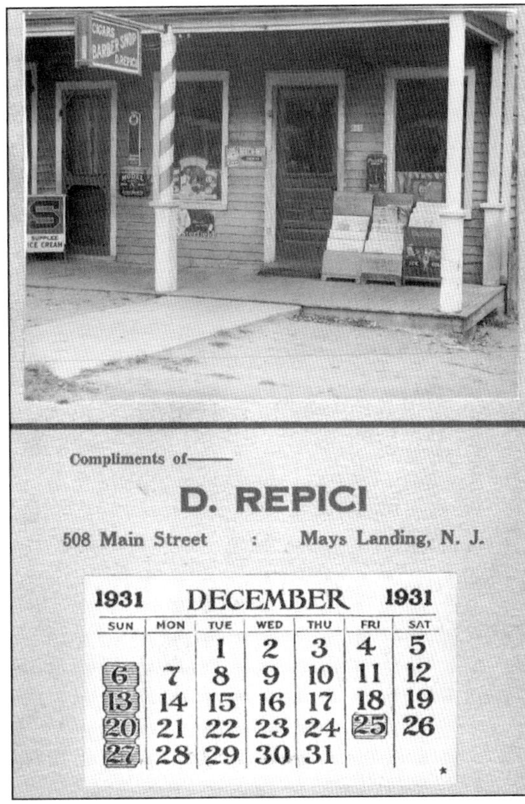

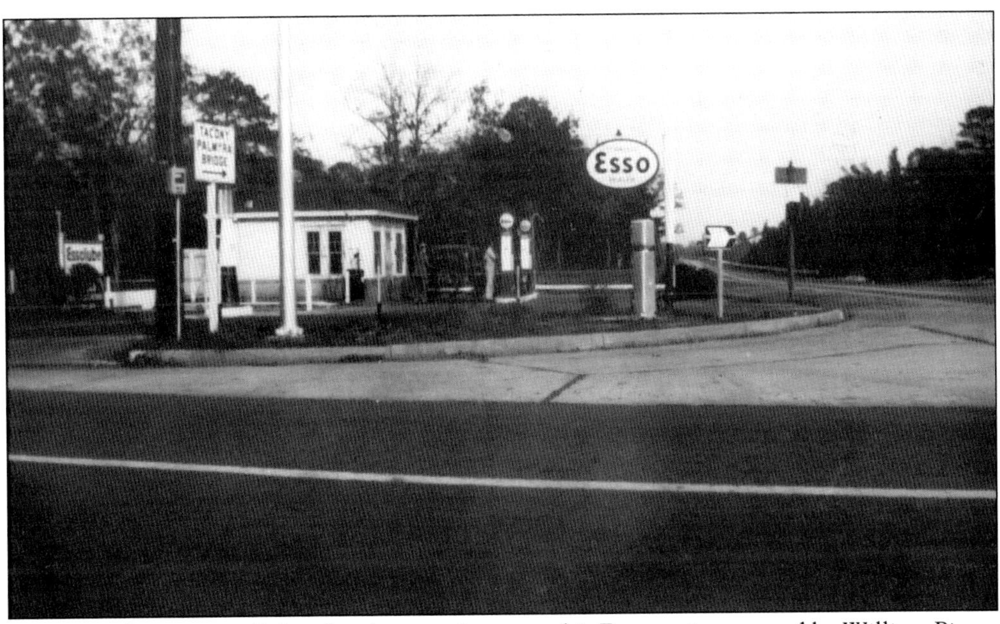

The Postville section of Mays Landing was home to this Esso station, owned by William Pierce c. 1940. It was located at the corner of Routes 40 and 50 and Mill Street.

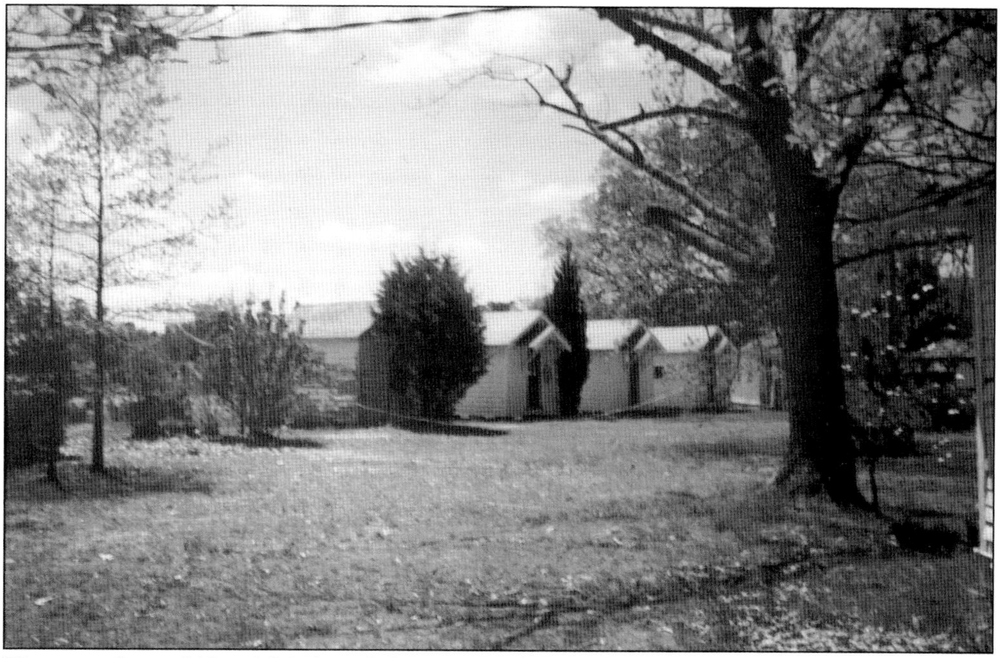

This view shows Abbott's Modern Cabins on Harding Highway in Mays Landing. Built in 1927, they are now on the New Jersey Register of Historic Places.

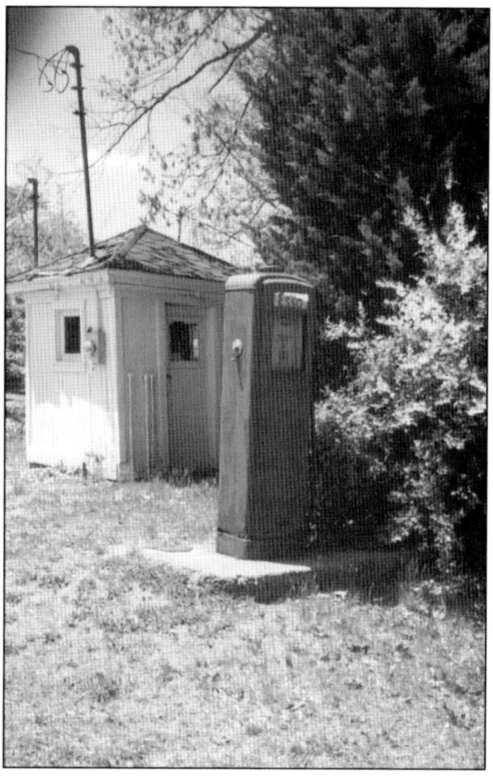

Many will recall early gas pumps such as this one at Abbott's.

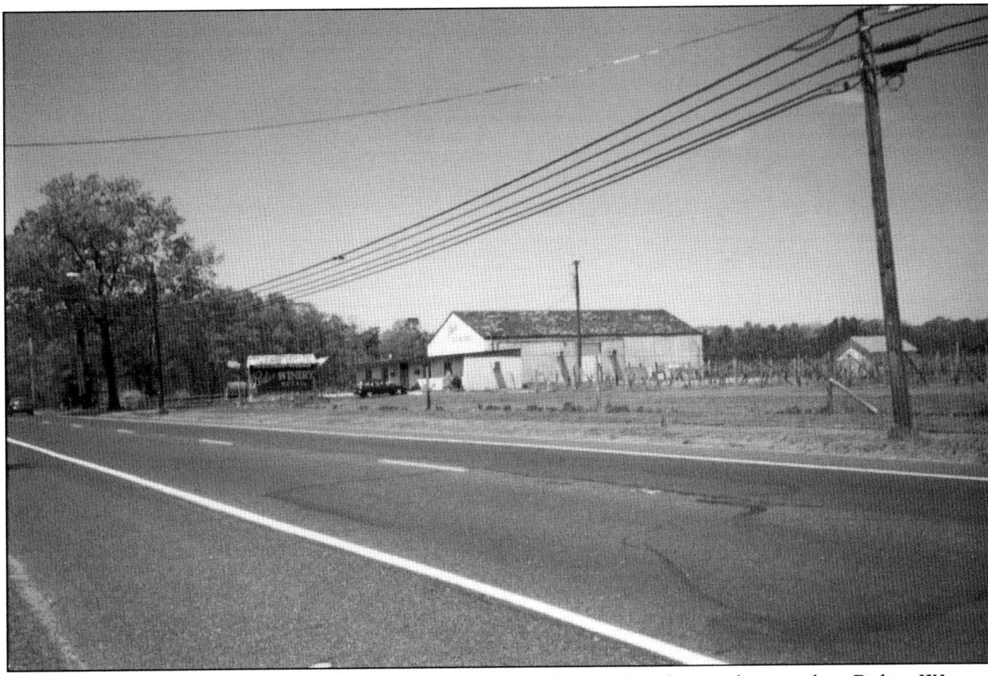

This view, looking down Harding Highway in Mays Landing, shows the Balic Winery and vineyard.

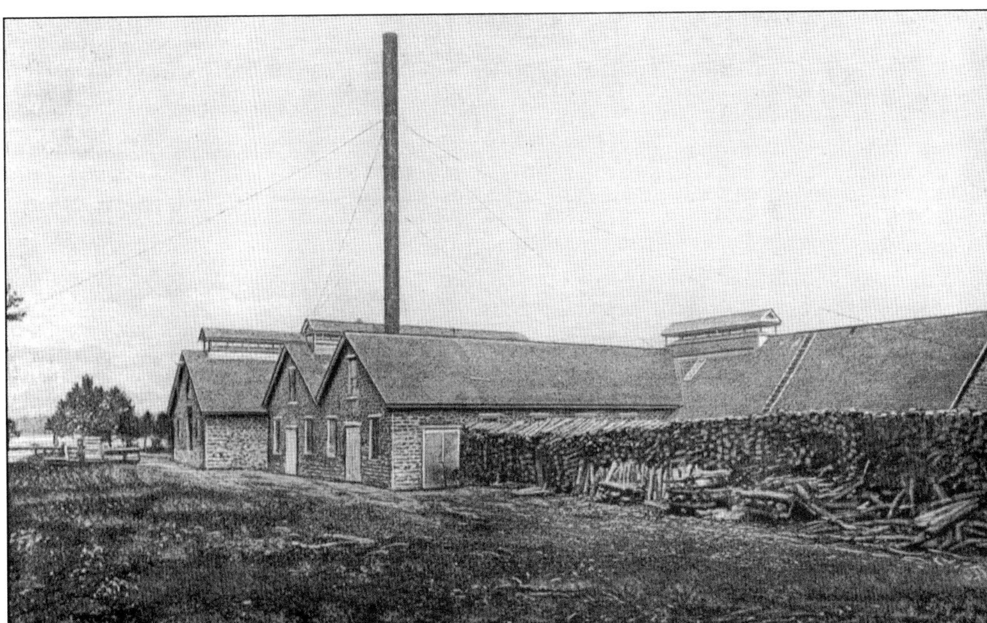

A paper mill was established in 1868 on the site of the former Weymouth Iron Furnace in the Weymouth section of the township.

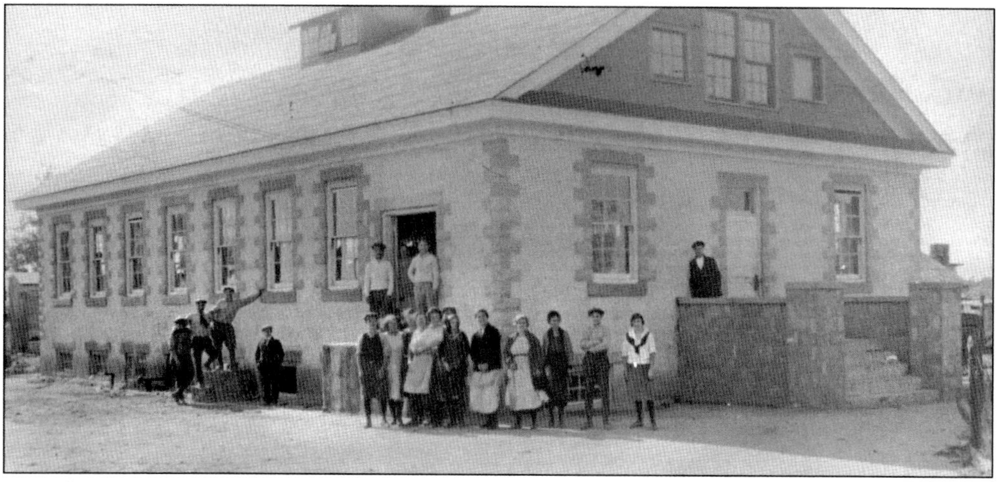

Mizpah Coat Factory employees take a break from their work to be photographed. The factory was located in the Mizpah section of the township. During World War II, the factory was involved in the manufacture of uniforms for American servicemen. At one point, it employed at least 100 local residents.

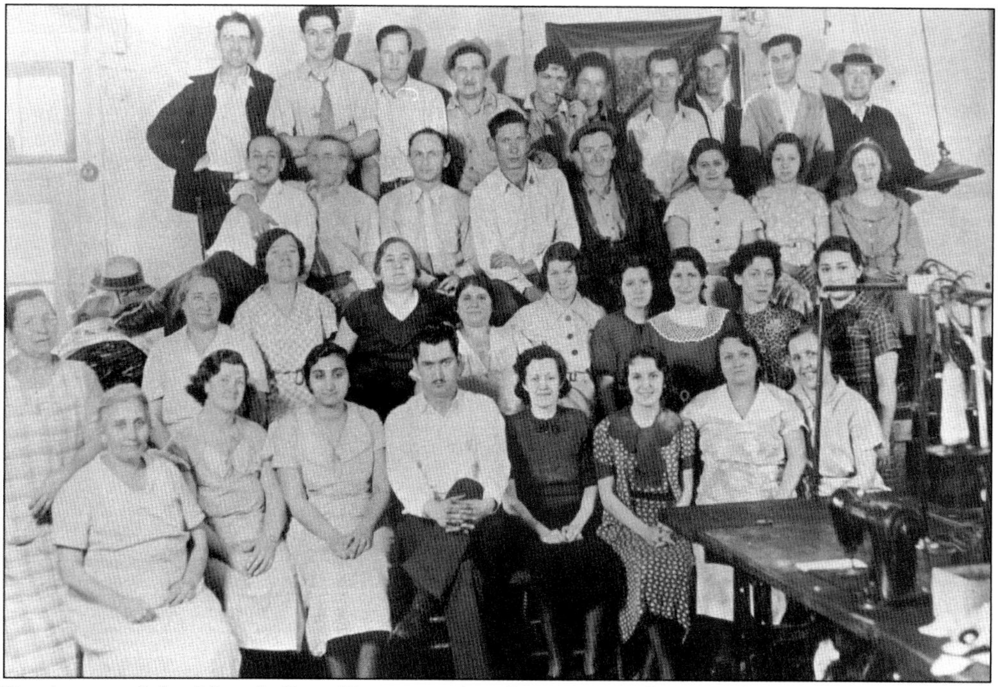

Employees of the Mizpah Coat Factory gather for a group photograph c. 1940. From left to right are the following: (first row) Rose Pagano, ? Hayes, Katie Messina, Joe Messina, Margaret Aaron, Antoinette Biancarosa, ? Pizza, and ? Monfredo; (second row) ? Mattero, Peretta, ? Sauerwald, ? Rettino, ? Biancarosa, Barbara Hayes, Rosa (Messina) Spero, Paulino (Pappalardo) Sipala, Mary Cincotti, and Antoinette (Messina) Peraneo; (third row) William Fontanaza, Andy Messina, Anthony Spero, ? Wagner, George Sauerwald, Frances (Hunt) Cerino, Jenny Mattero, and Helen (Cerino) Musso; (fourth row) Jim Farrel, unidentified, ? Wagner, Sam Peretto, Joe Perri, ? Barbagallo, unidentified, John Signarella, Frank Biancarosa, and ? Messina.

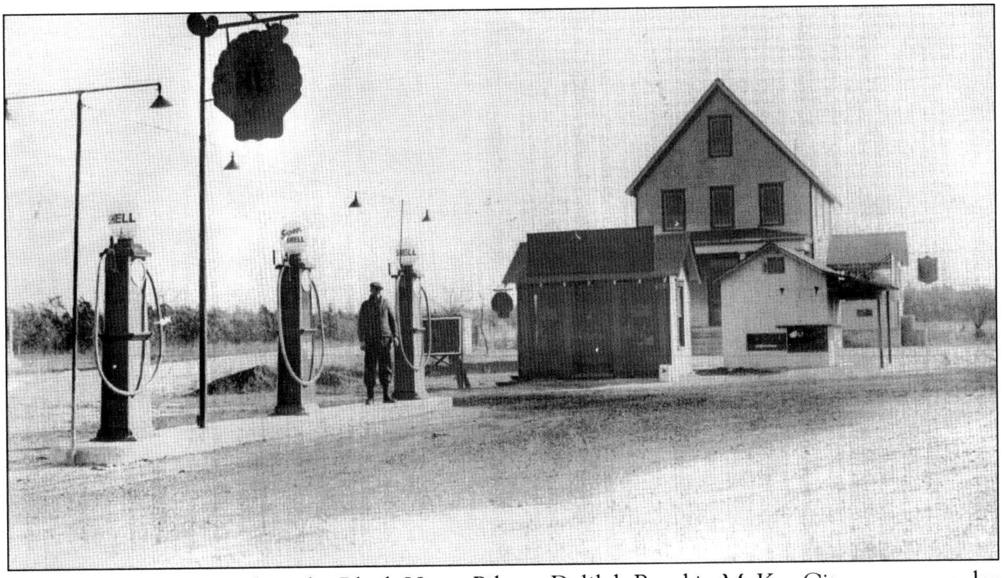

The Gables Inn, located on the Black Horse Pike at Delilah Road in McKee City, was a popular eatery dating back to 1929. In 1960, Charles and Rita Zaberer purchased the inn, changed its name to Zaberer's, and opened for business on June 12, 1961. Over the years, many rooms and a gift shop were added. The restaurant became a huge success with its advertising motto, "Minutes Away," on signs often located as far away as Pennsylvania. Charles, who died in 1971, is immortalized by the words engraved on his tombstone, "Minutes Away." Zaberer's continued serving its famous dinners and "Zaberized" (king-sized) cocktails until the early 1980s, when the opening of the casinos in Atlantic City took business away. The property was later sold and the buildings demolished.

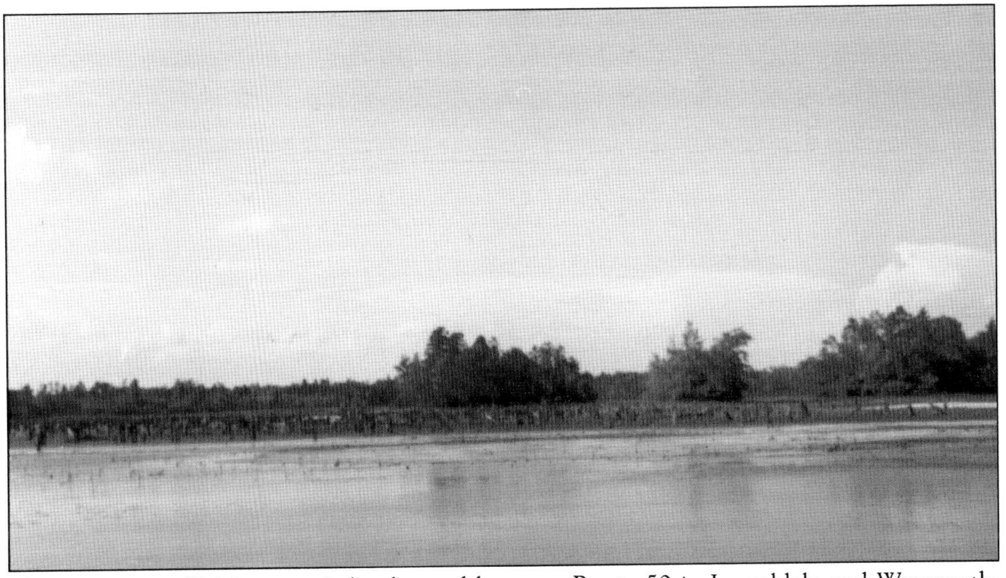

This is a view of Makepeace Lake, located between Route 50 in Laureldale and Weymouth. The lake has been used as a water supply for nearby cranberry bogs and for the Atlantic Blueberry Company.

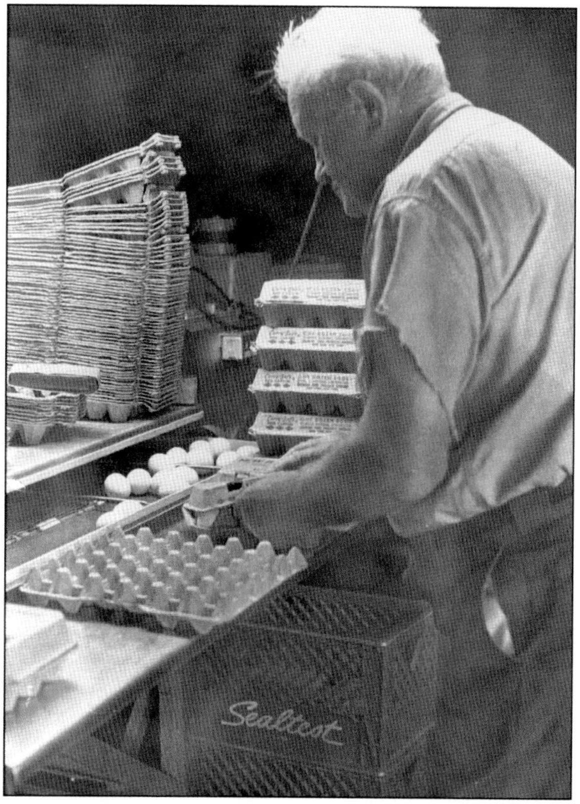

John Ysewyn, poultry farmer, is shown packing eggs on his Laurel Street farm in the Laureldale section of the township.

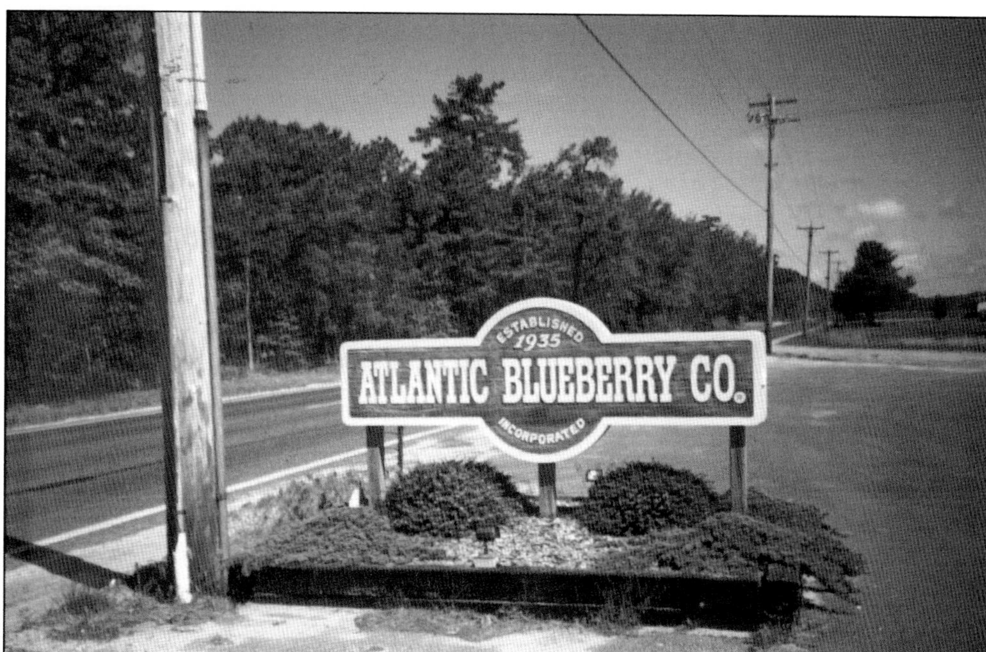

Established in 1935, the Atlantic Blueberry Company is the largest blueberry farm in the world. It is located on Weymouth Road in DaCosta.

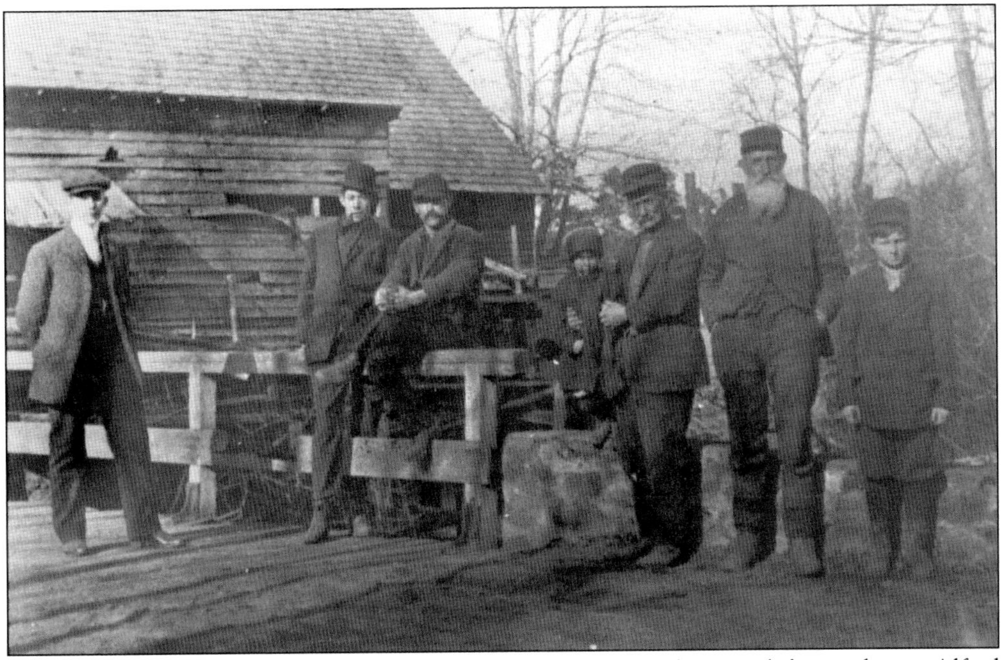

Employees of the Gravelly Run Saw Mill pause for a photograph. From left to right are Alfred Joslin, John A Thomas Sr., William S. Thomas, Joe Ireland, Bob Glover, Ancil Crowell, and Somers Ireland.

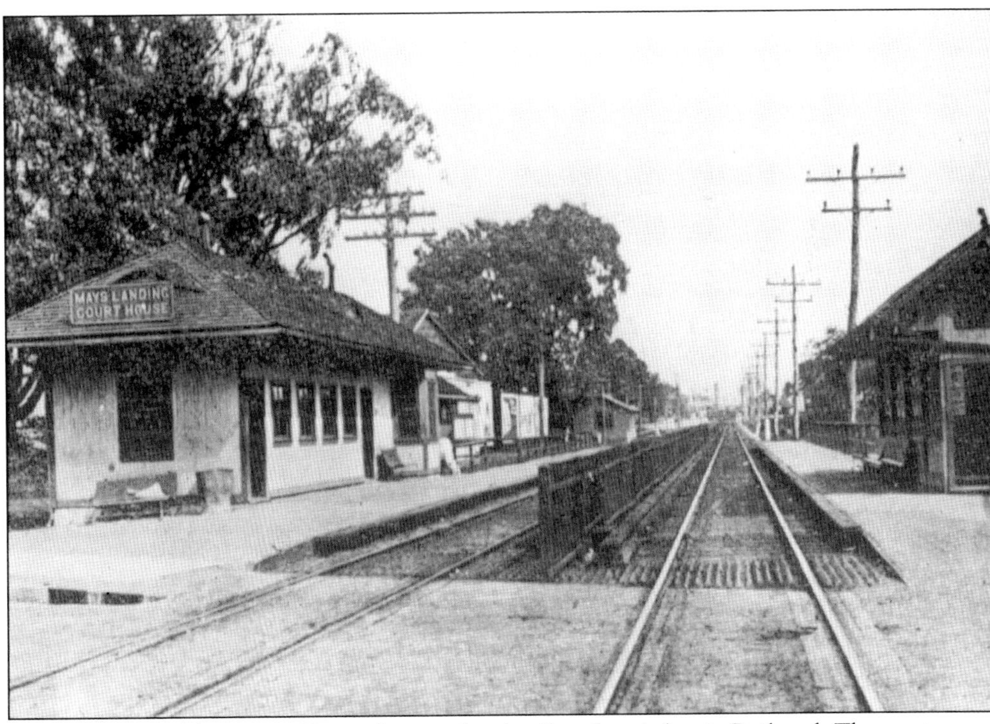

This is a view of the Court House Station for the Camden-Atlantic Railroad. The station was located on Farragut Avenue in Mays Landing and also served the West Jersey Railroad.

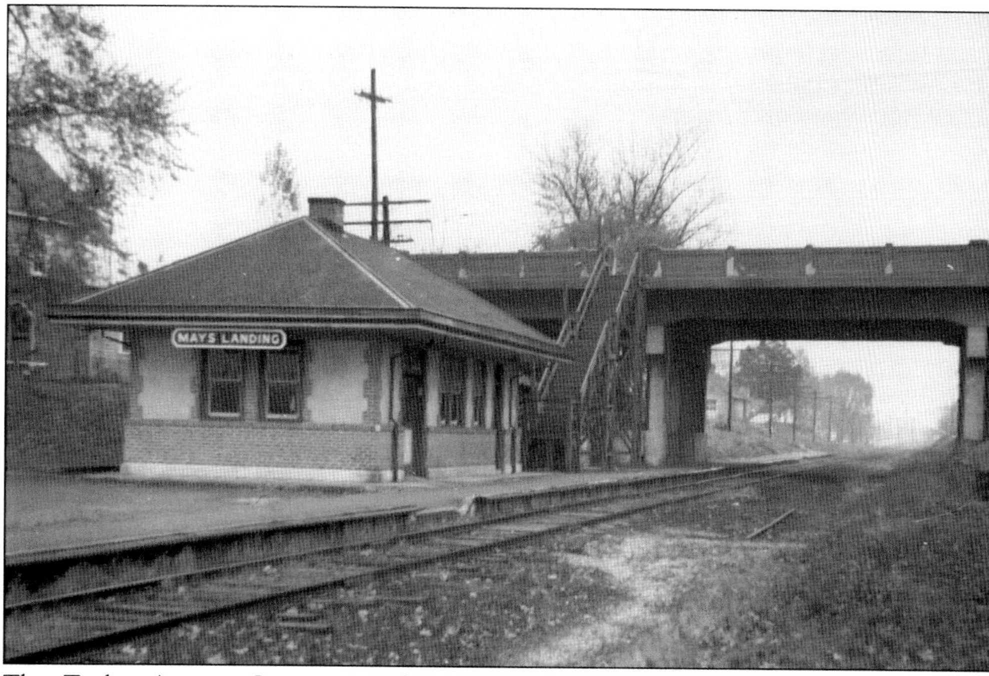

The Taylor Avenue Station was located at the base of the Route 50 overpass in Mays Landing.

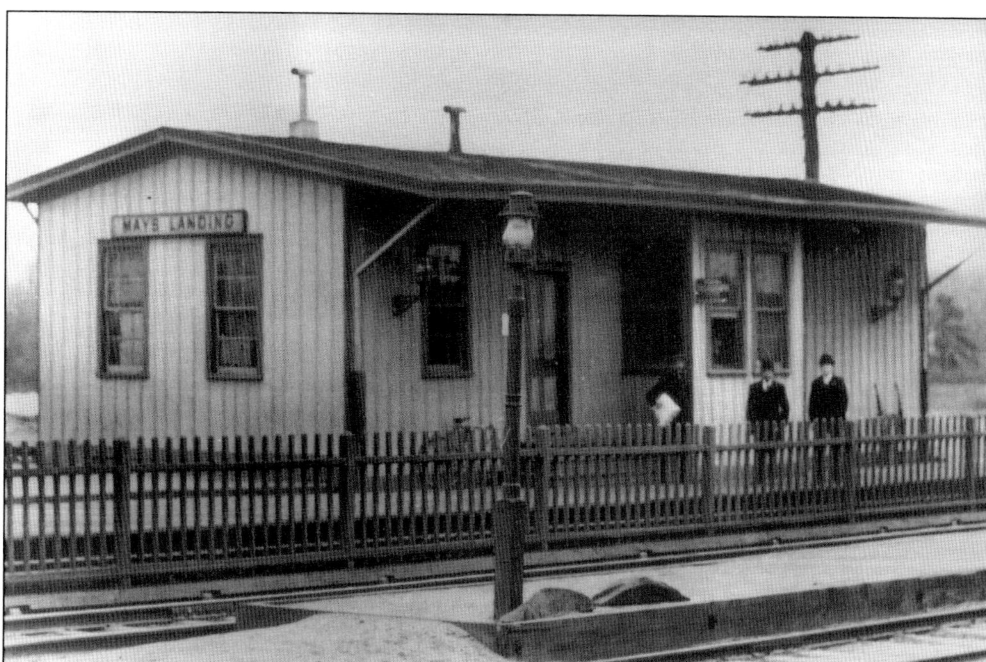

The Uptown Station for the West Jersey & Southern Railroad was located on Railroad Avenue in Mays Landing.

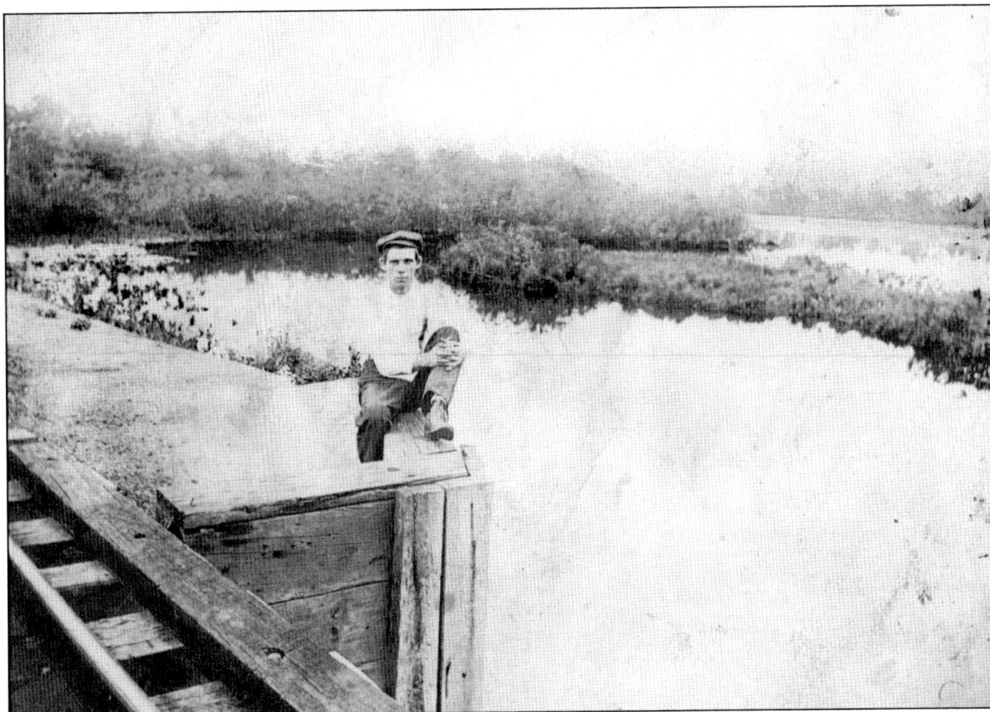

A young man perches on the railroad trestle over the Great Egg Harbor River, as viewed from Taylor Avenue in Mays Landing.

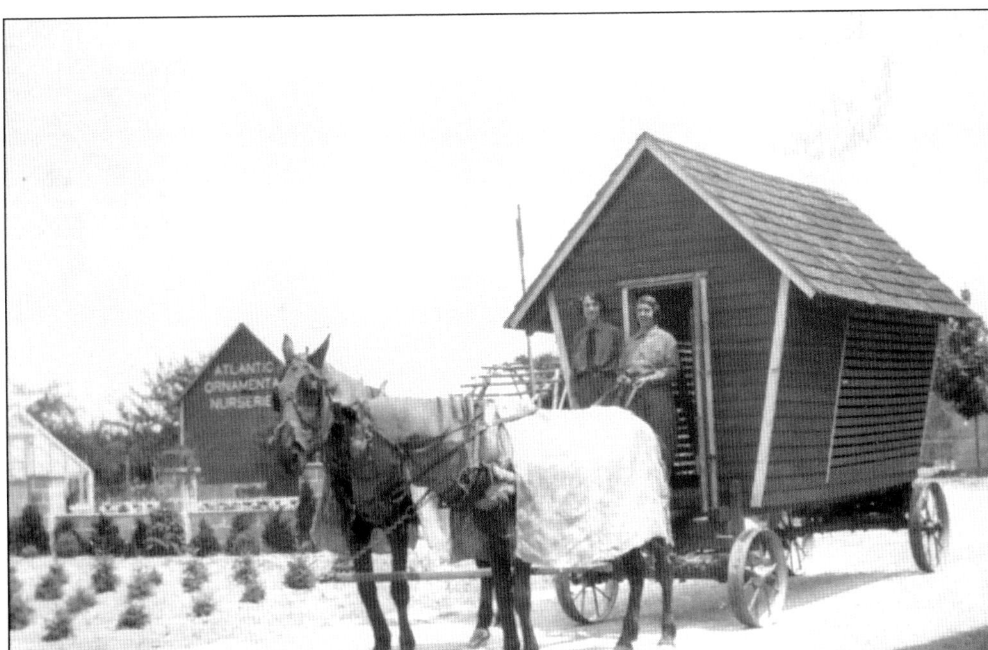

Caroline and Theresa Foell are shown on a horse-drawn cart with a corncrib they were hauling on George H. Liepe's Nursery, Cologne Avenue, Cologne.

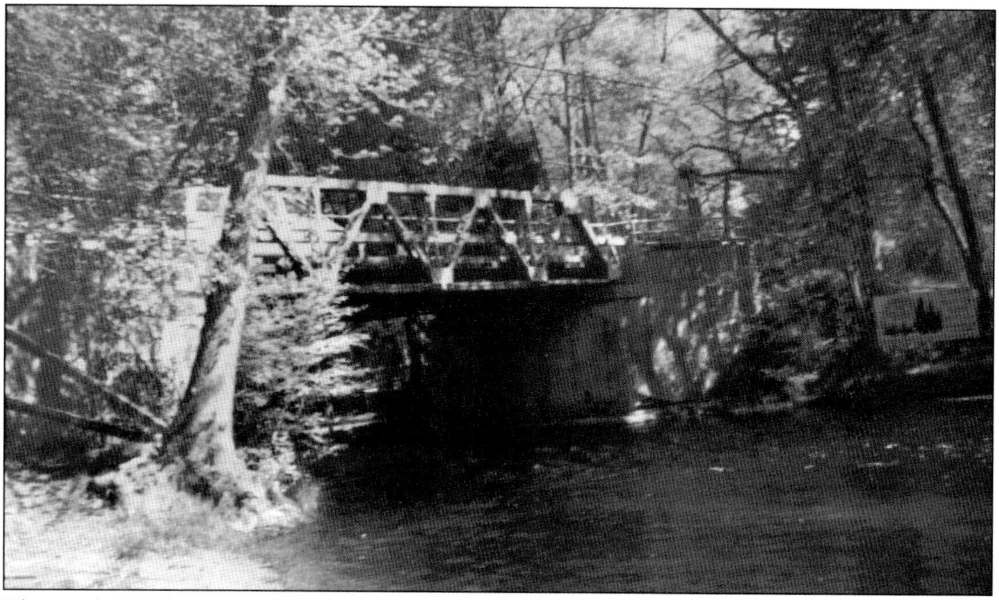

This is the bridge over the Great Egg Harbor River at the Weymouth Iron Works. It is a Warren pony truss bridge and was recently placed on the New Jersey Register of Historic Places. This bridge design was patented in 1848 by James Warren and Willoughby Monzoni.

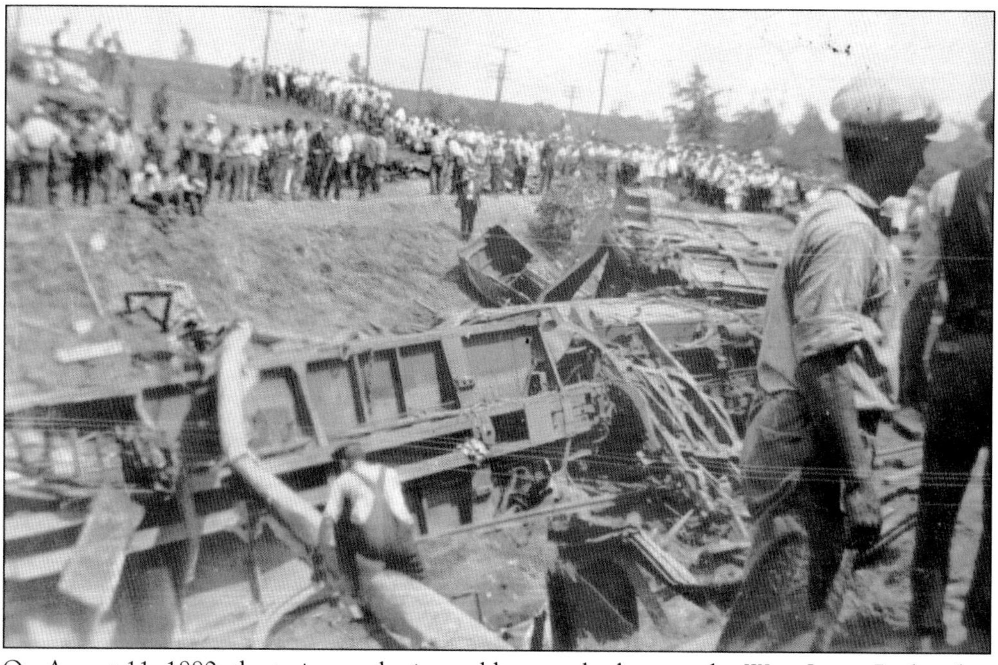

On August 11, 1880, the train wreck pictured here took place on the West Jersey Railroad at the intersection of Main Street in Mays Landing, killing 27 and injuring 40 more. Steam from the locomotive filled the crashed coach, and those not killed by the impact were scalded. The passengers were members of St. Ann's Literary Society of Philadelphia who had been enjoying an excursion to the New Jersey shore. The wreck occurred only a few weeks after the railroad was officially opened.

Three

EDUCATION AND RELIGION

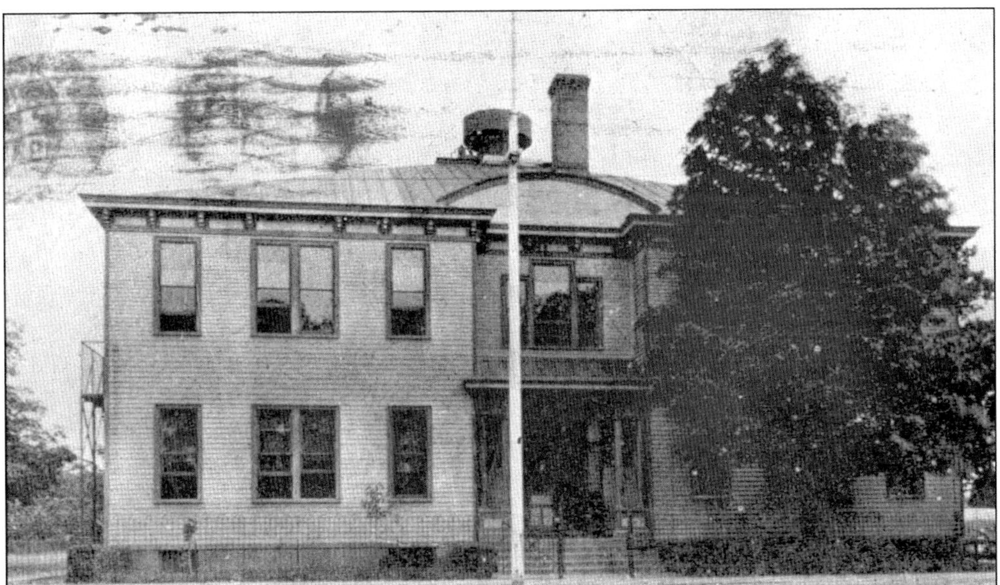

The two-room Old Wooden School was located between Second and Third Streets facing Farragut Avenue in Mays Landing. It was built in 1868 and was enlarged to three rooms in 1874. By early 1890, it had four rooms. It was rebuilt in 1908–1909, ultimately containing eight rooms, an assembly room, and a principal's office.

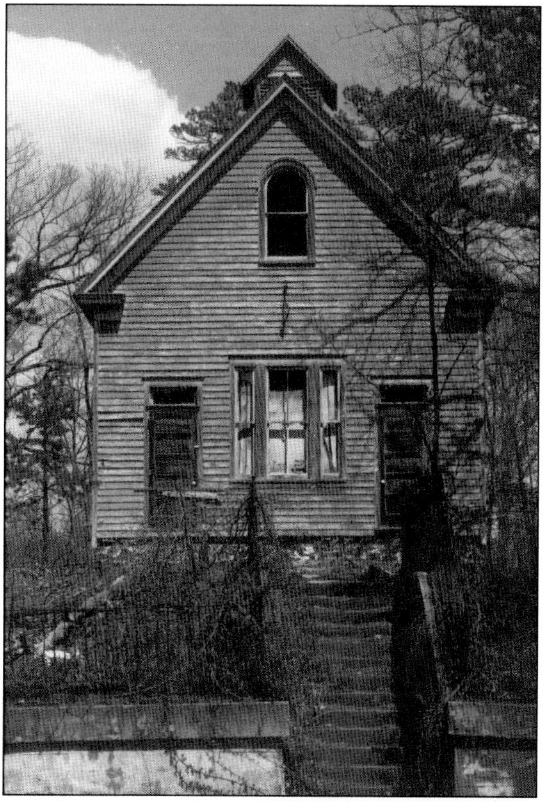

Built *c.* 1887 on property deeded by the Honorable Charles T. Abbott, the Gravelly Run School on Mays Landing-Somers Point Road, Route 559, served local schoolchildren until 1916. It is now a private home.

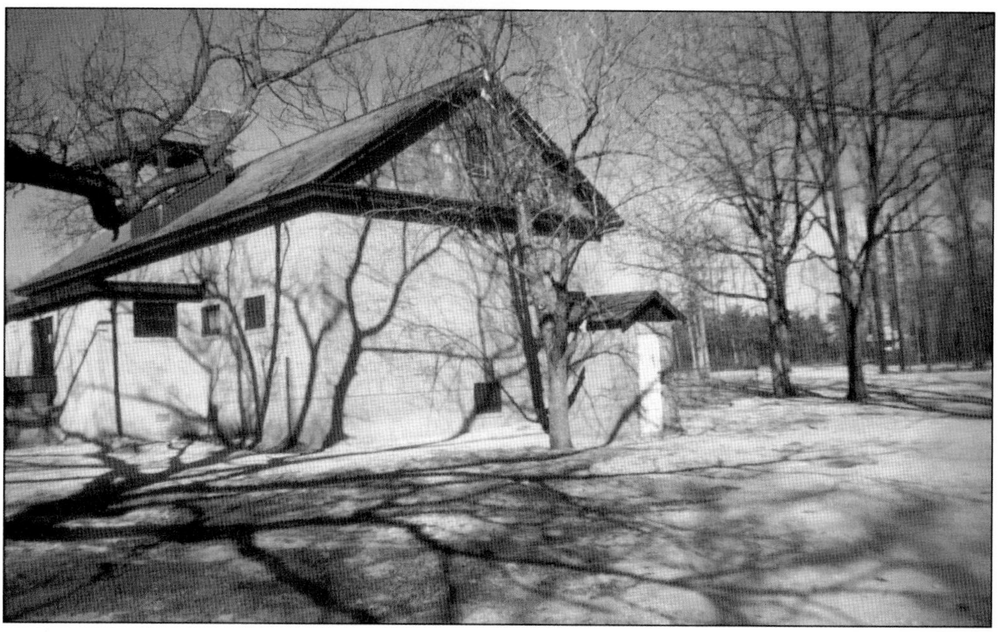

In the 1930s, there were four grades in each of the two-rooms of the Mizpah School House, located on DeHirsch Avenue in the Mizpah section of the township. Mizpah was named by the original Russian Jewish immigrants. According to the Bible, the word means, "May the Lord watch over thee while we are absent from one another."

Students from the Cologne School No. 9 pose for a photograph *c.* 1911. From left to right are the following: (first row) Marie McKeever, Ada Rice, Phyllis Rice, Anna Eaton, Emilie Bruckner, and Gregory Hagel; (second row) Katie Liepe, Marjory Schaab, Gertrude Schmidt, Edna Baur, and Mary Rice; (third row) August Baur, George Corbett, and Theresa Hagel; (fourth row) William Rice, Albert Gainsford, and Fred Liepe; (fifth row) Herman Liepe, George Liepe, Edward Corbett, and their teacher, Miss Whitman.

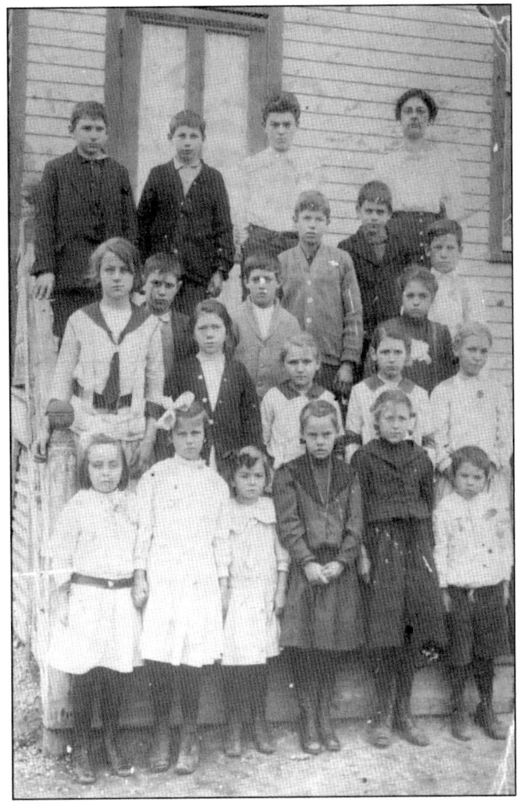

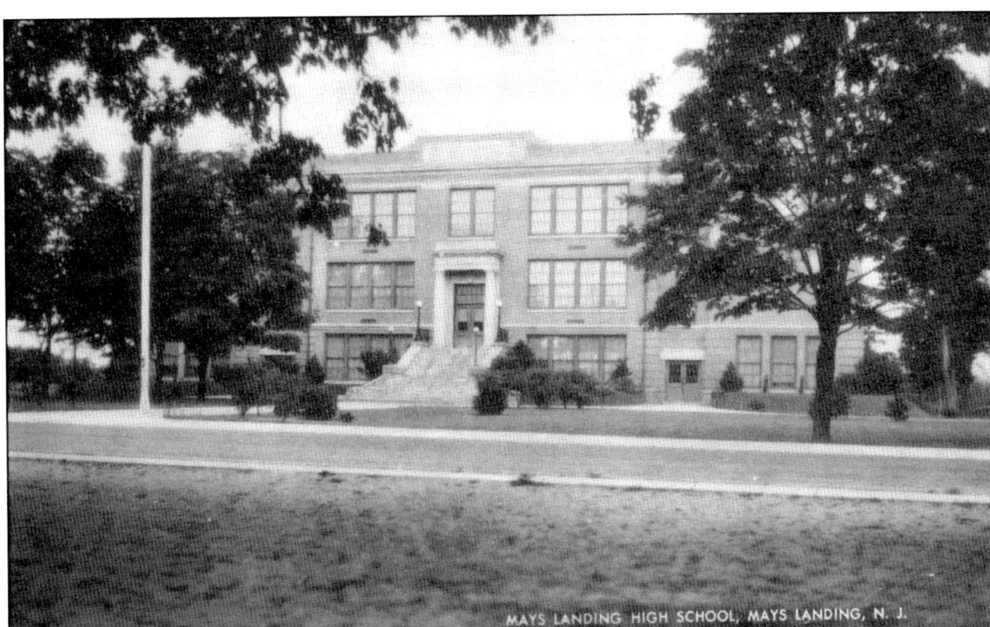

Built in 1928, this school housed kindergarten through 10th grade and was called Mays Landing High School. It became an elementary school in 1947 and was dedicated to J. Harold Duberson in 1972.

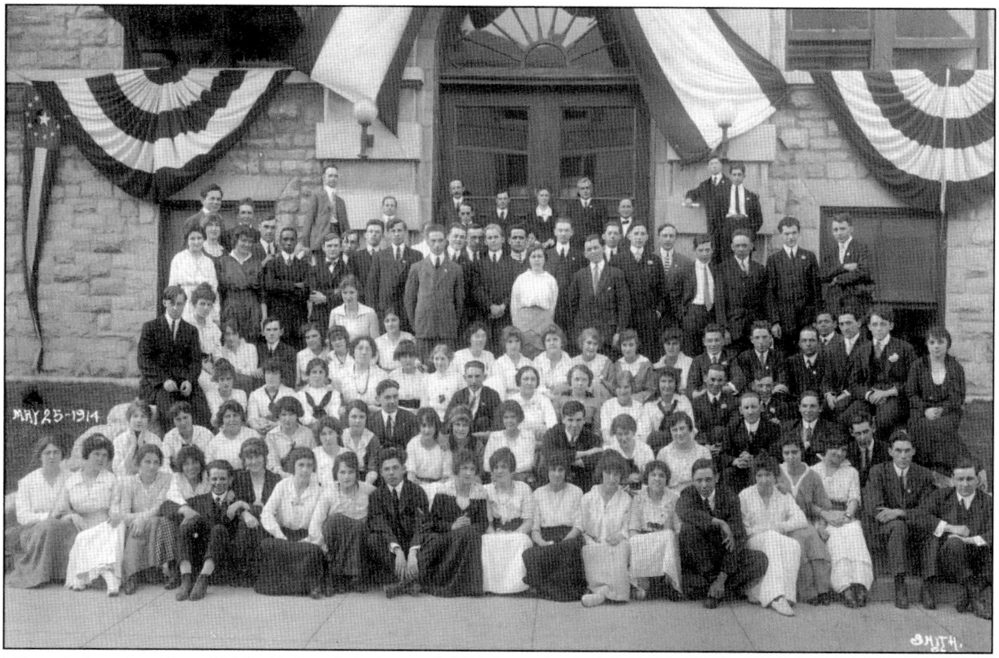

The Atlantic City High School Class of 1914 included many students from Mays Landing. Mays Landing High School (now Duberson) included only up to the 10th grade. For subsequent grades, Mays Landing students commuted to Atlantic City by train.

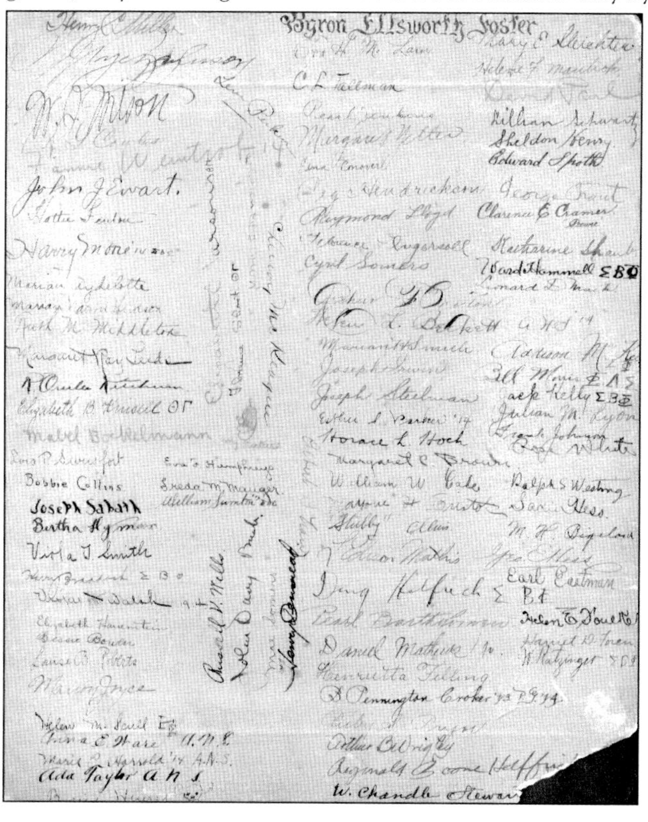

According to tradition, each graduate signed the reverse side of the class photograph, much as students in later years signed yearbooks. These are the signatures of the Class of 1914.

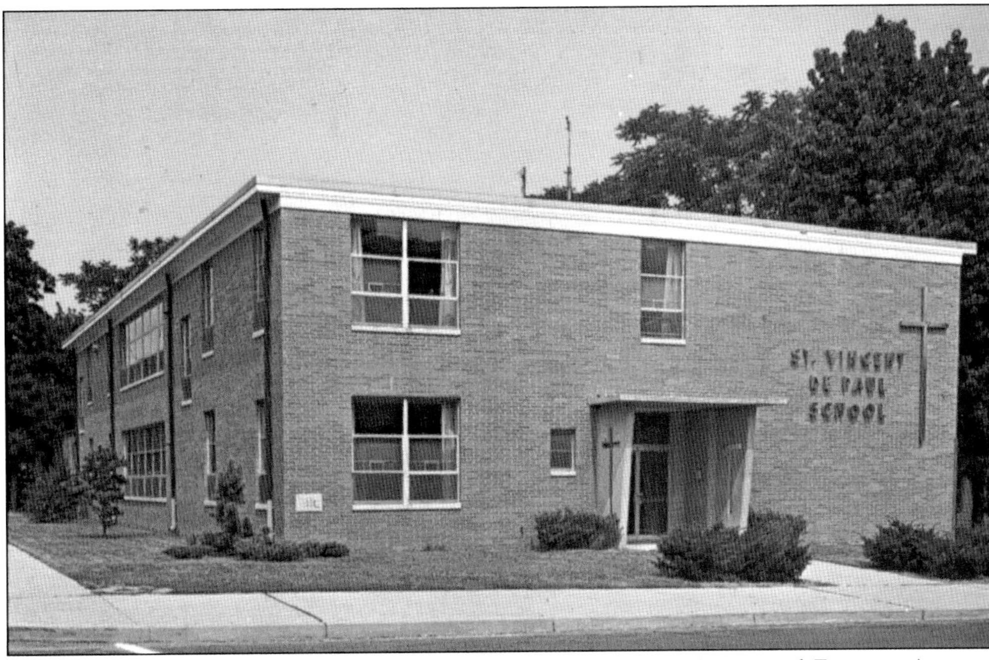

The St. Vincent De Paul Elementary School, located at Main Street and Farragut Avenue, opened in 1961. It stands on the site of the former Bethlehem Inn and Underhill's Store.

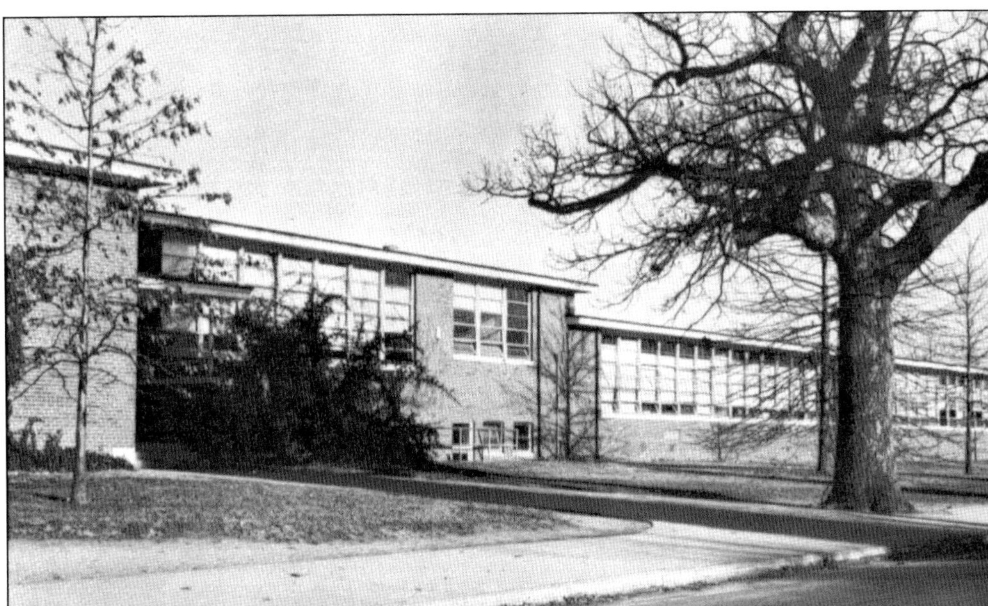

Shaner School, an elementary school, was built in 1957. Located on the corner of Third Street and Farragut Avenue in Mays Landing, it is named in honor of Joseph C. Shaner.

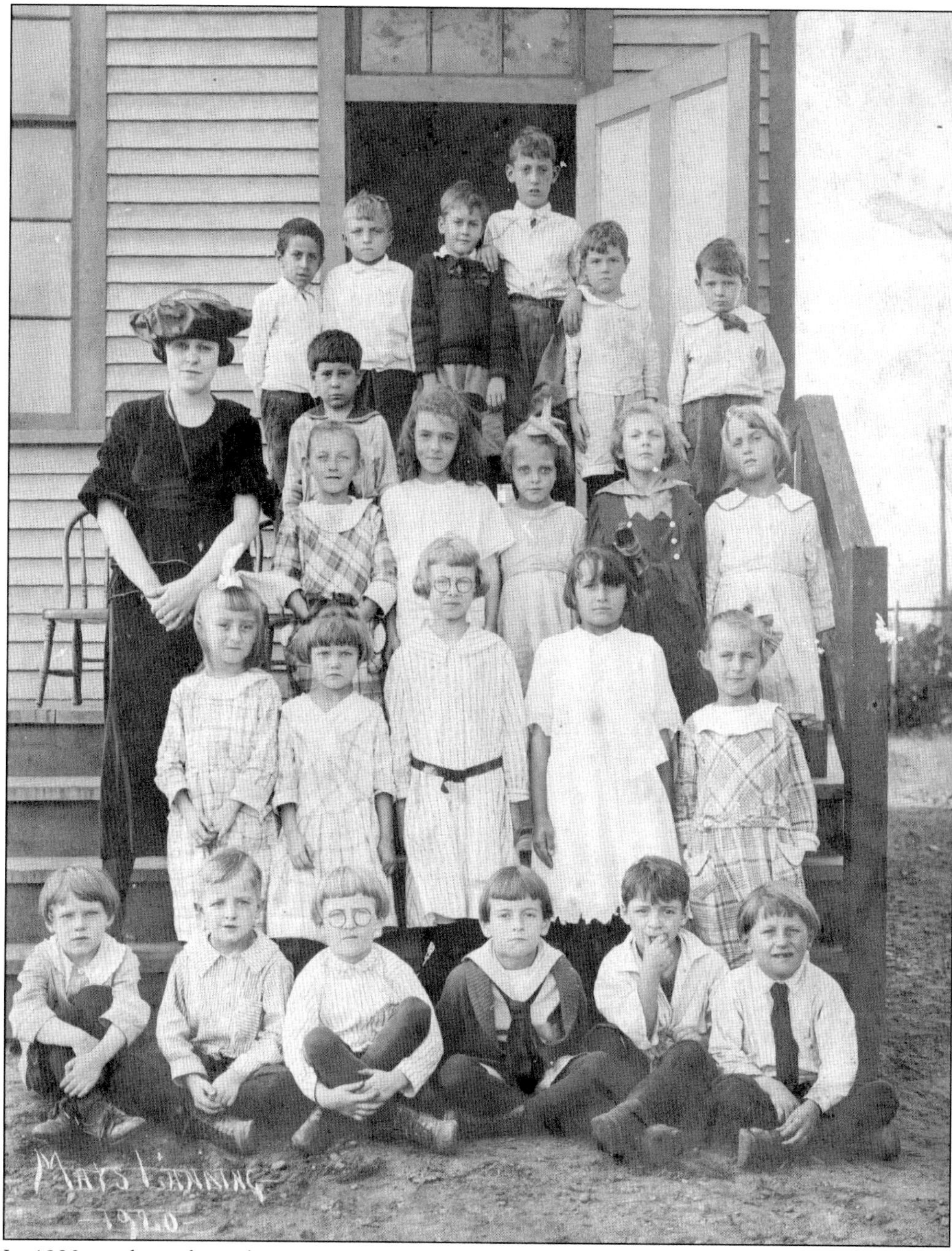

In 1920, students from the Uptown School in Mays Landing pose in front of their Little Red School House. The building is now the home of the Township of Hamilton Historical Society. Pictured, from left to right, are the following: (first row) Joseph Sorrentino, Howard Titus, ? Bruce, Donald Cline, Louis Sorrentino, and Frank Onda; (second row) Anna Barry, Geneva Coventry, Sarah Schenck, Margaret Lorenz, and Gladys Fisher; (third row) Verna Applegate (teacher), Frances Fisher, Elizabeth Haines, Bertha Titus, Emma Lashley, and Rose Lorenz; (fourth row) Joseph Bush; (fifth row) John Francisco, Mike Bozak, Paul Taylor, Louis Grob, John Leach, and ? Turp.

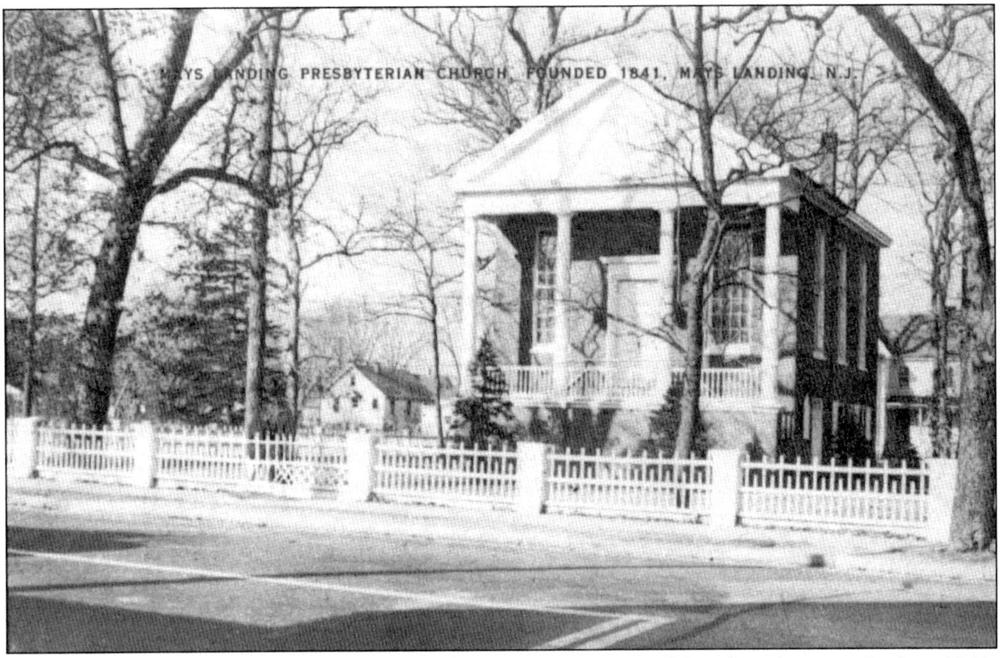

The cornerstone of the Presbyterian church on Main Street in Mays Landing was laid in 1841. The church was built on land donated by Samuel Richards and was dedicated in 1844. In 1866, the building was used for a church-sponsored school. It is still in use today and is on the New Jersey Register of Historic Places.

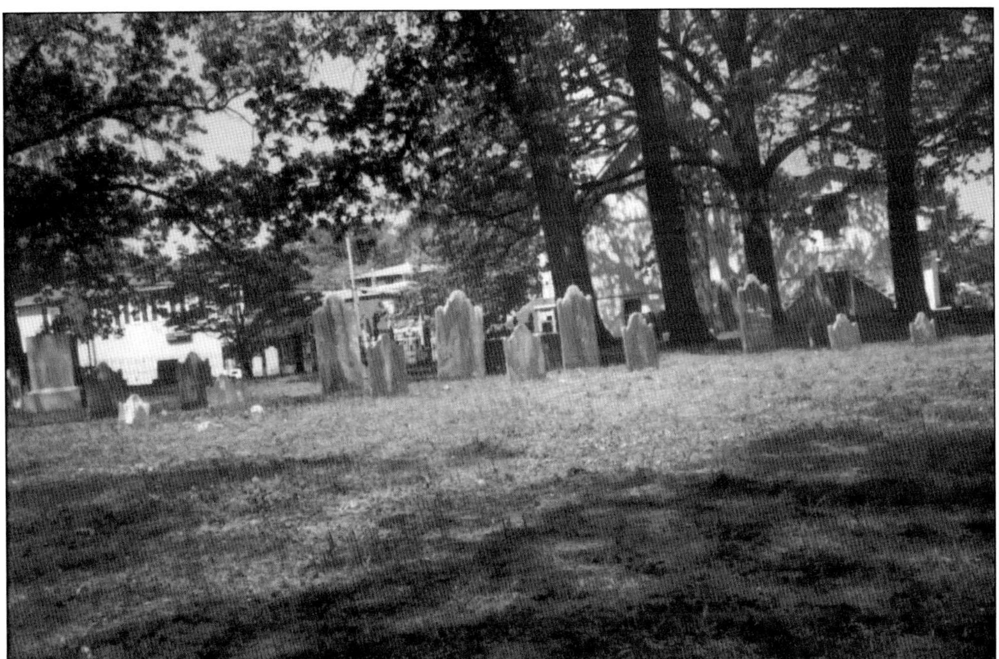

The Wescoat Free Burial Ground is located between the Methodist and Presbyterian churches on Main Street in Mays Landing.

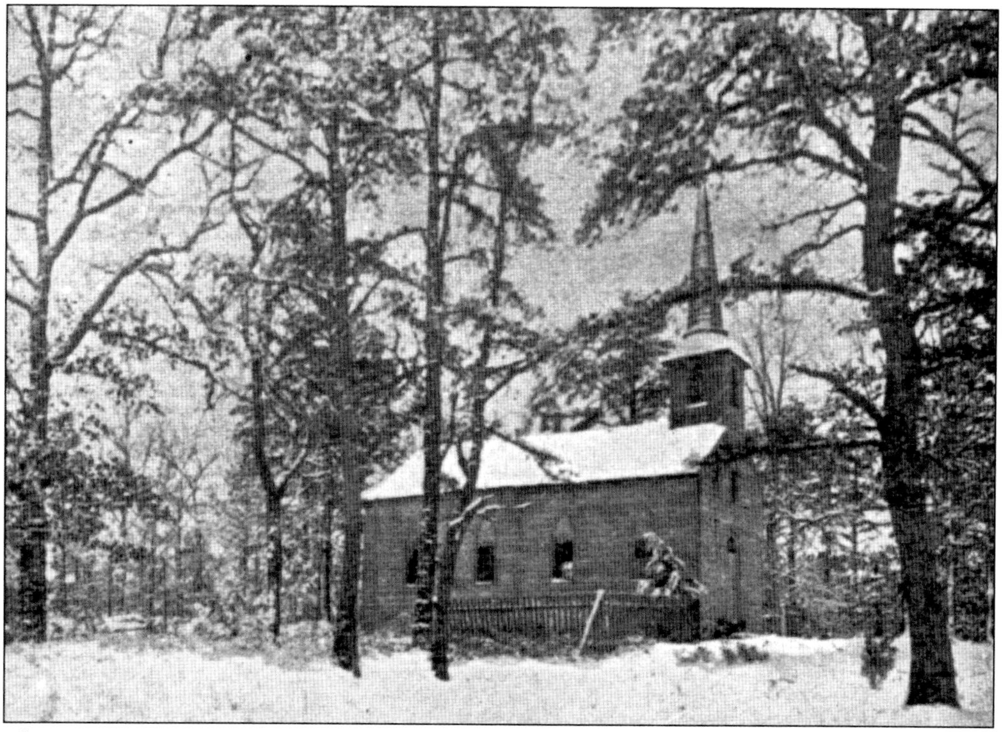

This picturesque scene includes the Catawba Church, located in the Catawba section of the township.

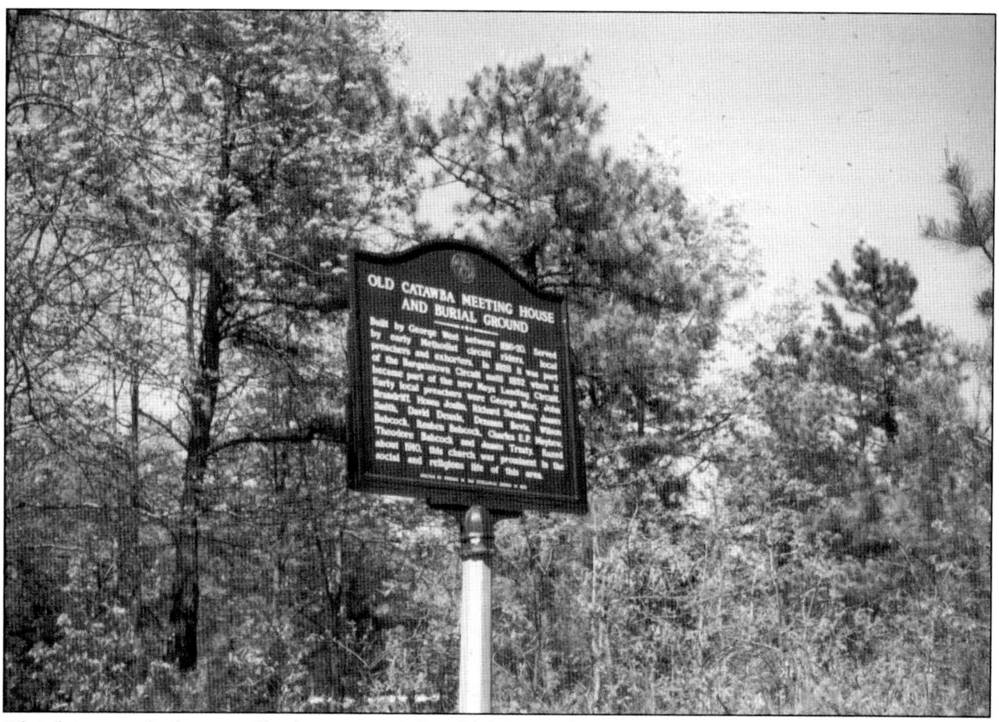

This historical plaque tells the story of the Old Catawba Meeting House and Burial Ground.

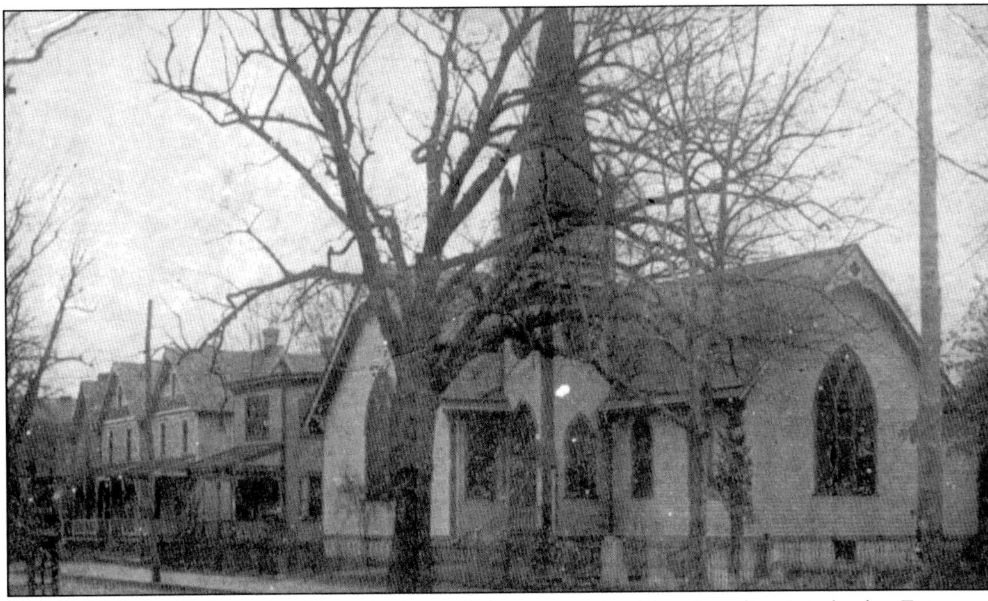

The First United Methodist Church, formerly known as the Mays Landing Methodist Episcopal Church, was completed in 1848. It was later destroyed by fire and, in 1888, was rebuilt. It is located on Main Street in Mays Landing.

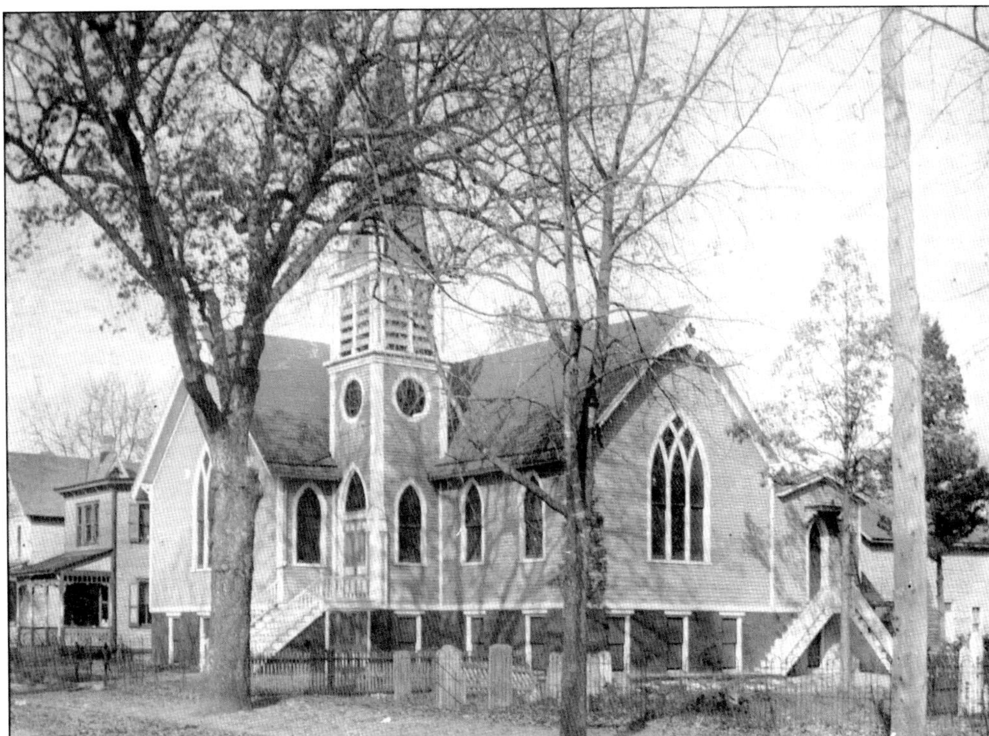

In 1910, the First United Methodist Church building was elevated to provide basement classrooms for Sunday school sessions. The building was remodeled in 1924. Today, the church is known as the United Methodist Church.

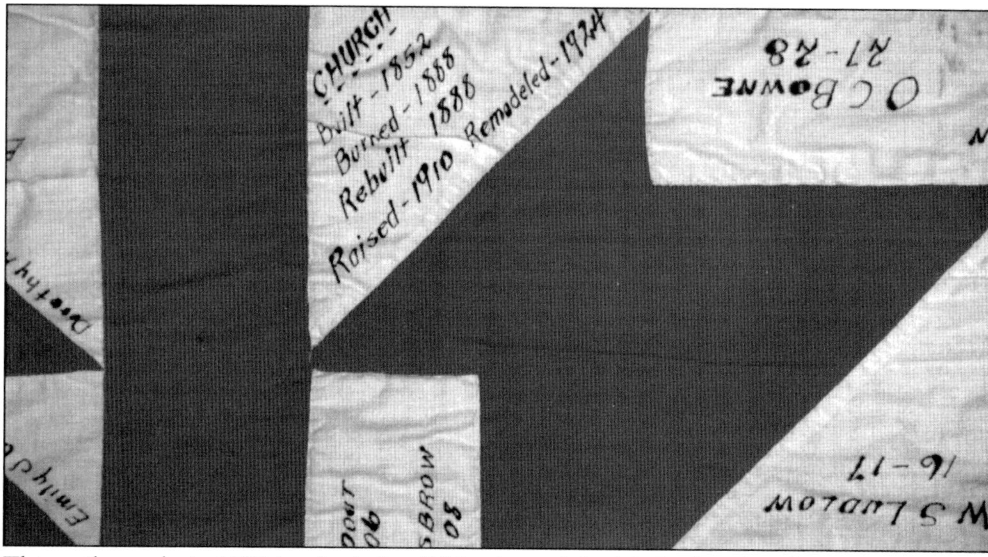

This quilt, made in 1928 by the ladies Bible class of the Methodist church, was created as a fundraiser. Individuals paid a nominal fee to have their names included on the quilt. It was then auctioned off, purchased by Burton A. Gaskill. It is now the property of the Township of Hamilton Historical Society.

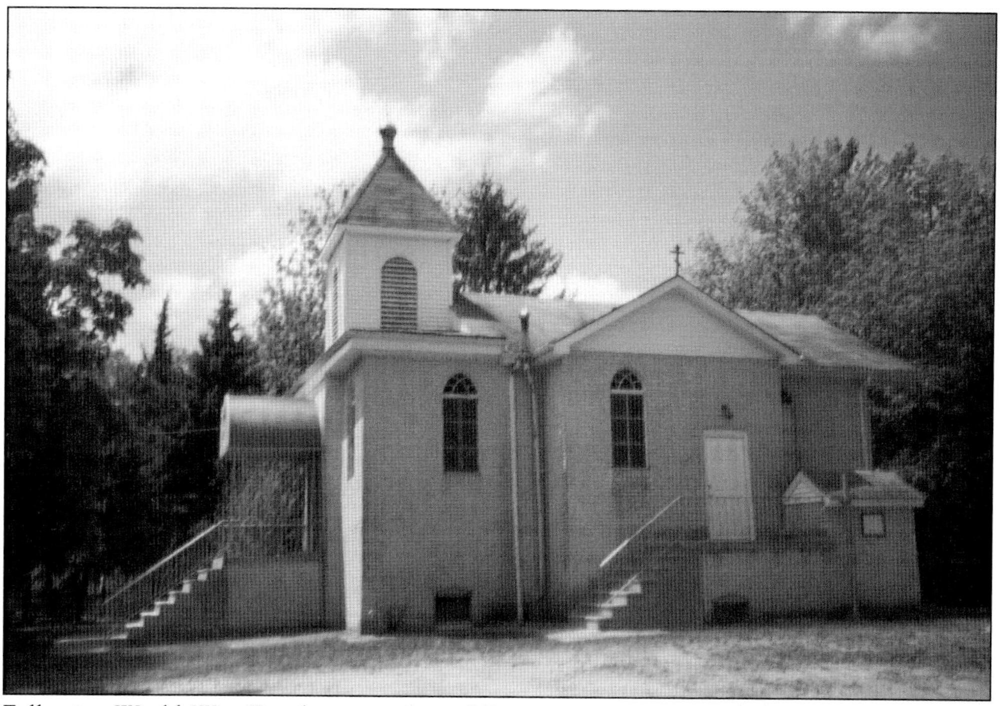

Following World War II, a large number of Russian immigrants settled in the Township of Hamilton. Wasily and Valentina Fursin purchased the 115-year-old American Hotel on Main Street in Mays Landing from Michael Suprin on October 14, 1954. The hotel subsequently became known locally as the Russian Hotel or the Russian Embassy. This photograph shows the Russian Orthodox Church of the Mother of God, located on Hudson Street in Mays Landing.

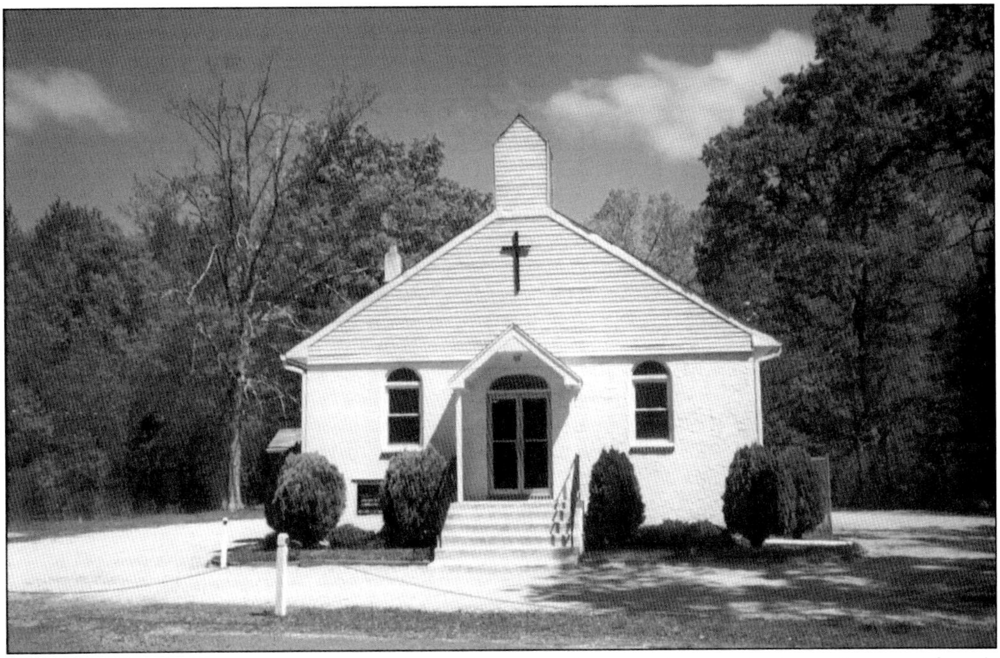

The Bears Head section of the township is home to the New Mount Calvary Baptist Church on Millville Road.

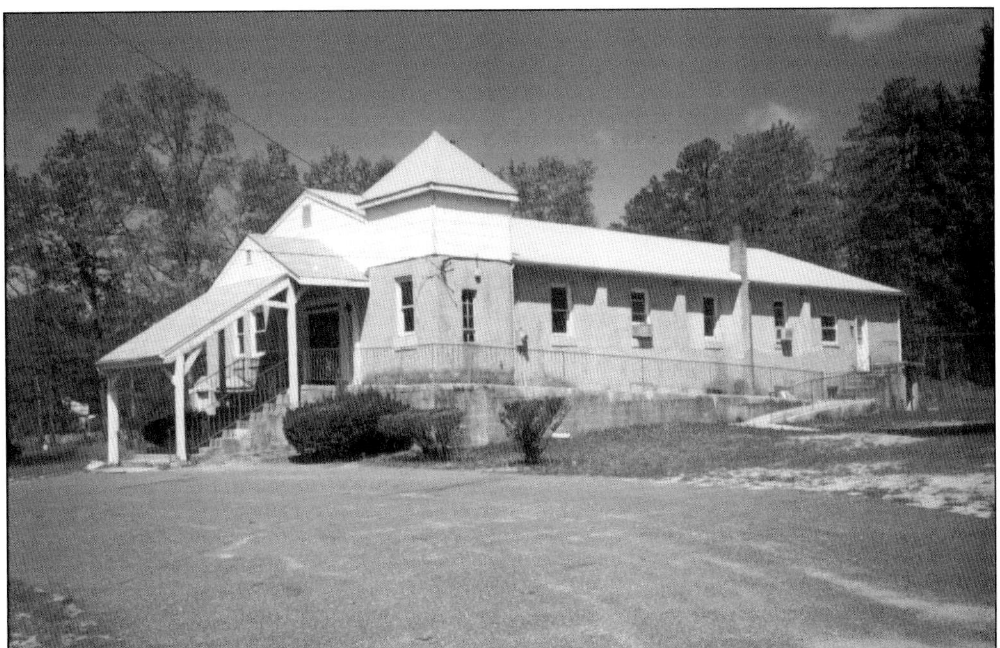

The St. James AME Church is also located on Millville Road in the Bears Head section.

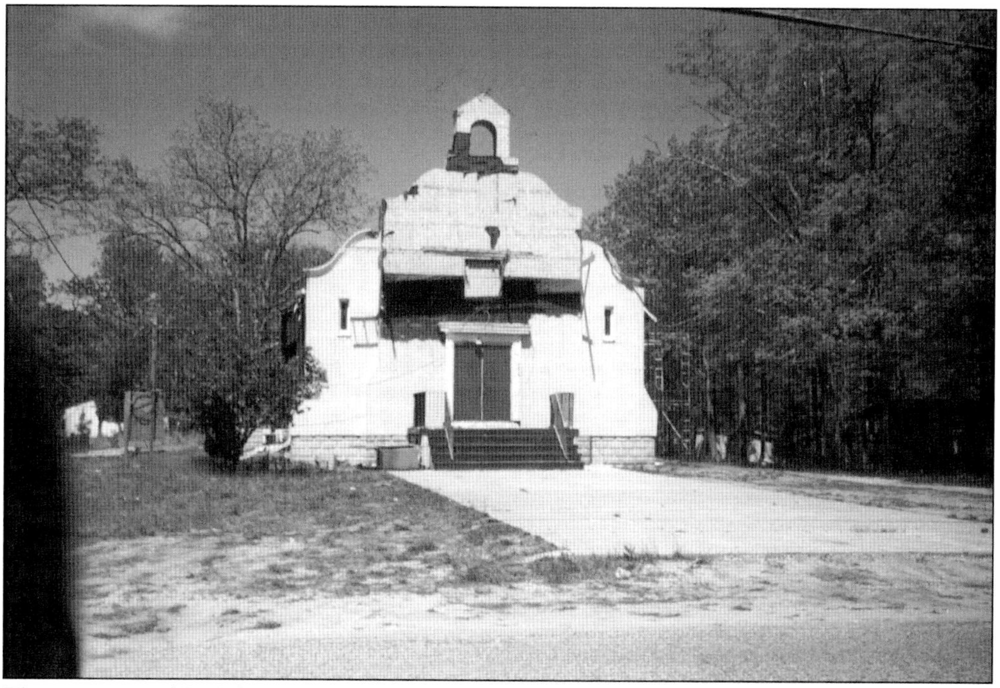

This is a view of St. John's Catholic Church on DeHirsch Avenue in the Mizpah section. It is currently undergoing renovation.

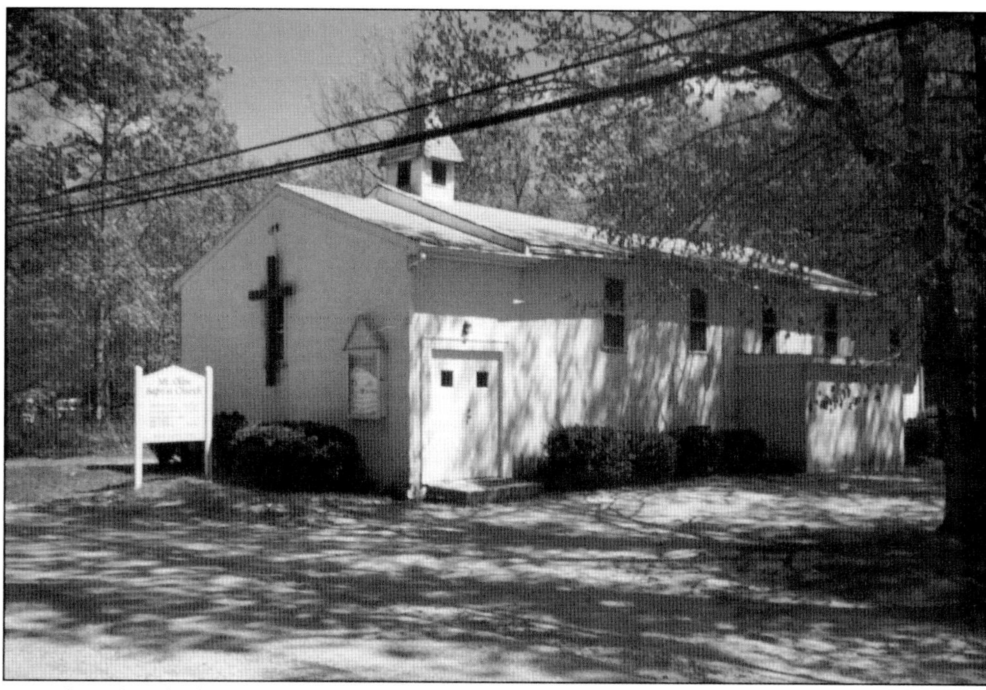

Mizpah is also the home of the Mount Olive Baptist Church, located on Strand Avenue.

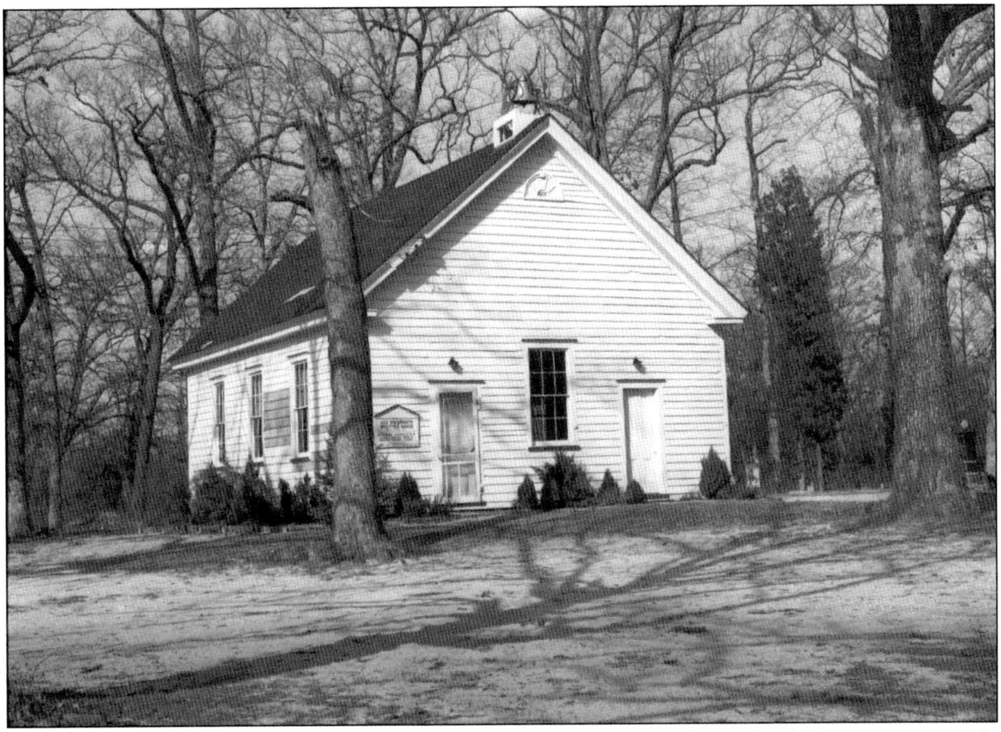

The United Methodist Church at Weymouth was built in 1805 by Samuel Richards primarily for the workers at the Weymouth Iron Furnace. Services are still held there each Sunday. The adjoining cemetery contains many graves of iron foundry workers and some markers made from Weymouth iron.

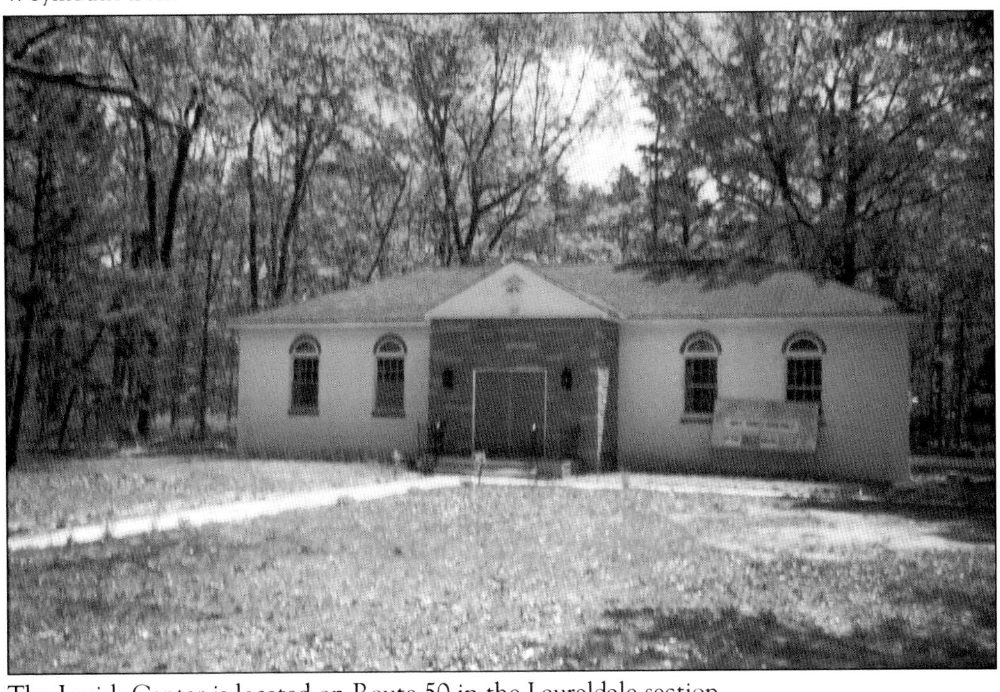

The Jewish Center is located on Route 50 in the Laureldale section.

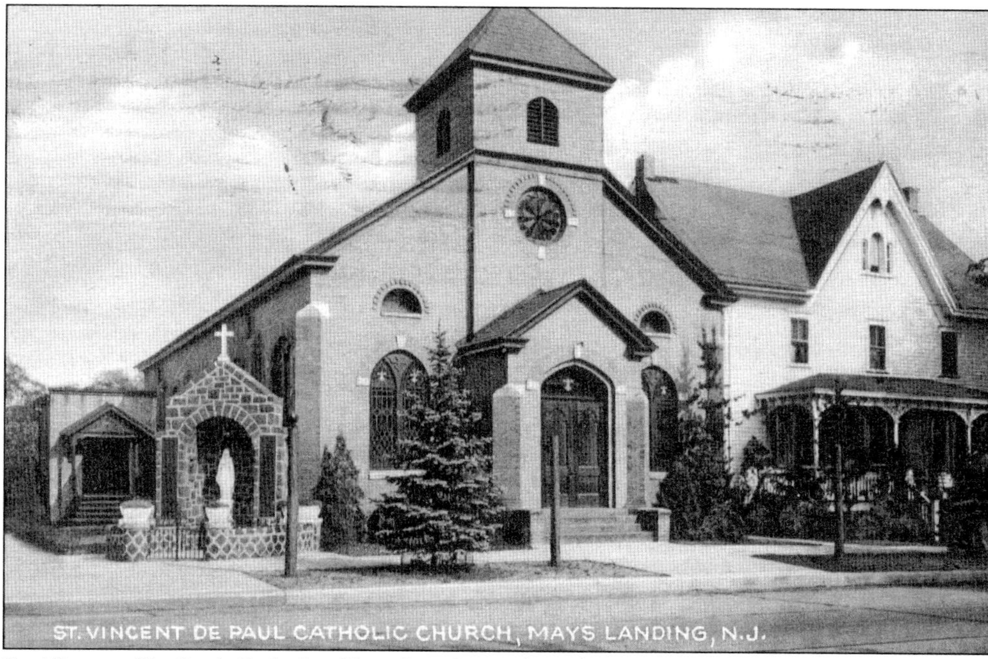

St. Vincent De Paul Catholic Church is located at the corner of Second Street and Cape May Avenue in Mays Landing. The rectory once served as the home of the Atlantic County sheriff when it was located on Farragut Avenue. The church's cornerstone was laid in 1907 and dedicated in 1908.

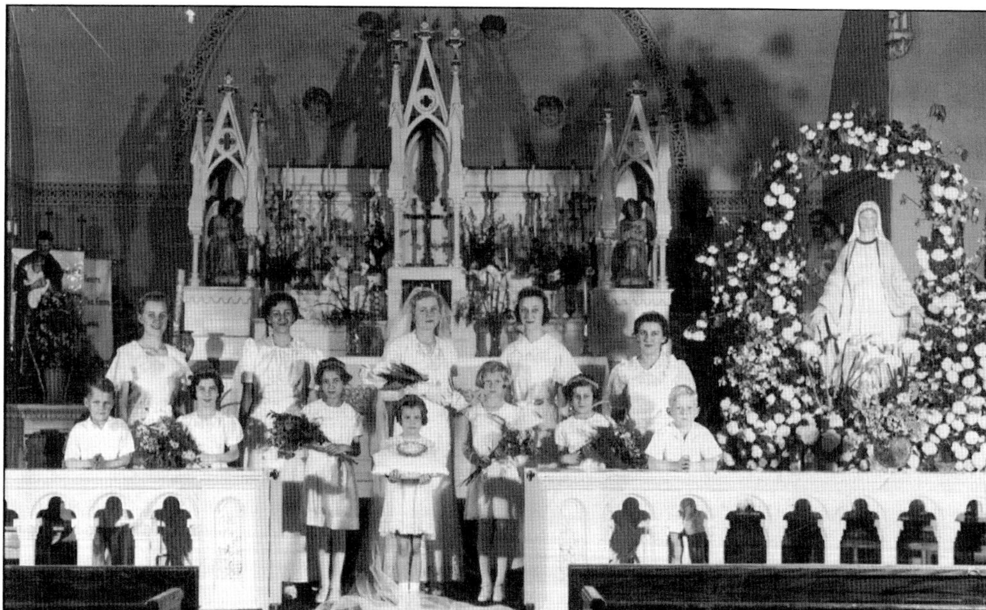

Inside St. Vincent De Paul Catholic Church, a May crowning ceremony was held in front of the ornate altar. Pictured, from left to right, are the following: (front row) unidentified, Rita Cahill Anderson Ricci, Mary Piriello, unidentified, unidentified, Antoinette Cristinzio, and unidentified; (back row) unidentified, unidentified, Agnes Boreyko Petusky, Anna Barry, and Elizabeth Wagner.

Four

Recreation and Sports

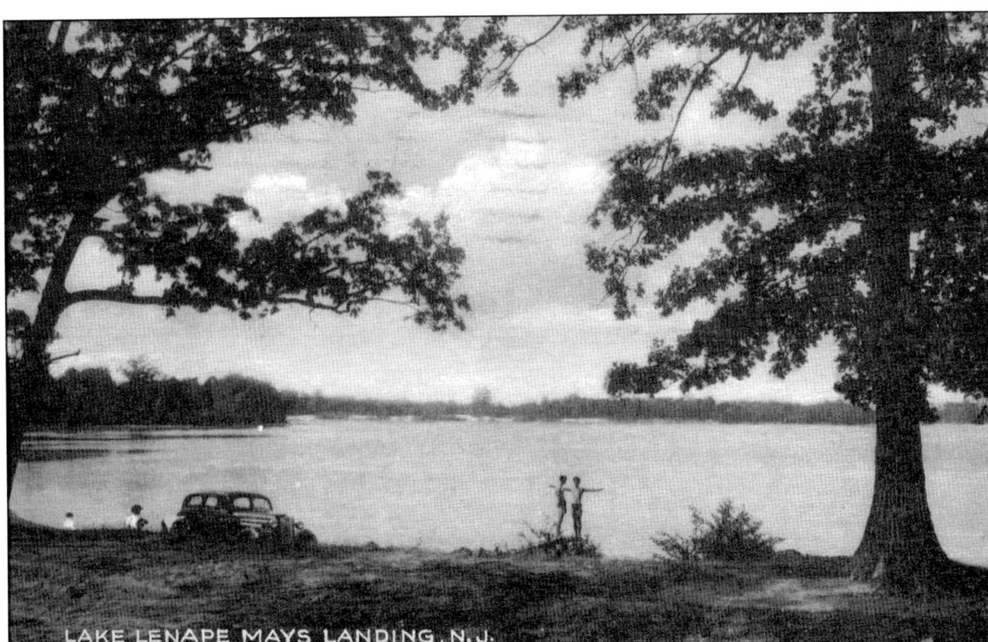

Since its formation in 1844, Lake Lenape has provided year-round water sports and entertainment, not only for local residents but also for many visitors to the region.

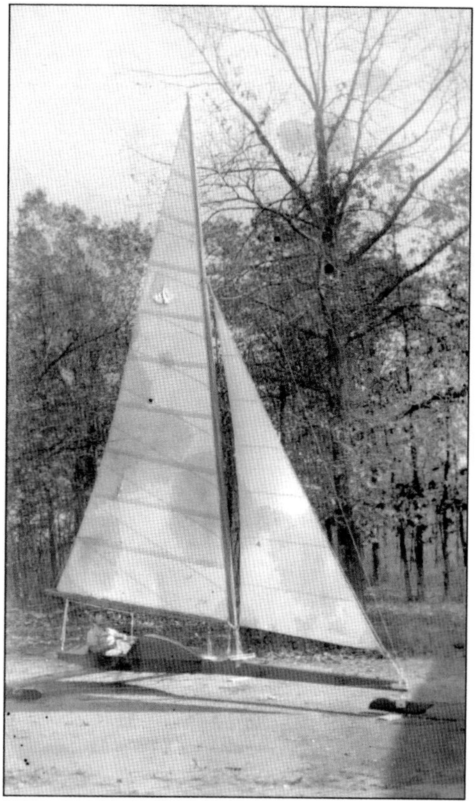

As shown by this iceboat on the beach at Lake Lenape, the coming of winter was also a welcome opportunity for enjoying the lake.

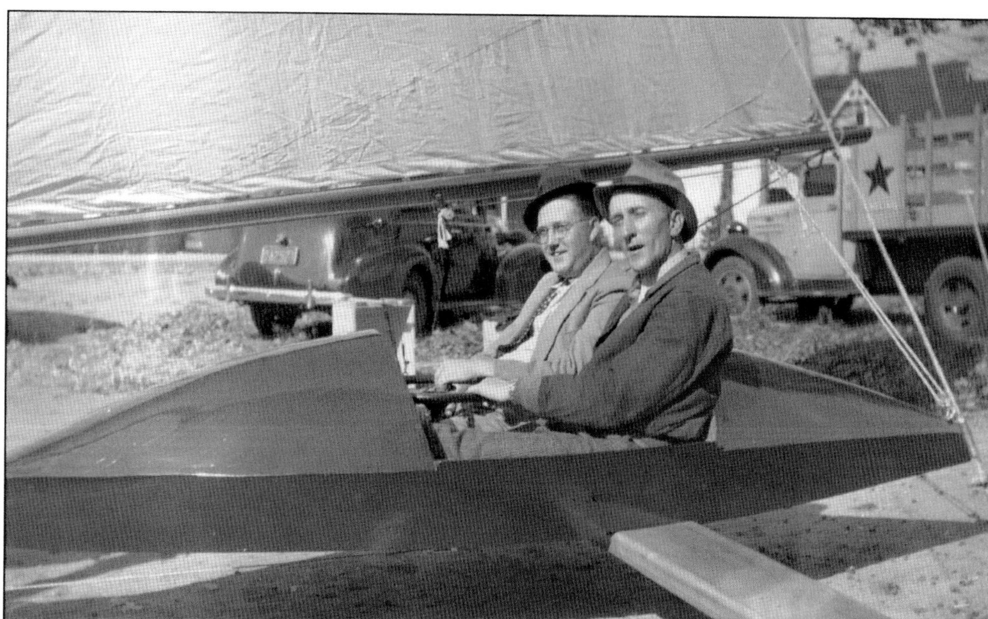

Tom Chard (left) and Joseph Kirkpatrick are ready to put their iceboat on Lake Lenape.

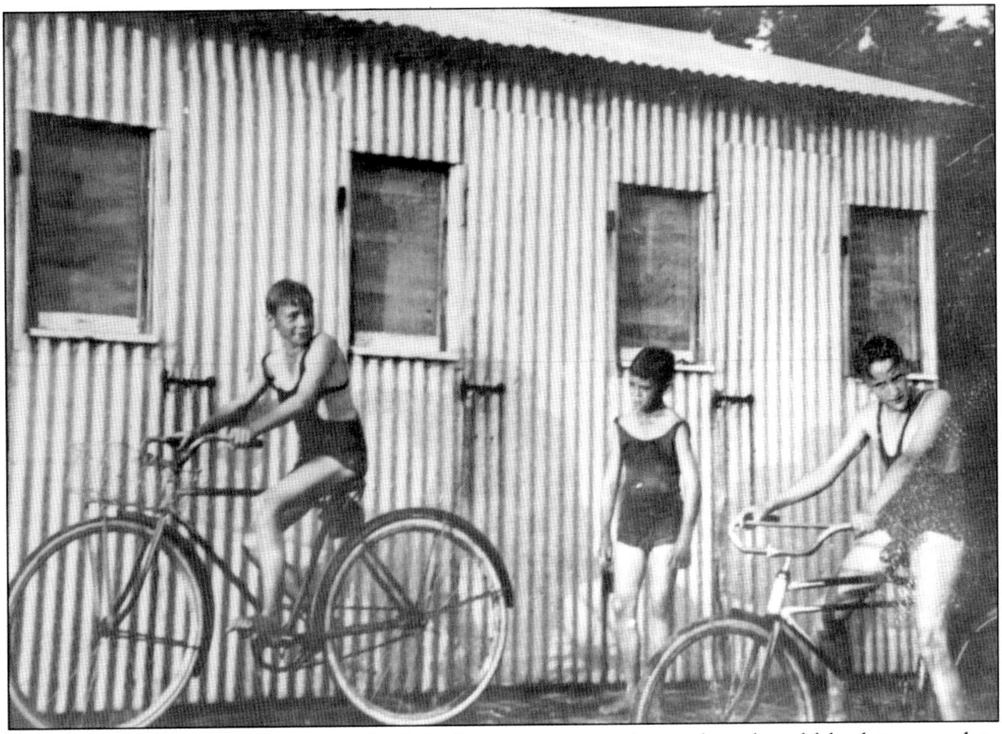

George H. Liepe's boathouse and bath locker rooms were located at the old bathing pond in Cologne. Pictured, from left to right, are Rudy Foell Jr., Dominic Hagel, and unidentified.

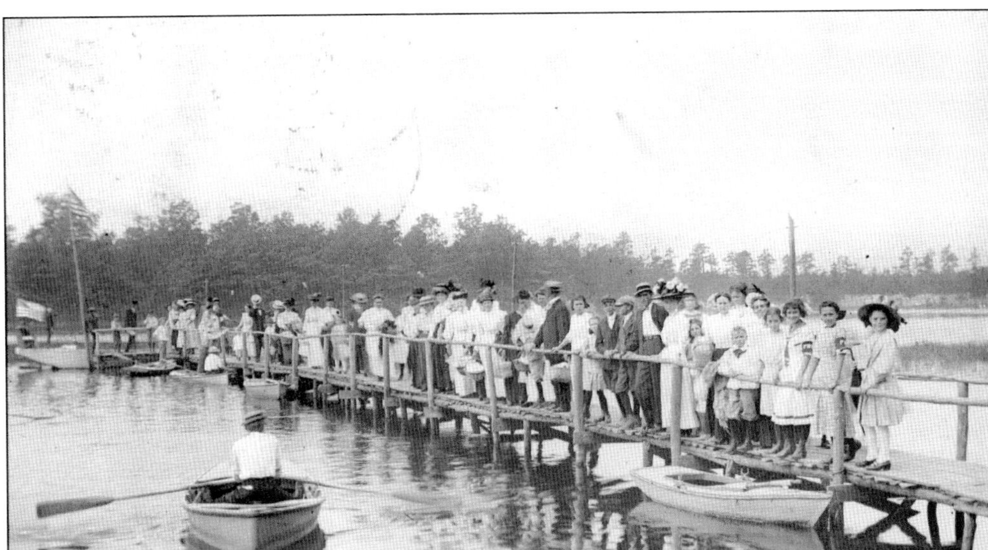

Lenape Park in Mays Landing, originally known as Leiling's Park, opened in 1906 and was the site of many excursions and group picnics. People visiting the park in the early days had to take a ride on Beach's Ferry Boat in order to access the lake area.

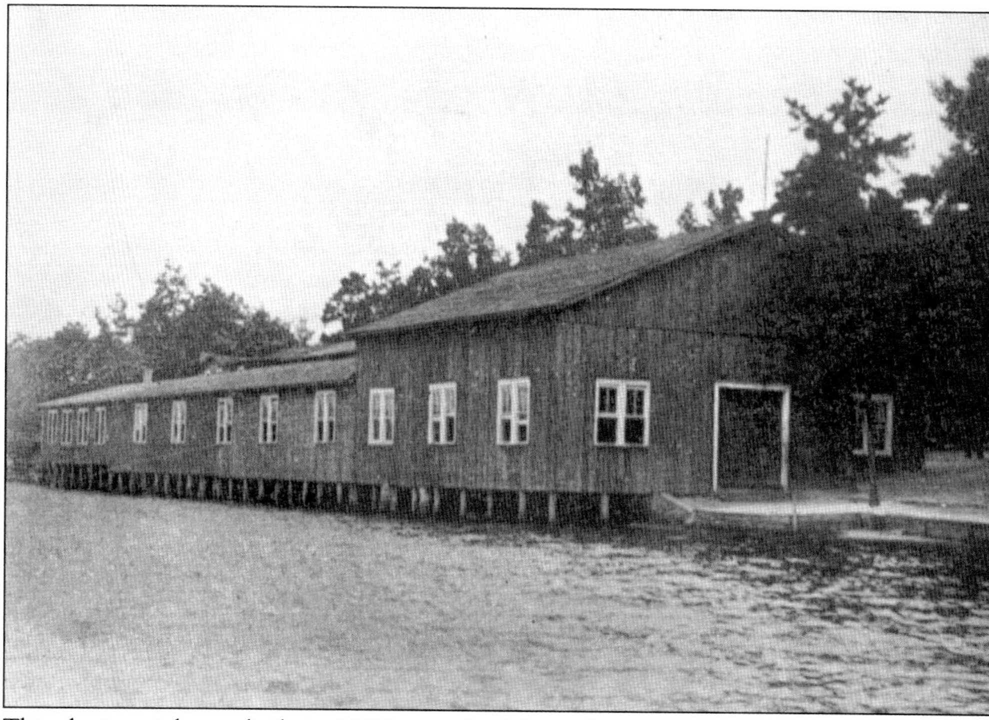

This skating rink was built in 1907 over the lake at Lenape Park. It featured an attached refreshment stand. Boarders could rent rooms on the second floor during the summers.

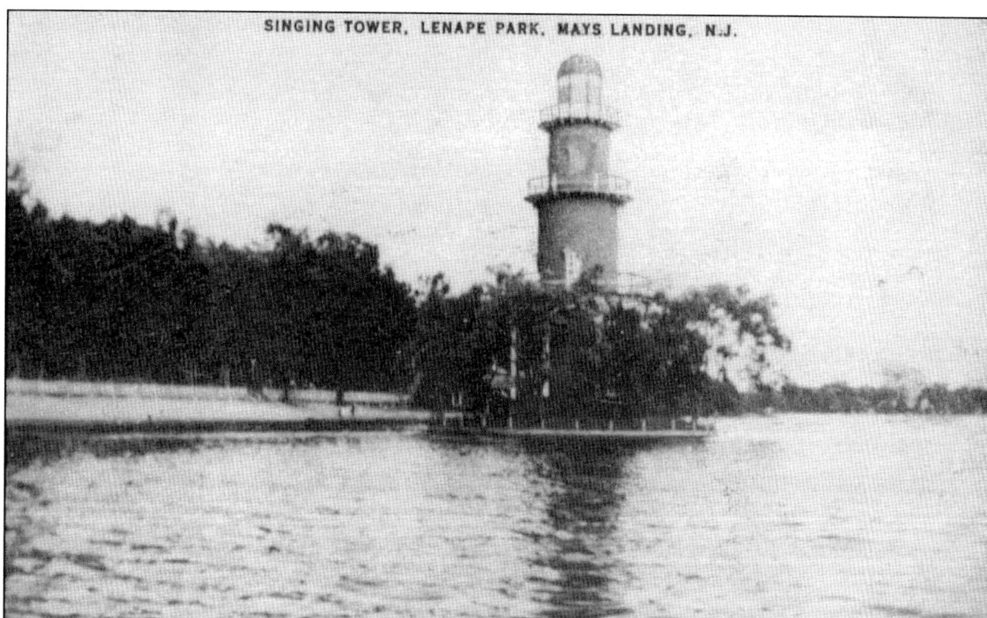

This structure has been called the Singing Tower and the Lenape Lighthouse. Completed in 1943, the tower is a landmark of Lenape Park. It was called the Singing Tower because of the music played by the owner throughout the Lenape Park summer seasons until 1960, when ownership changed.

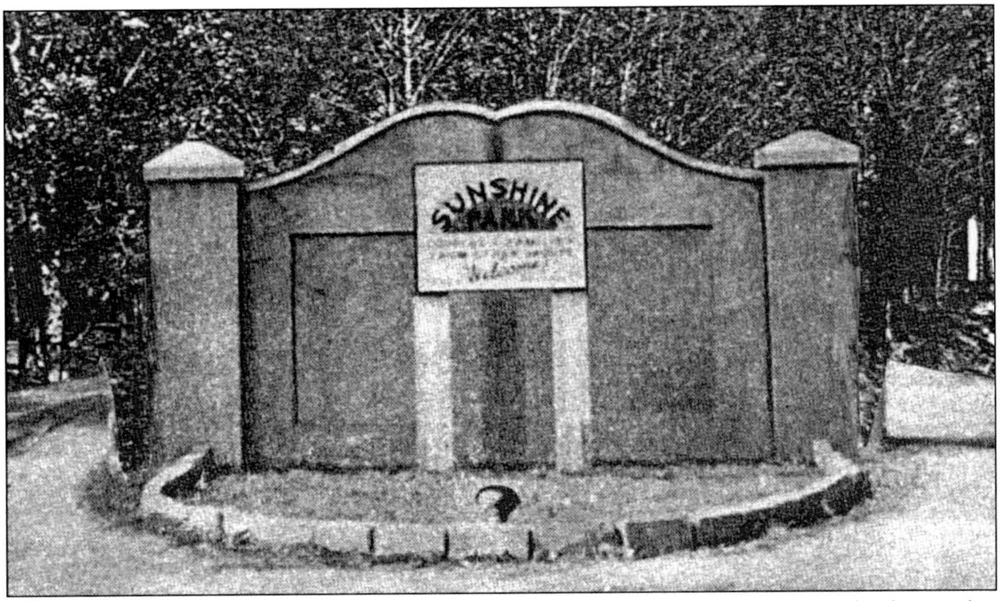

Sunshine Park, established by the Reverend Ilsley Boone in Mays Landing, was the first nudist resort in the United States. It offered a wide variety of sports facilities, housing accommodations, and excellent food. There was also an accredited private school, Sunshine Acres School, established in 1939–1940, serving preschool through high school. Reverend Boone's sister, Adeline L. Douglass, was dean of the school.

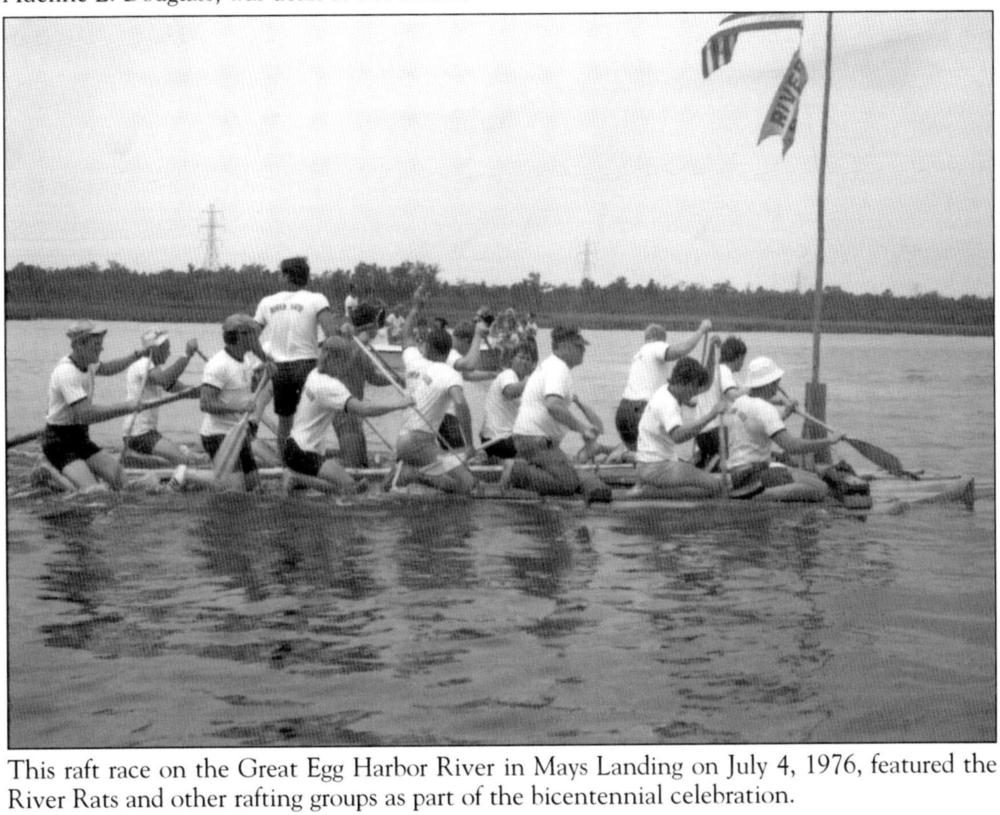

This raft race on the Great Egg Harbor River in Mays Landing on July 4, 1976, featured the River Rats and other rafting groups as part of the bicentennial celebration.

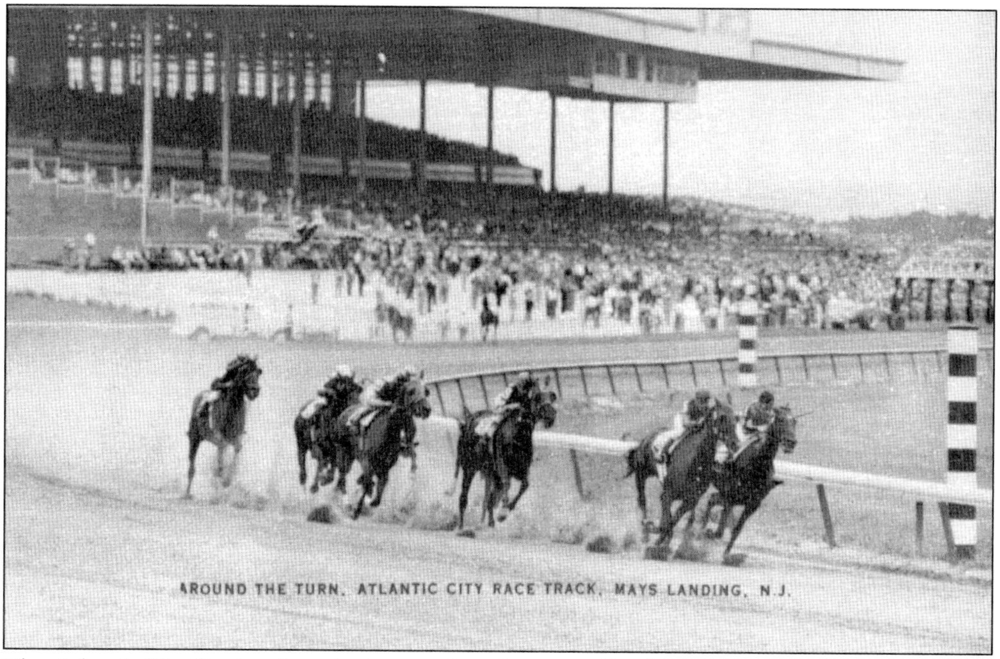

The Atlantic City Racing Association purchased a tract of land from the Township of Hamilton at the junction of Routes 40 and 322. The association, founded in 1944, counted among its original stockholders Bob Hope, Frank Sinatra, Kay Kyser, Phil Spitalny, Harry James, Xavier Cugat, and Sammy Kaye. John B. Kelly Sr., Olympic gold medal winner and father of the late Princess Grace of Monaco, was its first president.

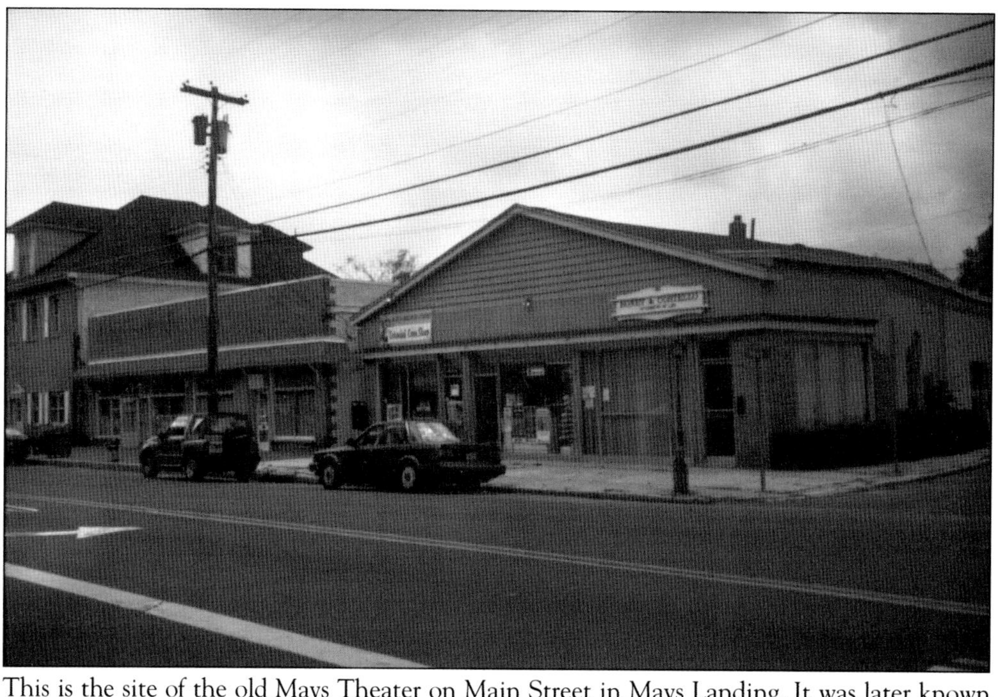

This is the site of the old Mays Theater on Main Street in Mays Landing. It was later known as the Ritz and is now occupied by several businesses.

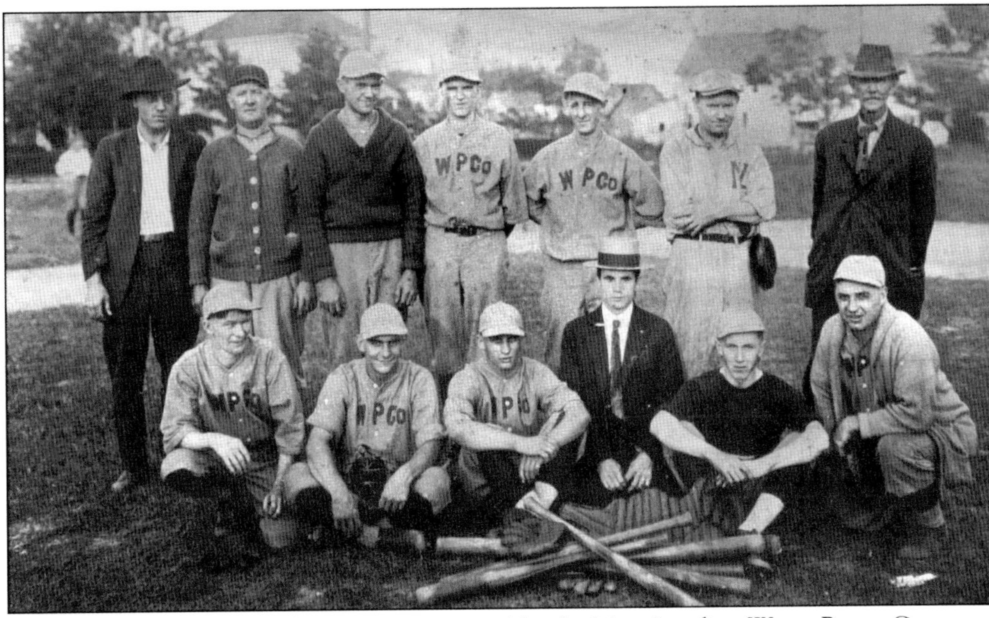

This Mays Landing baseball team was sponsored by the Mays Landing Water Power Company. The players are, from left to right, as follows: (front row) Jack Bonsall, Russell Peachey, Jack Kotansky, Robert Turp, Otis Luderitz, and Harry "Josh" Ingersoll; (back row) Jim Yanniello, Thomas Stewart, David Smith, Michael Morey, Charles Morris, Charles Coventree, and Wallace Coventree. Their field was located behind the Little Red School House on Mill Street in Mays Landing, the present site of the Township of Hamilton Historical Society.

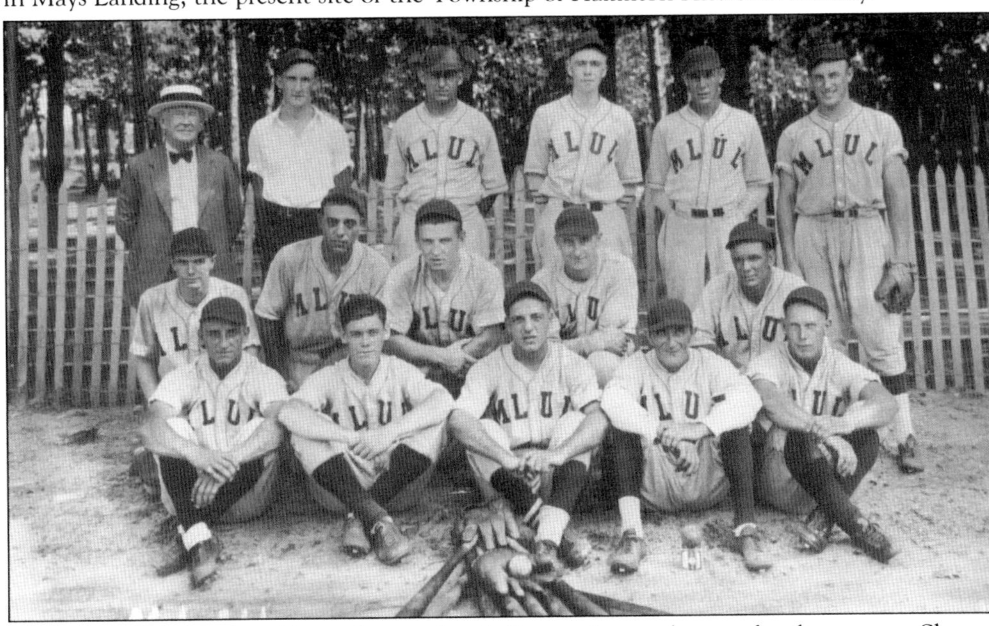

The 1934 Mays Landing Union League baseball team featured many familiar names. Shown, from left to right, are the following: (front row) Lou Kaenzig, John Slota, Carmen Yanniello, Mike Kotansky, and Gilbert Hill; (middle row) John Leach, Mike Yanniello, John Barry, Frank Onda, and Chick Kisby; (back row) coach Harry Wilson, pitcher Doug Kisby, John Lapihuska, Jack McCallum, Bill Kraus, and Jake Schusler.

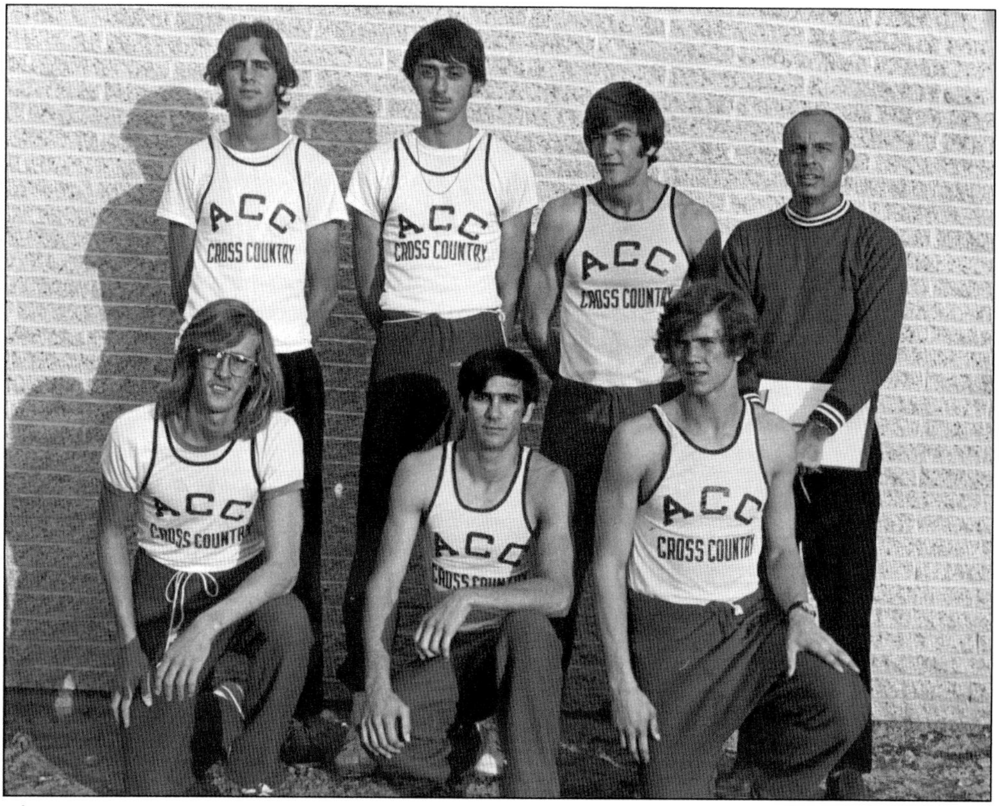

These cross-country athletes proudly represented the Atlantic Community College in Mays Landing, now known as Atlantic Cape Community College.

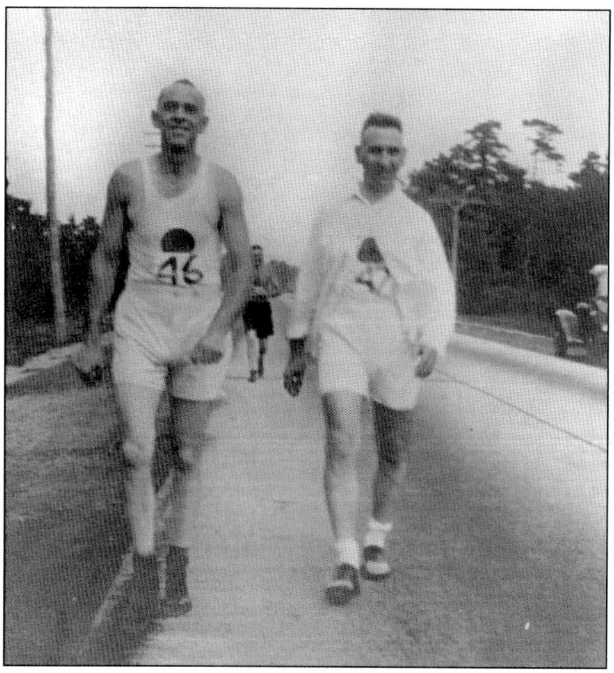

Township of Hamilton marathon runners Maurice Aaron and Henry Denmead are shown *c.* 1930.

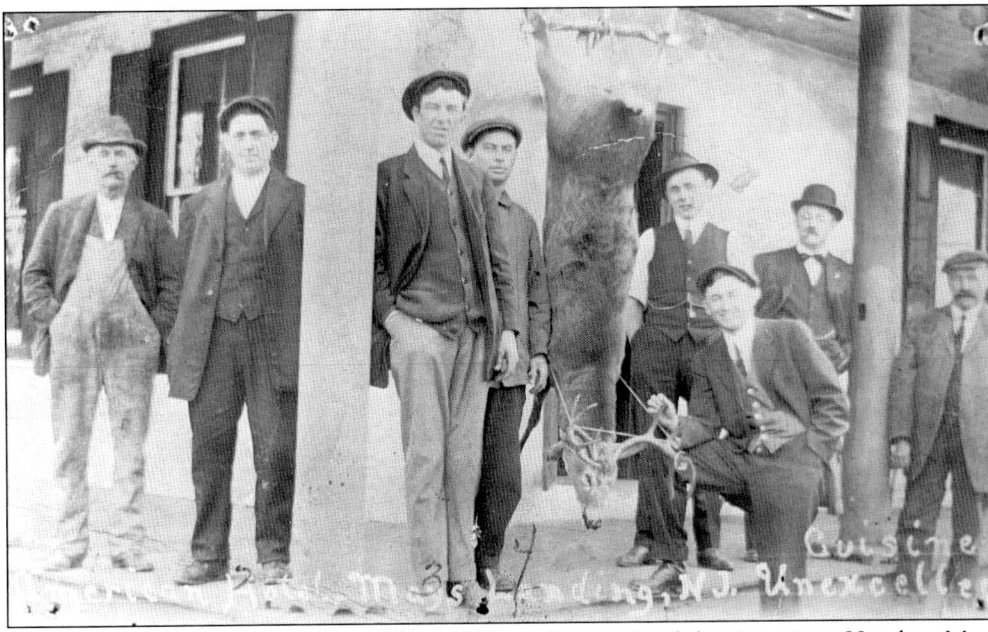

Local hunters proudly show their kill *c.* 1917 on the porch of the American Hotel in Mays Landing. Pictured, from left to right, are George Washington Norcross, Tony Aurelio, Bigee Ripley, Mart Ingersoll, ? Bastian and his two sons, and Lorenz Leiling.

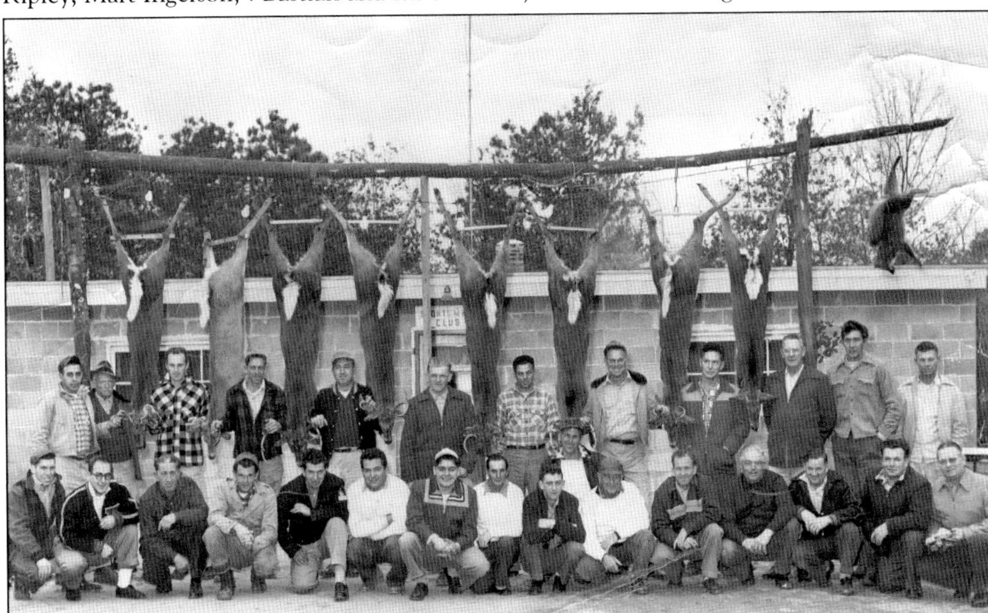

Hunters of the Mays Landing Sportsmen's Club pose in front of their clubhouse following a successful outing. From left to right are the following: (front row) Lou Panza, Bobby Pagano, Rudy Banner, Bob Ripley, Joe Pagano, Pete San Miguel, Pat San Miguel, Ronnie Emper, Jimmy Simpkins, Lou Emper, Toby Hoover, Earl Suran, unidentified, Stan Sokolski, and Ray Jansen; (back row) Big Moon Pagano, ? Scarann, Fred Ludcritz, Jess Simpkins, Joe Giabiatista, Ed Sokolski, Vince Cipolla, Jack Barnhart, Vince Emper, Bill Kraus, unidentified, and Greg Maruffi.

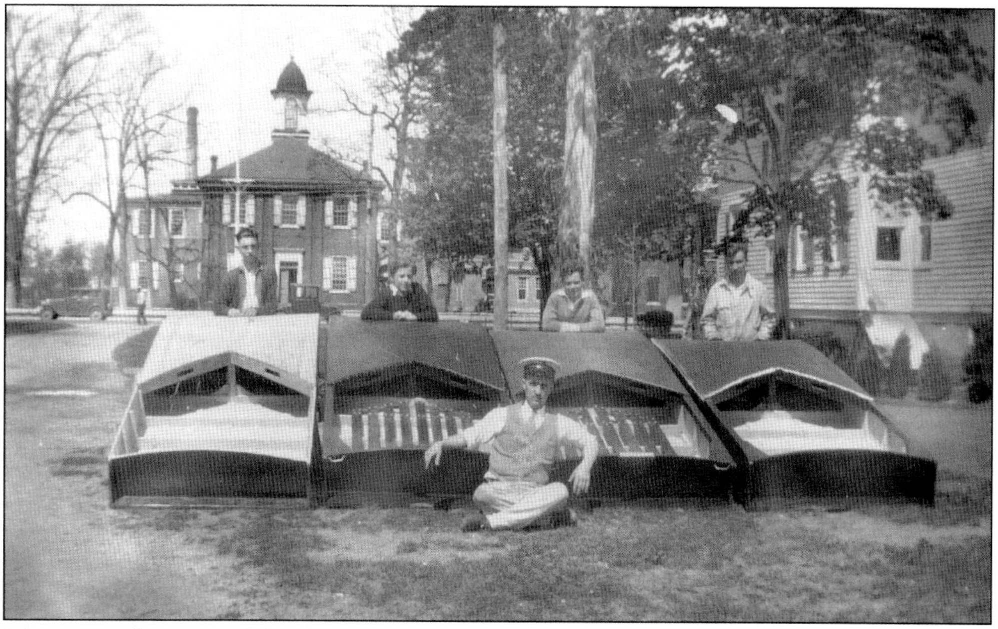

John C. Cook poses with his fleet of racing runabouts on the lawn across from the courthouse.

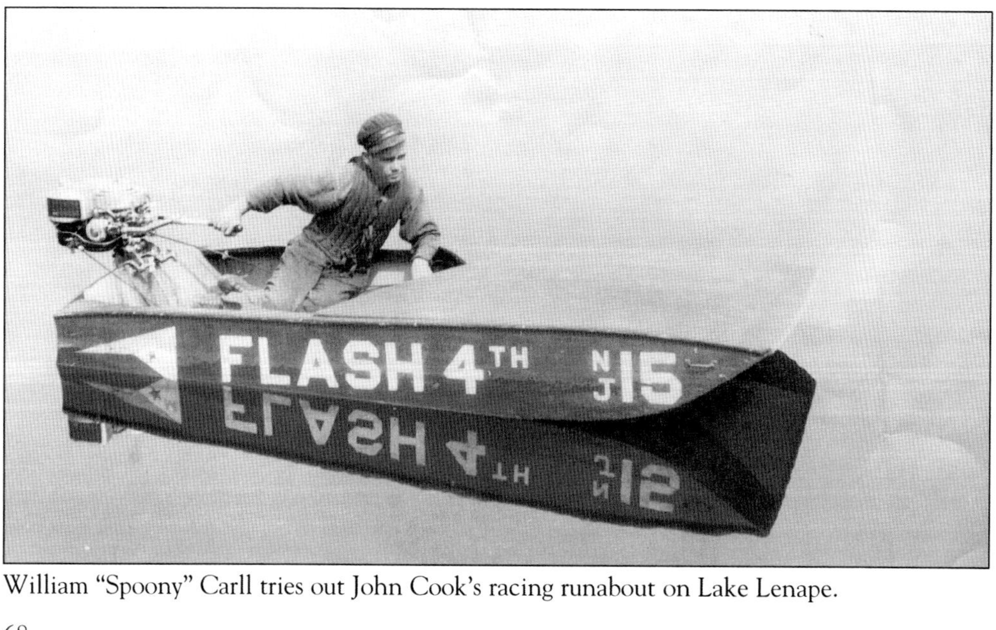

William "Spoony" Carll tries out John Cook's racing runabout on Lake Lenape.

Five

LODGING

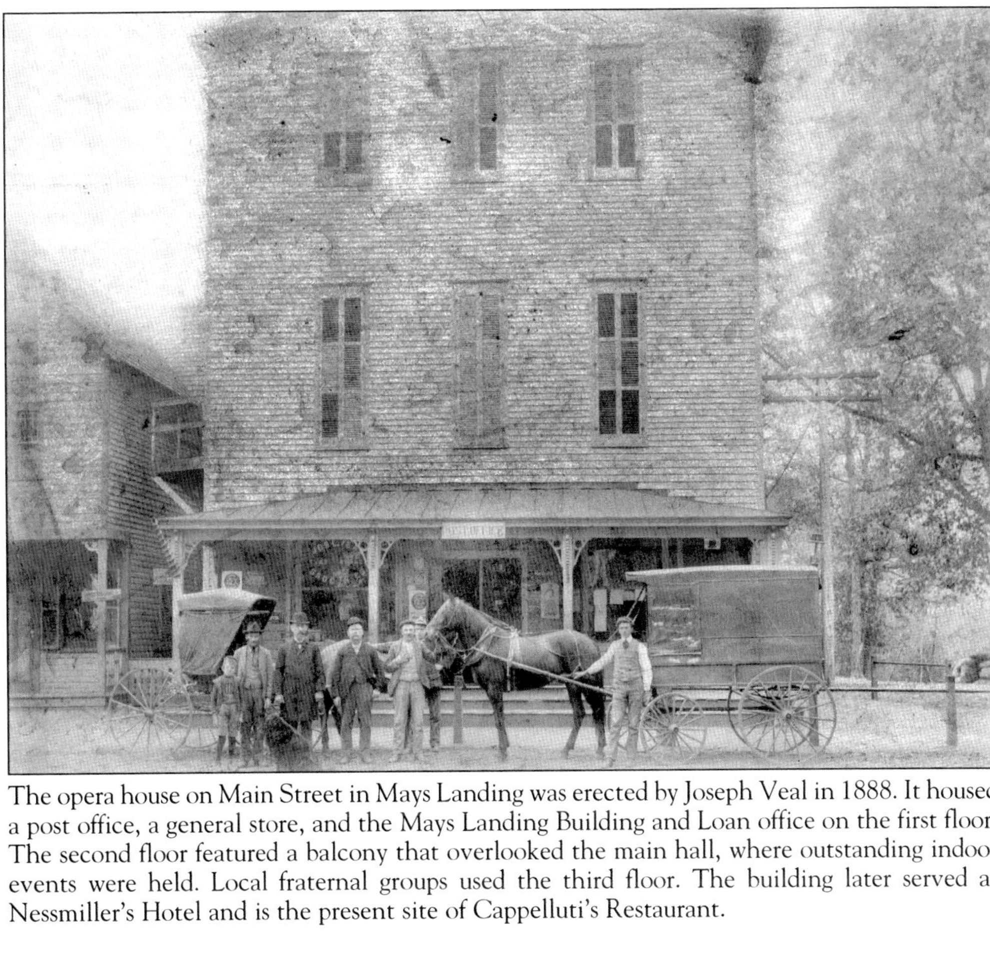

The opera house on Main Street in Mays Landing was erected by Joseph Veal in 1888. It housed a post office, a general store, and the Mays Landing Building and Loan office on the first floor. The second floor featured a balcony that overlooked the main hall, where outstanding indoor events were held. Local fraternal groups used the third floor. The building later served as Nessmiller's Hotel and is the present site of Cappelluti's Restaurant.

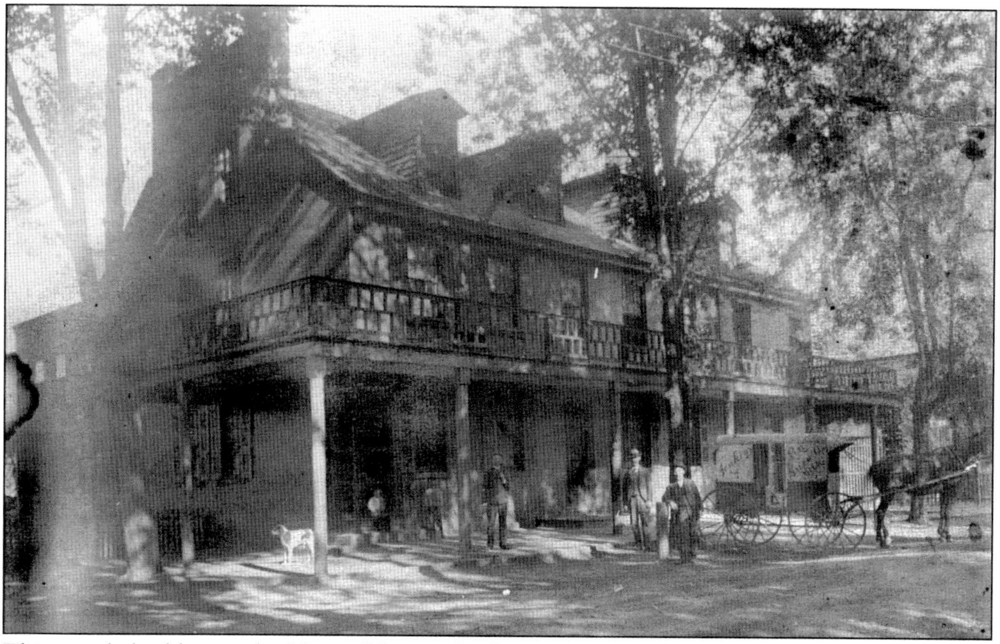

This stately building is the Union House, also known as Baker's Hotel, and was located at the corner of Mill Street and Weymouth Road in Mays Landing. The site is now a parking lot.

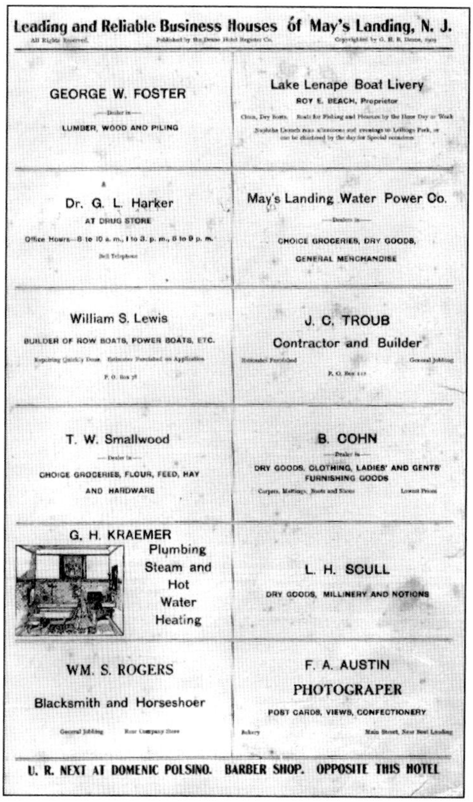

Leading and Reliable Business Houses of May's Landing, N. J.

All Rights Reserved.

GEORGE W. FOSTER —Dealer in— LUMBER, WOOD AND PILING	Lake Lenape Boat Livery ROY E. BEACH, Proprietor Clean, Dry Boats. Boats for Fishing and Pleasure by the Hour Day or Week
Dr. G. L. Harker AT DRUG STORE Office Hours—8 to 10 a. m., 1 to 3. p. m., 8 to 9 p. m. Bell Telephone	May's Landing Water Power Co. —Dealers in— CHOICE GROCERIES, DRY GOODS, GENERAL MERCHANDISE
William S. Lewis BUILDER OF ROW BOATS, POWER BOATS, ETC.	J. C. TROUB Contractor and Builder Estimates Furnished General Jobbing
T. W. Smallwood —Dealer in— CHOICE GROCERIES, FLOUR, FEED, HAY AND HARDWARE	B. COHN —Dealer in— DRY GOODS, CLOTHING, LADIES' AND GENTS' FURNISHING GOODS Carpets, Mattings, Boots and Shoes Lowest Prices
G. H. KRAEMER Plumbing Steam and Hot Water Heating	L. H. SCULL DRY GOODS, MILLINERY AND NOTIONS
WM. S. ROGERS Blacksmith and Horseshoer General Jobbing	F. A. AUSTIN PHOTOGRAPER POST CARDS, VIEWS, CONFECTIONERY Bakery Main Street, Near Boat Landing

U. R. NEXT AT DOMENIC POLSINO. BARBER SHOP. OPPOSITE THIS HOTEL

A 1909 advertisement page from the Baker's Hotel logbook features "Leading and Reliable Business Houses of May's Landing, N.J."

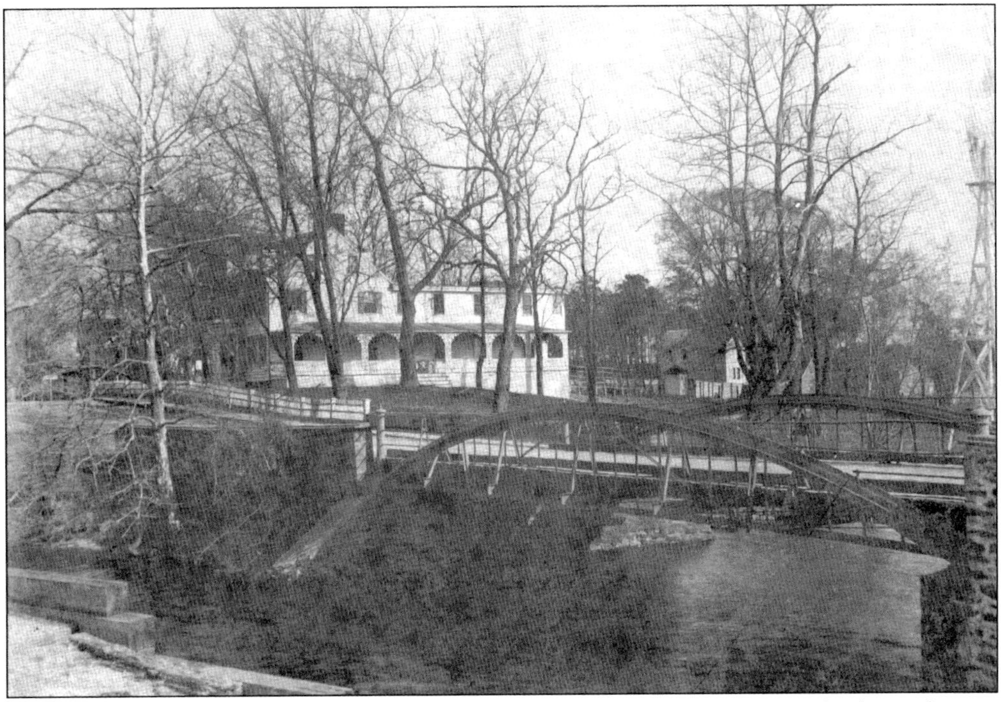

This is an early view of Abbott Villa, later Moore Mansion, showing an iron bridge and tower in the foreground. It is now the site of the Inn at Sugar Hill in Mays Landing.

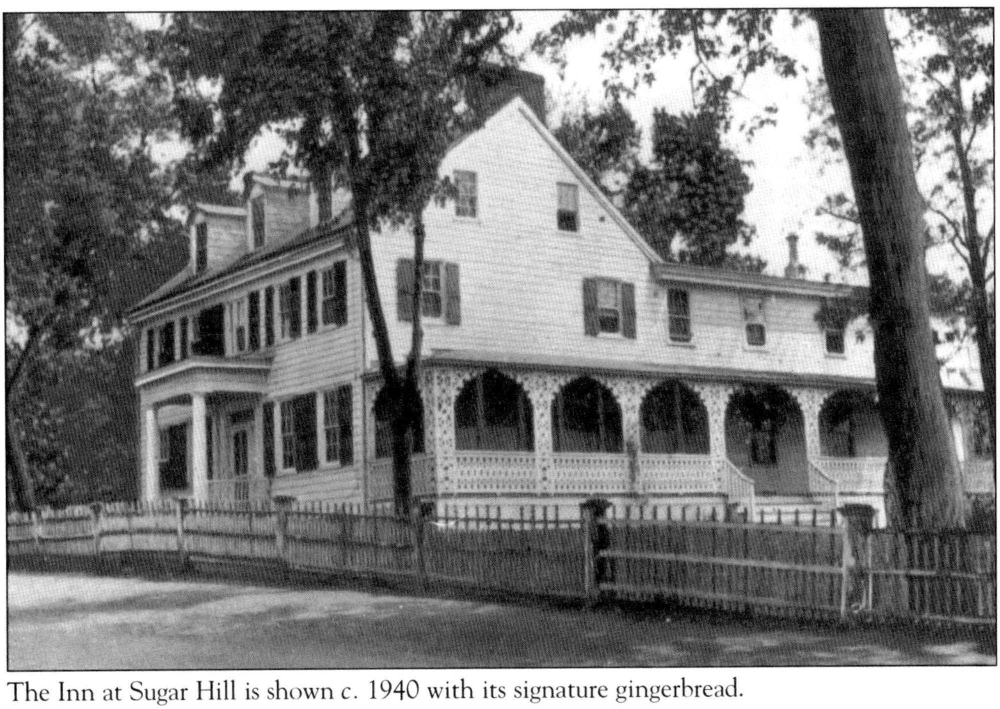

The Inn at Sugar Hill is shown *c.* 1940 with its signature gingerbread.

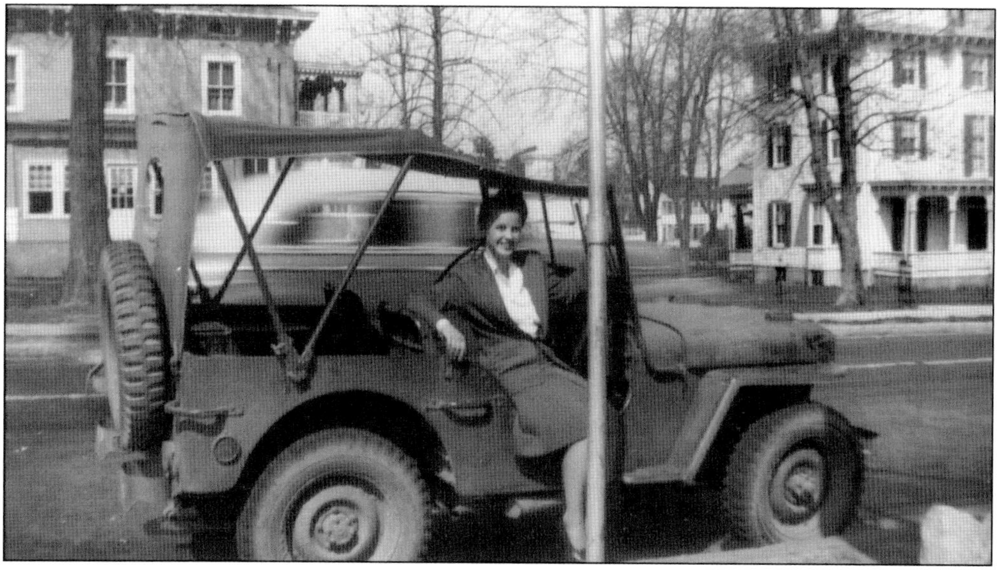

Shown *c.* 1943, Stella Chiola rests in a jeep belonging to soldiers who were stationed in Mays Landing during World War II. In the left background is the Bethlehem Inn, which was owned and operated by the Heiney family. The inn was razed to make way for the St. Vincent De Paul School. On the right is the home of Anna Corson, a descendant of one of the oldest local families. It is now the convent of St. Vincent De Paul.

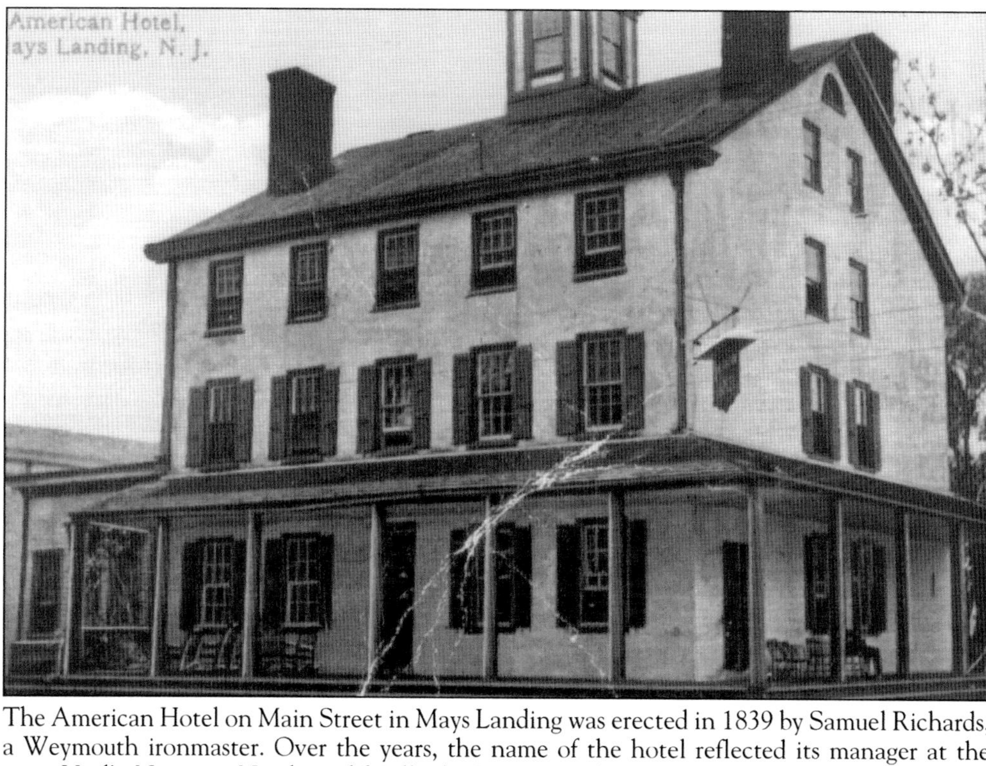

The American Hotel on Main Street in Mays Landing was erected in 1839 by Samuel Richards, a Weymouth ironmaster. Over the years, the name of the hotel reflected its manager at the time: Veal's, Norcross, North, and finally the Russian Embassy. It is currently incorporated into the Mays Landing Branch of the Atlantic County Library.

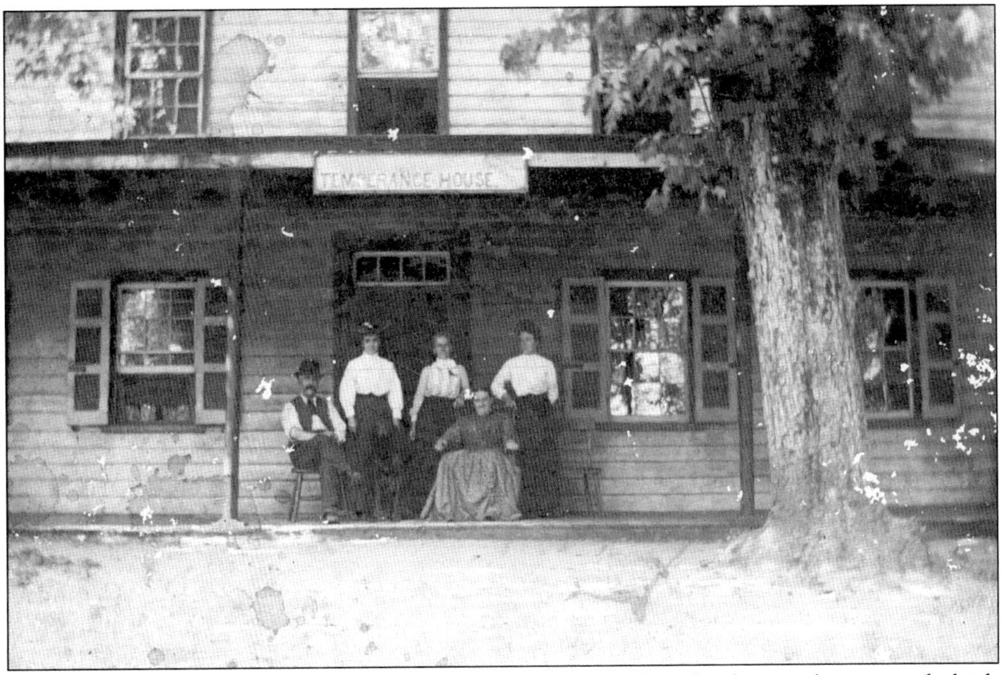

Temperance House, on Main Street in Mays Landing, was a boardinghouse, the name of which reflected its no-alcohol policy.

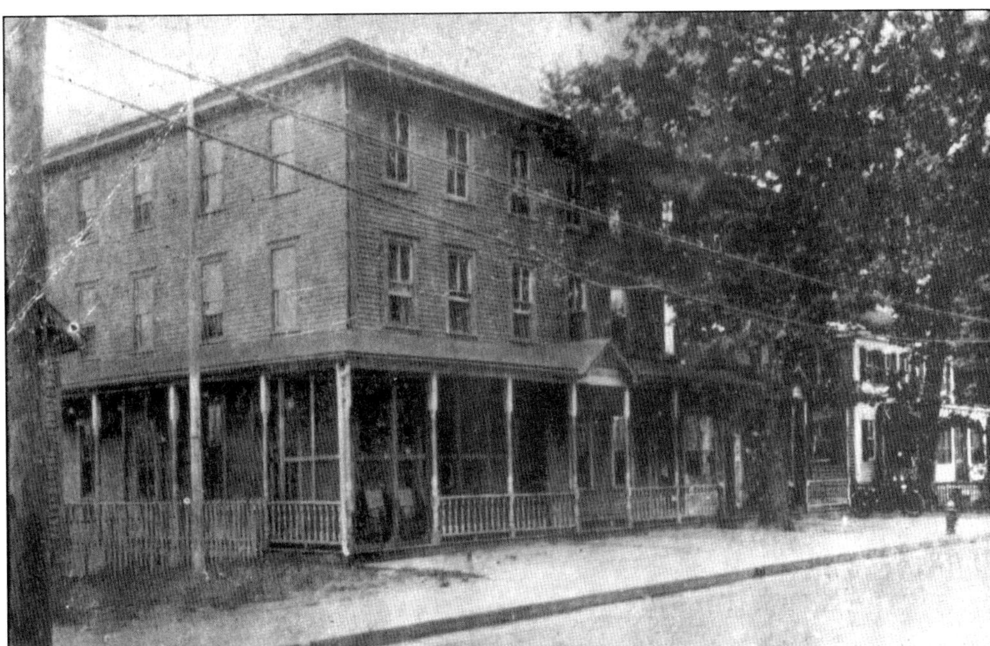

The Coleman Mansion, an important part of late-19th-century Main Street in Mays Landing, was subsequently known as the Madison House and Jackson House. It is now the Homestead, site of several small businesses and lodging.

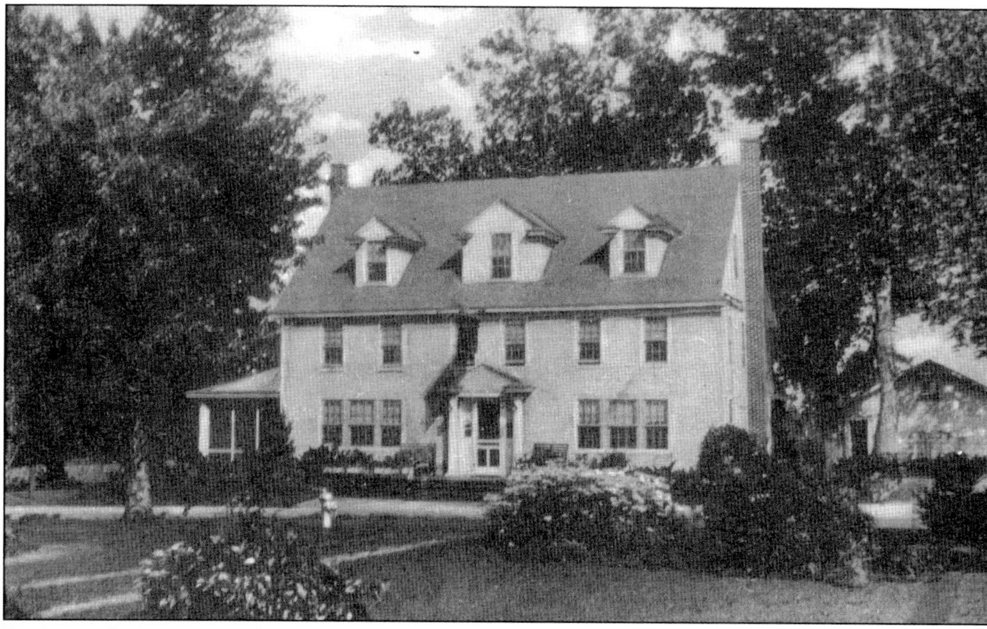

Built on former Rape family property, this building on Mill Street in Mays Landing was renovated in 1925–1926 and became the Lafayette Hotel in 1927. The top floor was also used as a schoolroom. It is now the site of Donny's Inn.

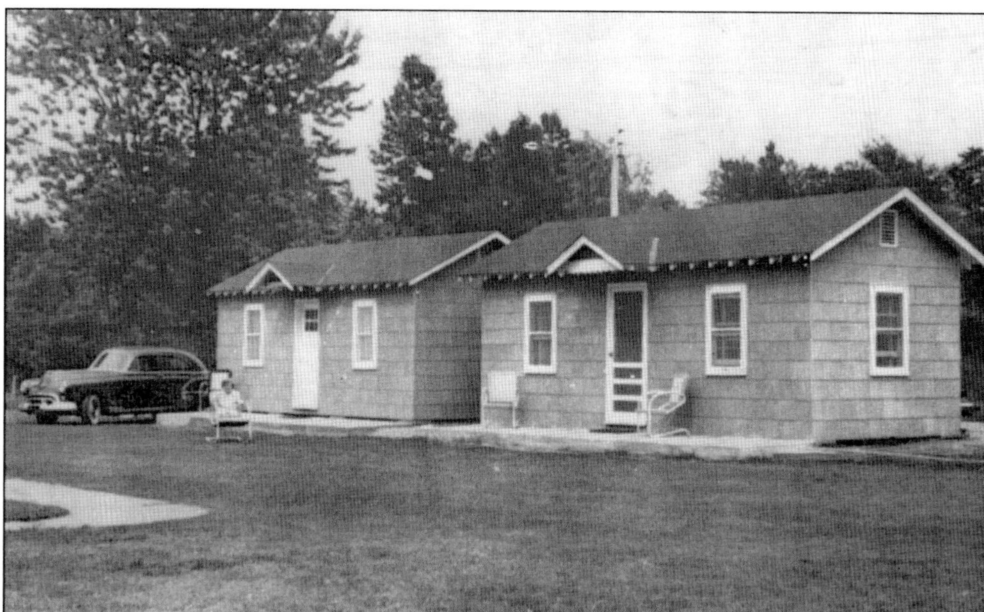

A resting place for travelers, the Betty Lou Motel was located on East Main Street near the Babcock Bridge intersection in Mays Landing.

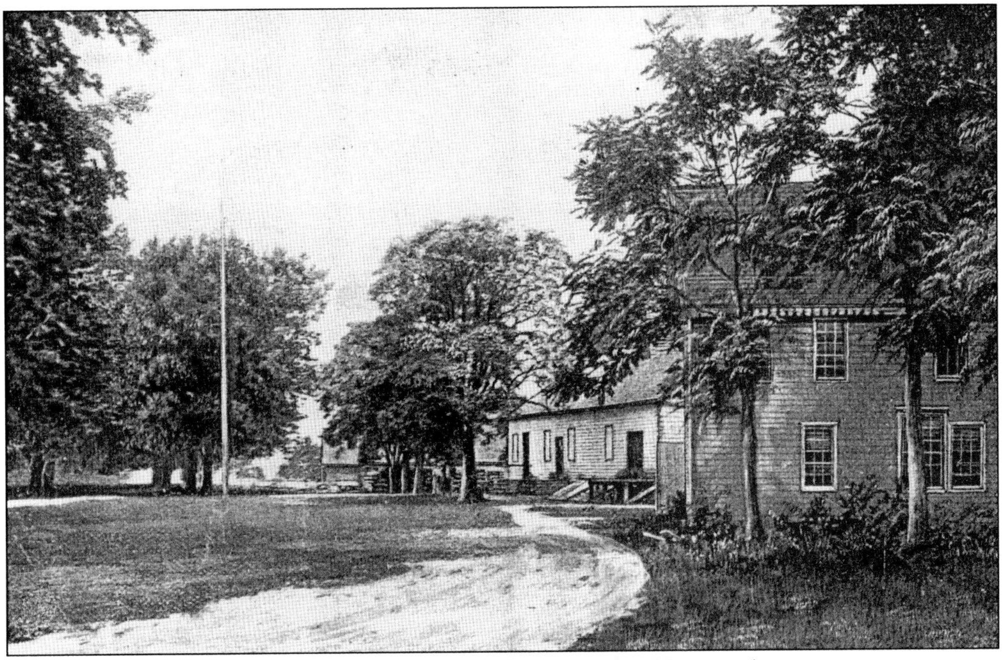

Shown are the company store and the boardinghouse in the Weymouth section.

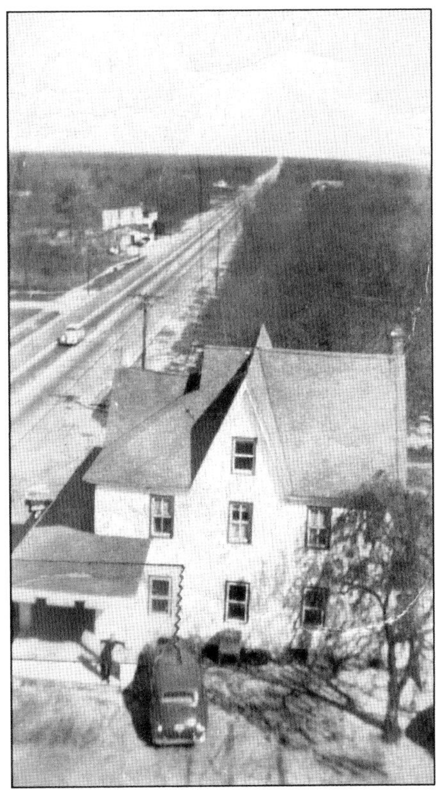

This aerial view of the Mizpah Hotel looks east on Harding Highway.

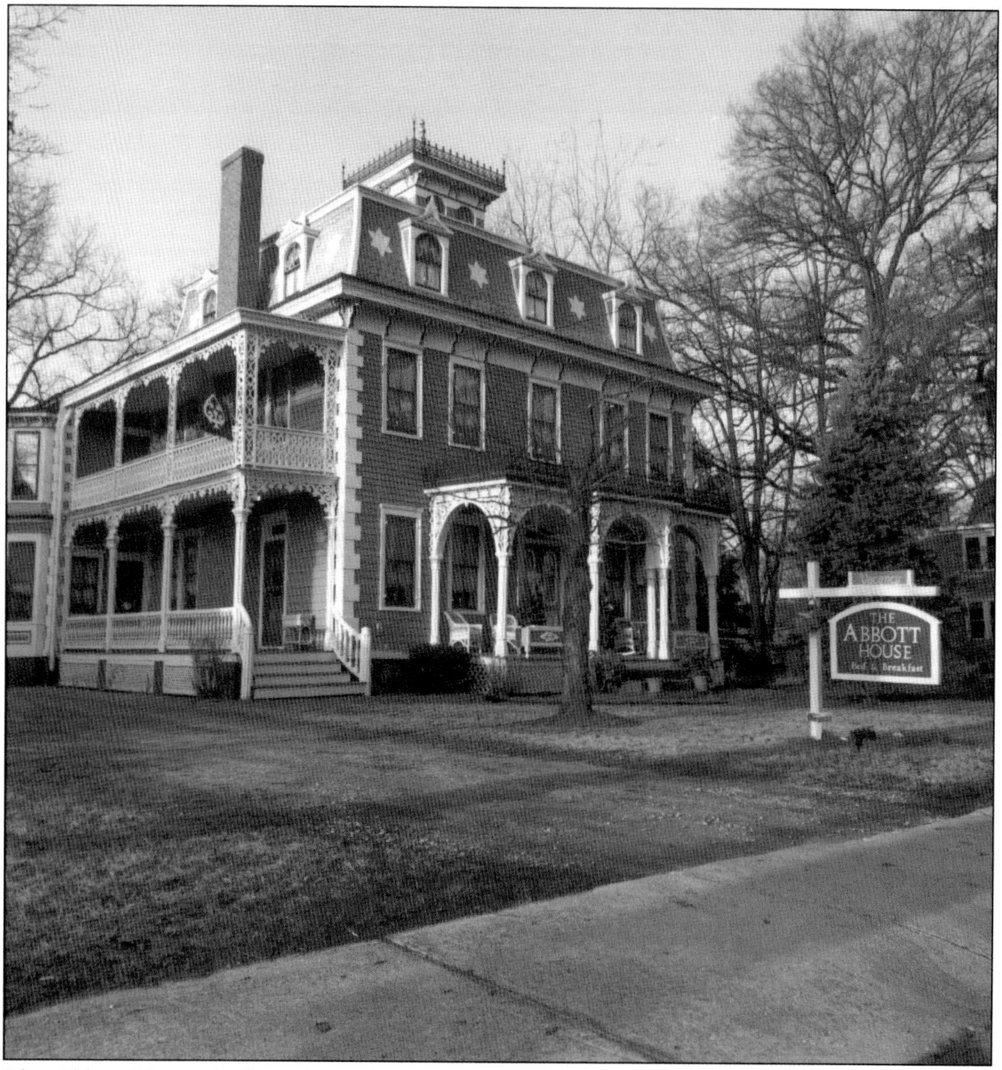

The Abbott House, built in the early 1860s on Main Street in Mays Landing, was the home of J.E.P. Abbott, a local attorney. Roy E. Beach purchased the home in 1920. Today it is a popular bed-and-breakfast and one of the most photographed houses in the township.

Six

Guardians of Our Nation and Community

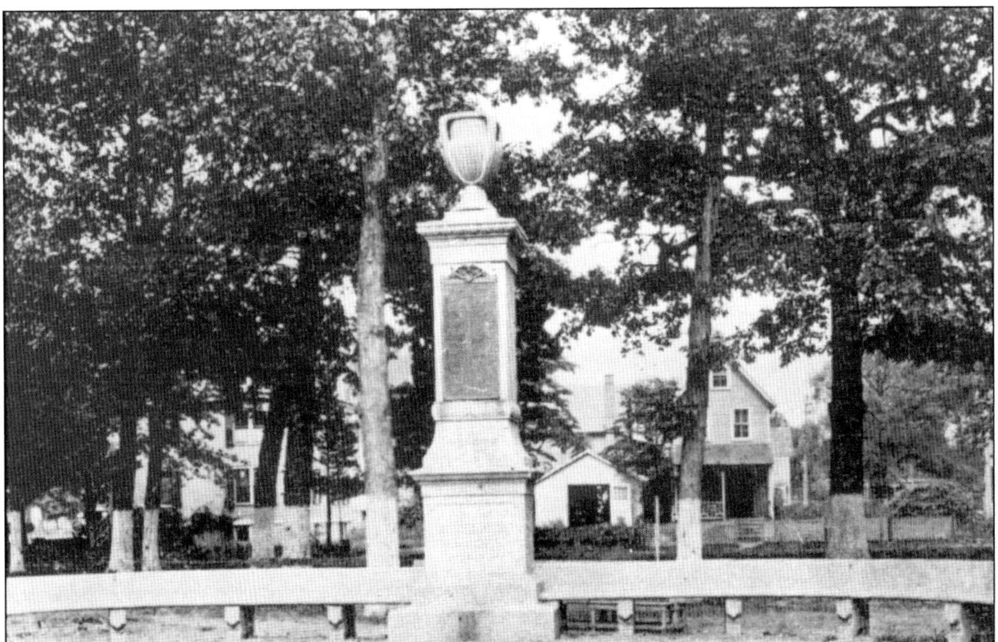

The Township of Hamilton honors its citizens who served their nation with the Memorial to All Wars Park on Main Street in Mays Landing. Its monument bears the names of those who gave their lives and is the site of annual Memorial Day commemorative ceremonies.

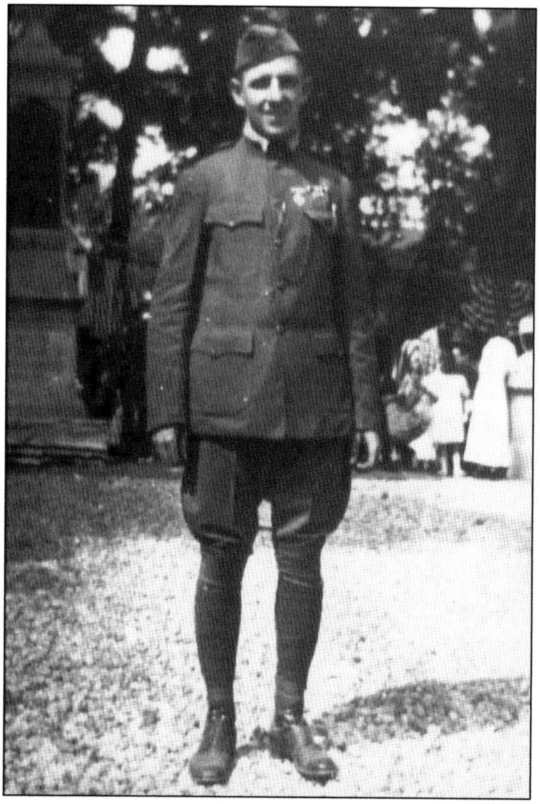

A veteran who served in World War I, Henry W. Denmead, was the tax collector for the Township of Hamilton as well as its historian.

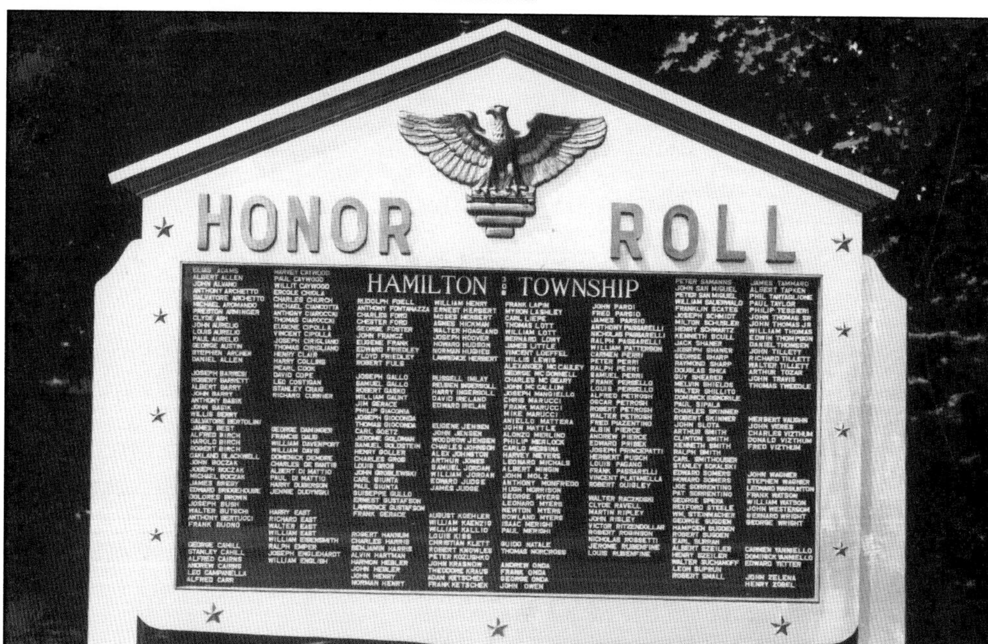

This honor roll bears the names of the township's World War II veterans. It was originally located in Memorial Park in Mays Landing. It was replaced by a monument honoring veterans of all wars.

Norman "Chippy" Hughes served his township and his country well. He was a sergeant during World War II, an active member of the Mays Landing Fire Company, and a lifelong member of the Mays Landing Rescue Squad.

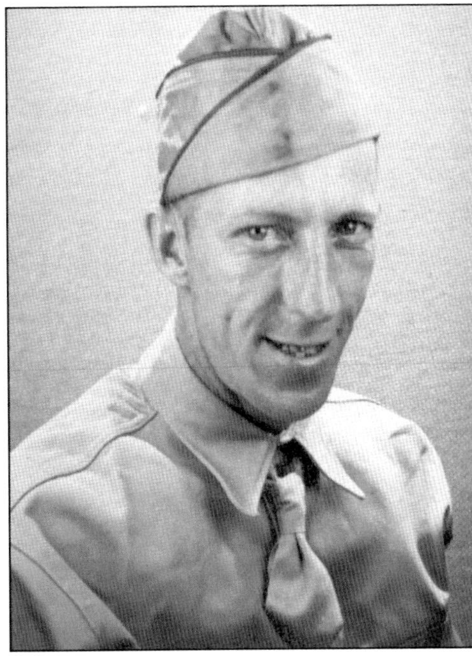

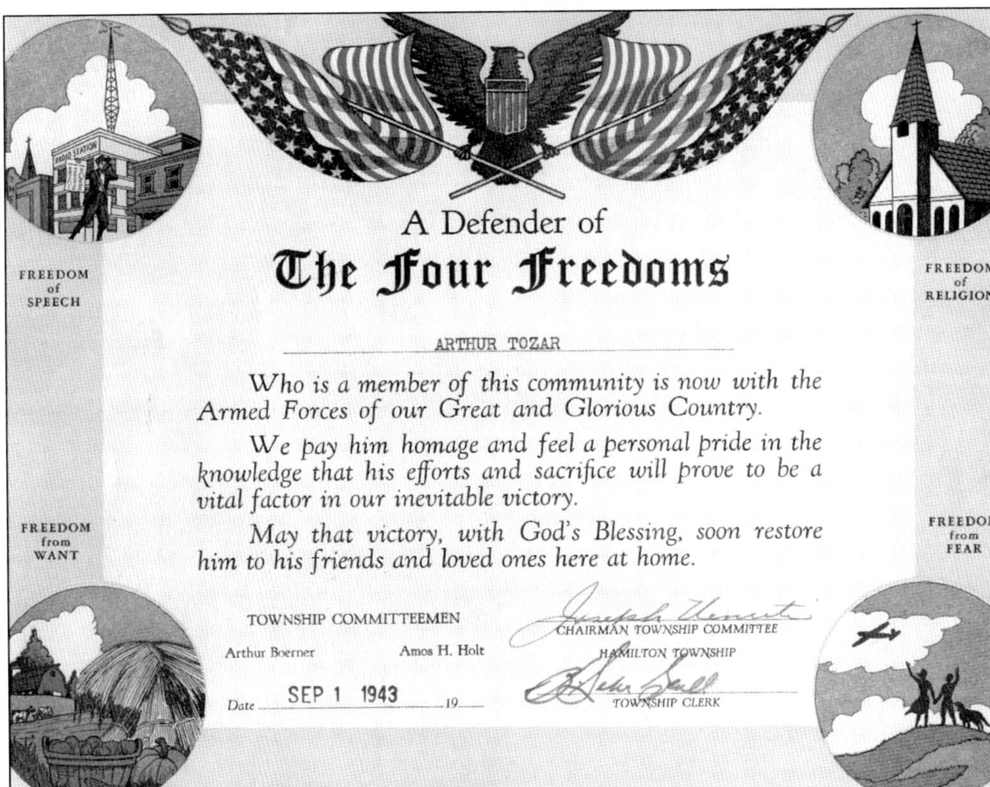

FREEDOM of SPEECH

FREEDOM of RELIGION

A Defender of

The Four Freedoms

ARTHUR TOZAR

Who is a member of this community is now with the Armed Forces of our Great and Glorious Country.

We pay him homage and feel a personal pride in the knowledge that his efforts and sacrifice will prove to be a vital factor in our inevitable victory.

May that victory, with God's Blessing, soon restore him to his friends and loved ones here at home.

FREEDOM from WANT

FREEDOM from FEAR

TOWNSHIP COMMITTEEMEN

Arthur Boerner Amos H. Holt

CHAIRMAN TOWNSHIP COMMITTEE

HAMILTON TOWNSHIP

Date SEP 1 1943 19

TOWNSHIP CLERK

The Township of Hamilton Committee issued this certificate on September 1, 1943, to Arthur Tozar, a "Defender of the Four Freedoms," paying him homage and expressing pride in his efforts and sacrifice during World War II.

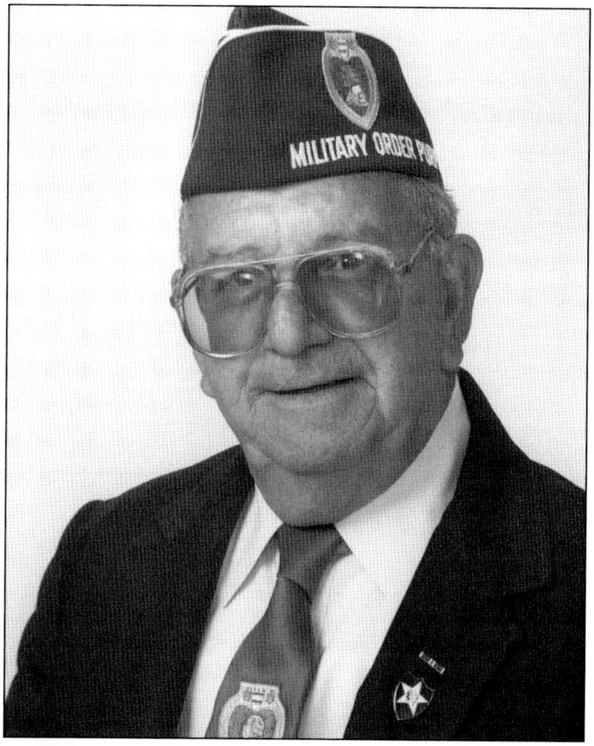

Purple Heart recipient Cpl. Walter Tweedle, a native of Mays Landing, was a member of the 9th Infantry, G Company, U.S. Army, fighting in Korea. His company, defending Little Gibraltar Hill, found they were out of hand grenades. Tweedle raced down the hill under enemy fire and carried a box of grenades to his company. Seriously wounded in the battle, he was given the Purple Heart for actions beyond the call of duty.

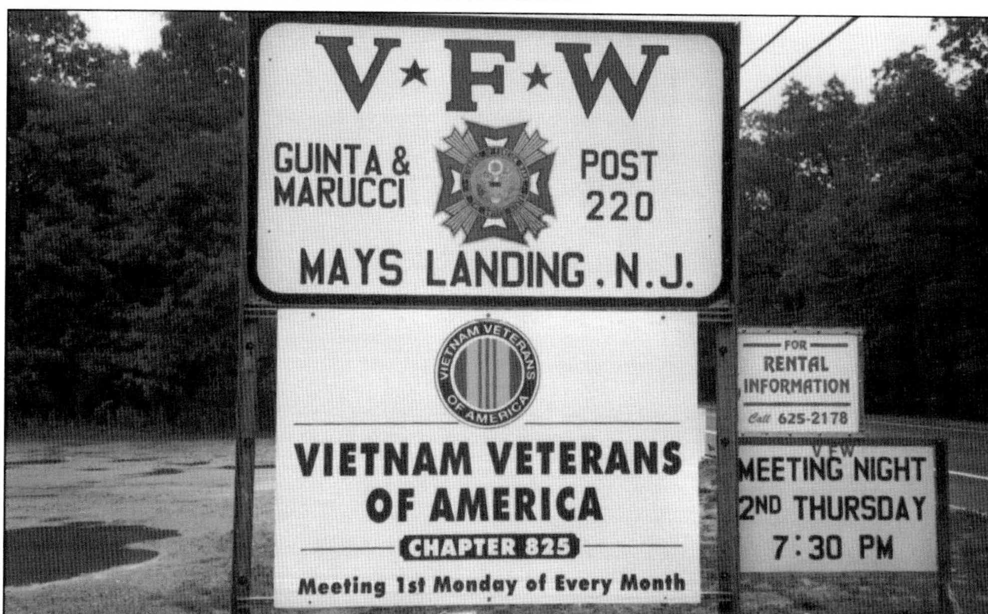

Harry Boyer Post No. 220, Veterans of Foreign Wars, was organized in the fire hall at Egg Harbor on May 22, 1936. The first commander was Emil Goebel. The first meetings were held at Aurora Hall in Egg Harbor, then in Laureldale and, in 1938, in Mays Landing. The name was changed to Guinta & Marucci in June 1946 and its meeting hall was moved to Route 50 in Mays Landing. The building also serves as the meeting place for Chapter 825 of the Vietnam Veterans of America.

The American flag and the POW/MIA flag are displayed with pride in front of the American Legion Post 254, located on Second Street in Mays Landing.

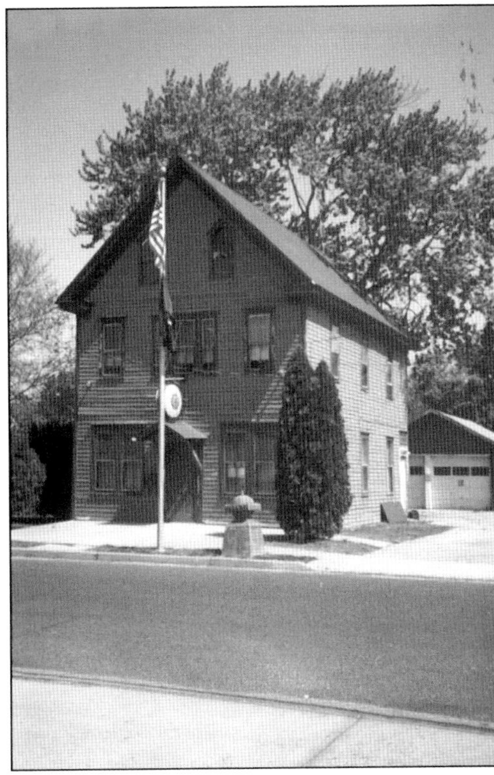

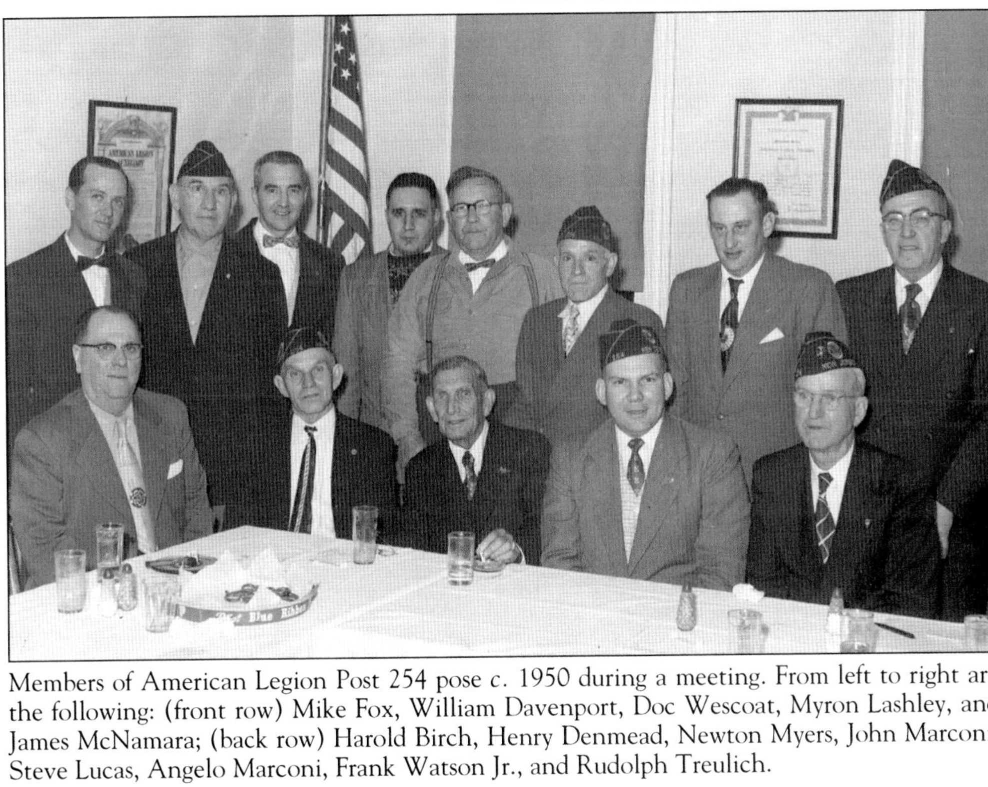

Members of American Legion Post 254 pose c. 1950 during a meeting. From left to right are the following: (front row) Mike Fox, William Davenport, Doc Wescoat, Myron Lashley, and James McNamara; (back row) Harold Birch, Henry Denmead, Newton Myers, John Marconi, Steve Lucas, Angelo Marconi, Frank Watson Jr., and Rudolph Treulich.

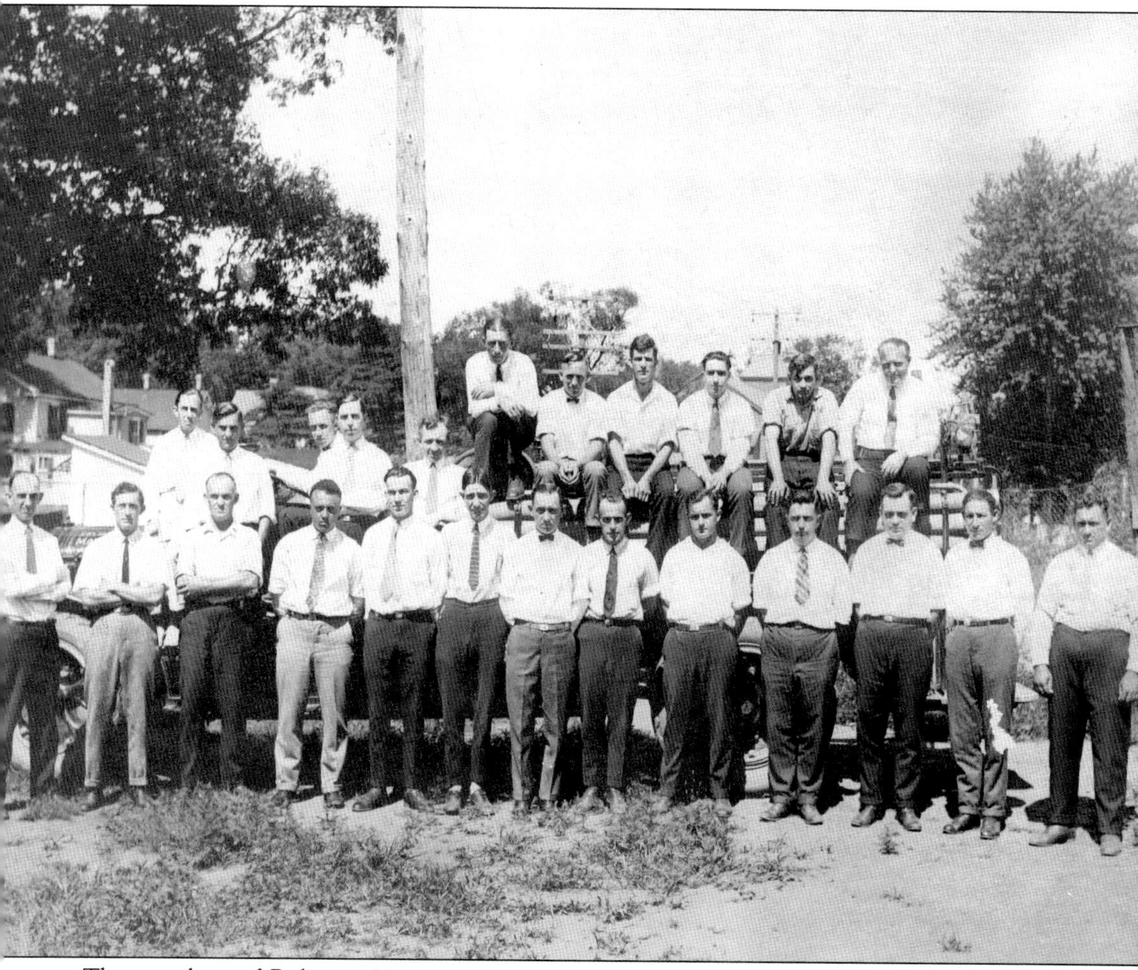

The members of Reliance Hose Company No. 1 posing in 1925 are, from left to right, as follows: (front row) Thomas J. Barrett, Mark Harris, Charles Voight Jr., Anthony Yanniello, Myron Lashley, Albert Hand, Walter Heffner, Joe Bridgehouse, Paul Machner, Joseph C. Shaner, William Carll, Reynolds Kraus, and Tony Aurelio; (back row) Melvin M. Ripley, George Yetter, Otis Luderitz, John McGeary, B. Lehr Scull, Arthur Thomas, Sam Keating, Paul Mangold, William Luderitz, Philip Tartaglione, and James Bridgehouse.

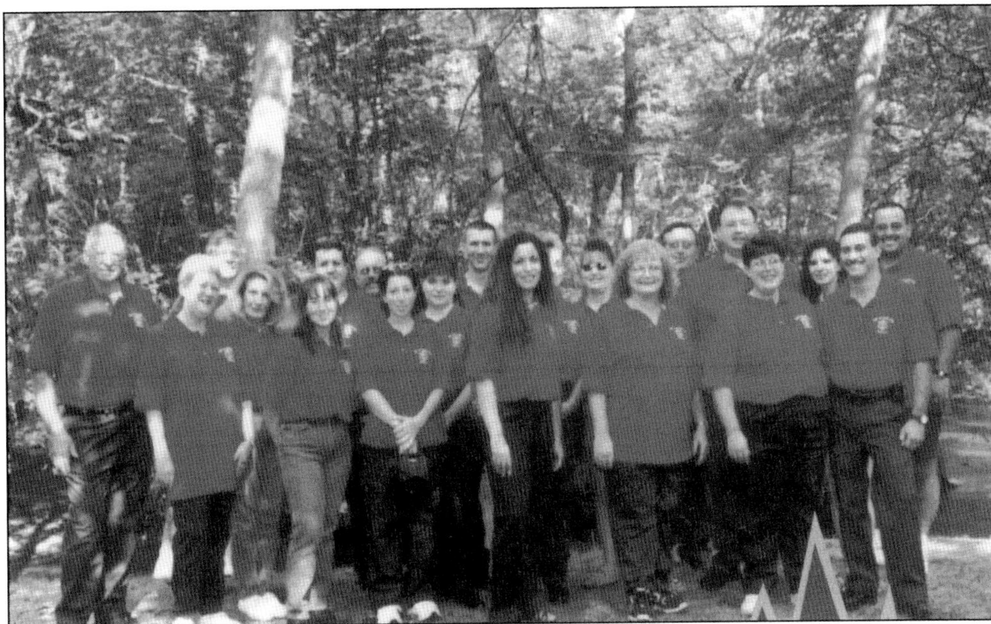

Members of the Township of Hamilton Volunteer Rescue Squad serve their community proudly.

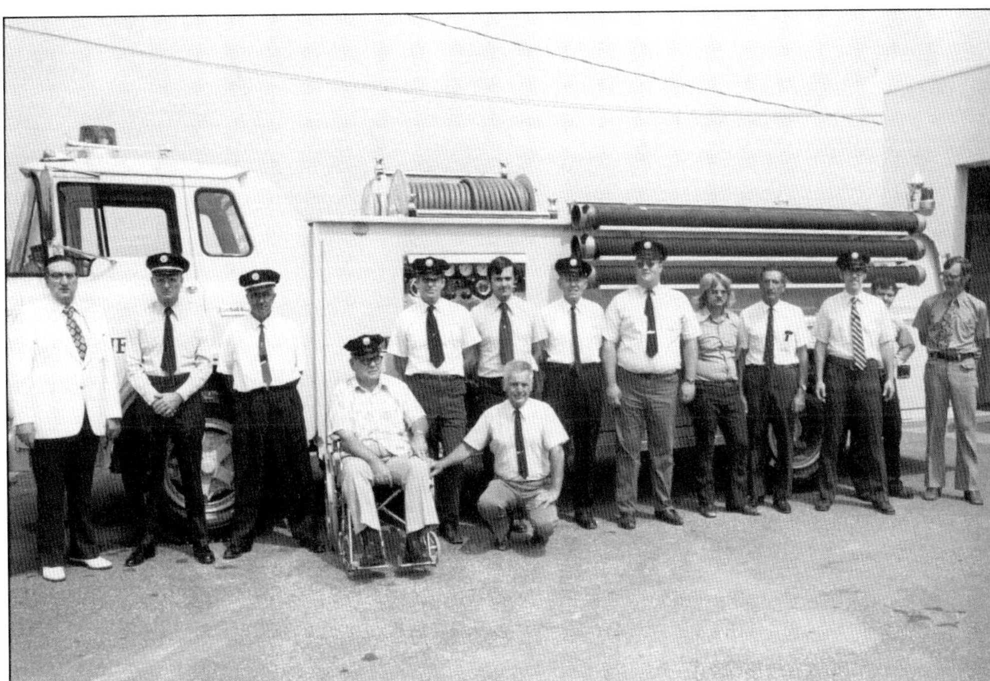

The Township of Hamilton also boasts the Cologne Volunteer Fire Company, members of which pose in front of one of their firefighting vehicles. This company began in 1960 through the efforts of Herman Liepe Jr. and others.

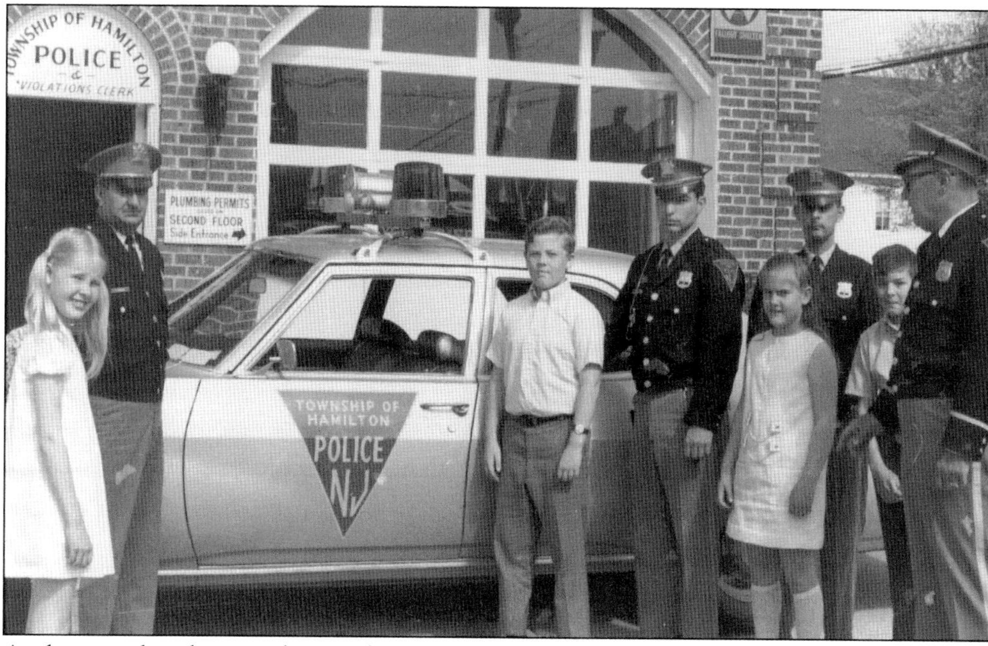

At the time this photograph was taken in 1967, the Township of Hamilton Police Department was located at the rear of the Old Town Hall on Cape May Avenue in Mays Landing. The location is now the site of the Summit Bank. The members of the police department shown here are, from left to right, Lt. Ted Gallo, patrolman Leo Foy, patrolman Ronald Martin, and director of public safety Jack Kertland. (Courtesy of the Ronald Martin Collection.)

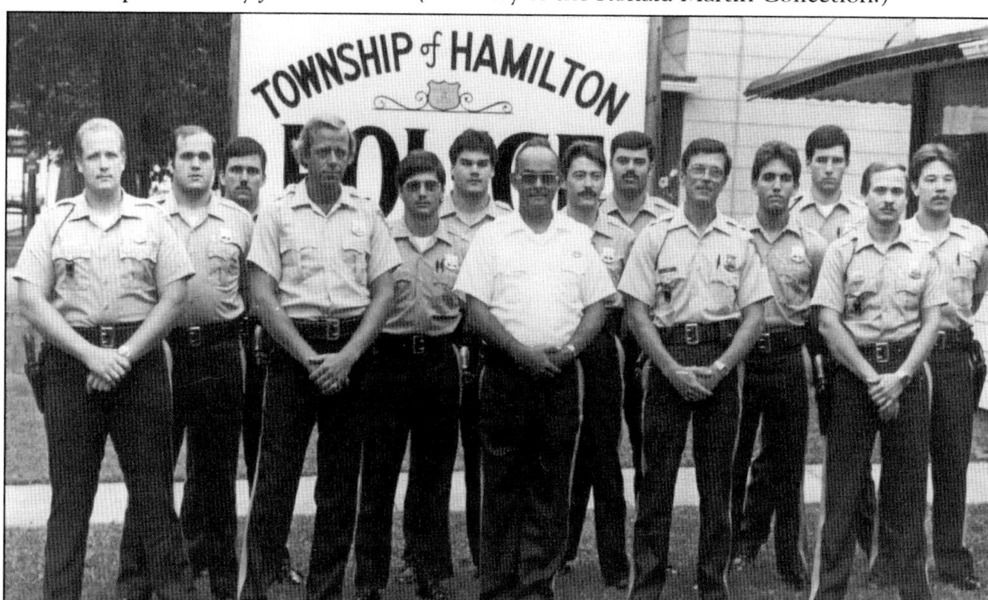

By 1978, the police department had expanded along with the township. From left to right are the following: (front row) Rick Frederiksen, Robert Birch, Steve Payne, Tony Garuffi, Capt. Ronald Martin, Pat Lentz, Frank Lentz, Marshall Cradock, and Sal Dilissio; (back row) Dave Cahill, Brian McCoy, James Linardo, Pat Purnell, and Joseph O'Donohue. (Courtesy of the Ronald Martin Collection.)

Seven

Fraternal, Civic, and Social Organizations

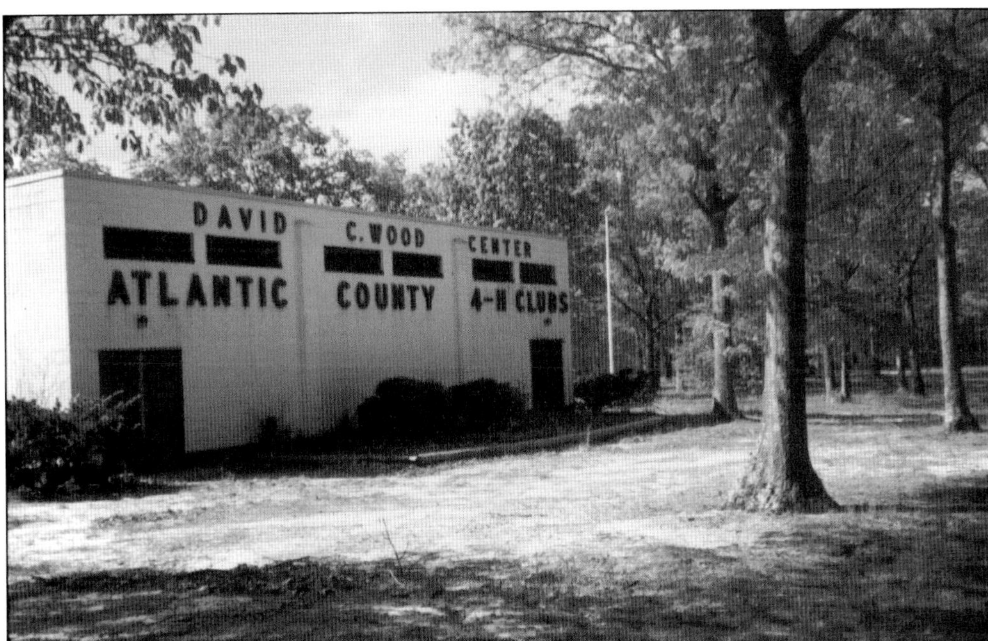

The Atlantic County 4-H Clubs Center is located partly in Galloway Township and partly in the Township of Hamilton. It was named after David C. Wood in honor of his longtime service as Atlantic County's 4-H agent.

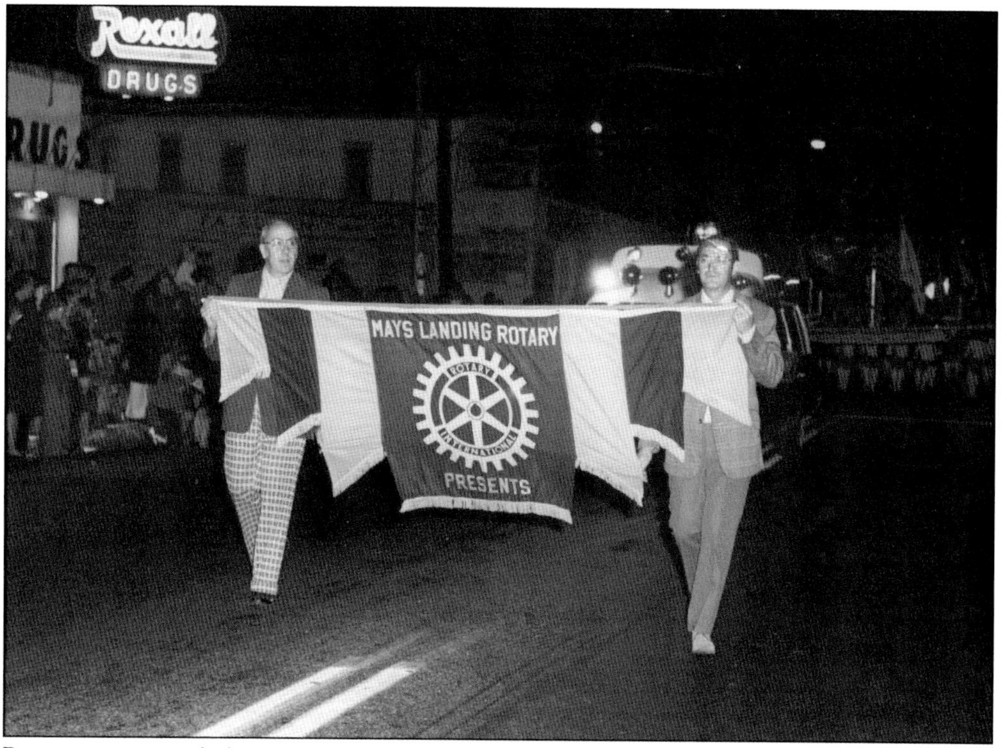

Representatives of the Mays Landing branch of the Rotary International display their organization's banner in a Halloween parade on Main Street.

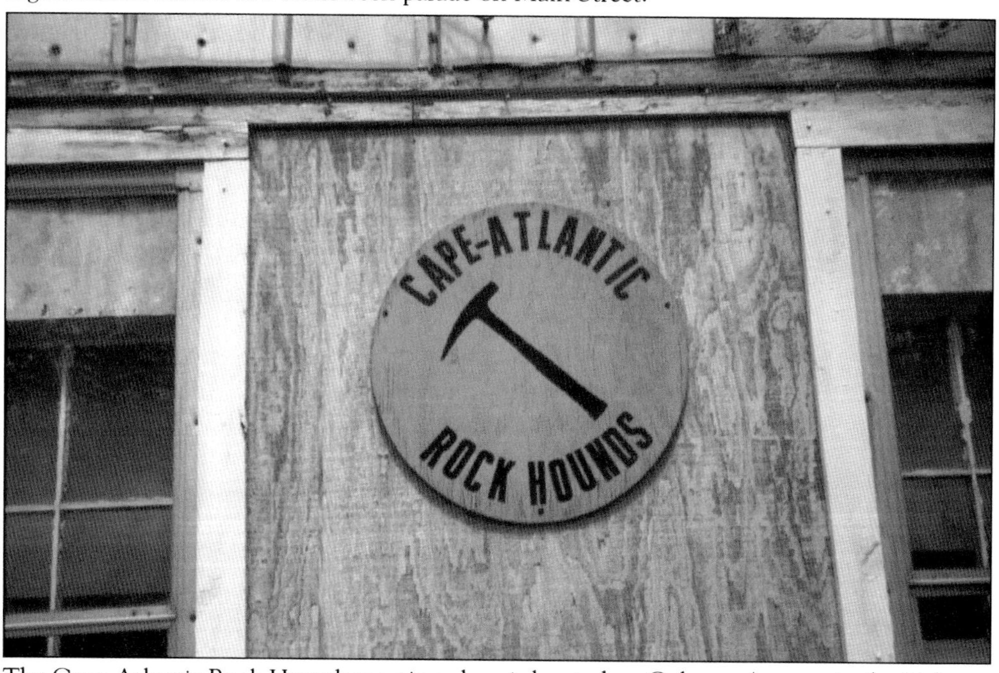

The Cape-Atlantic Rock Hounds meeting place is located on Cologne Avenue in the Cologne section of the township. Founded in 1962, the group is dedicated to spreading interest in geology by collecting specimens of rocks, minerals, and fossils.

This historic building, formerly the Mays Landing Water Power Company store on Mill Street, is now the home of Unity Lodge No. 96 of the Free and Accepted Masons.

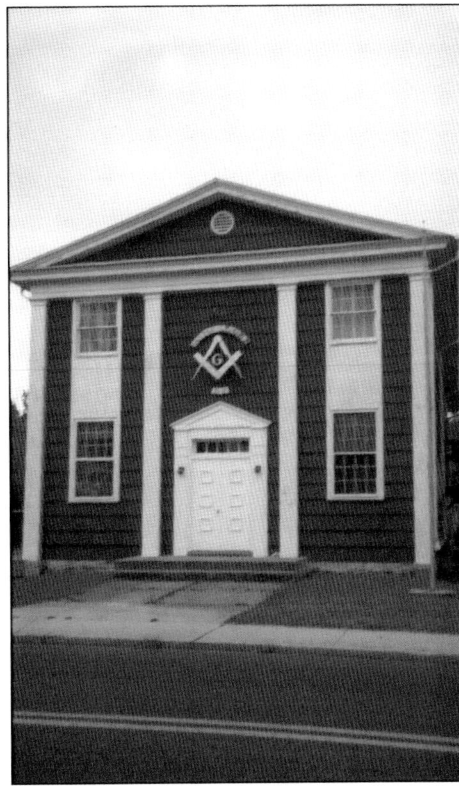

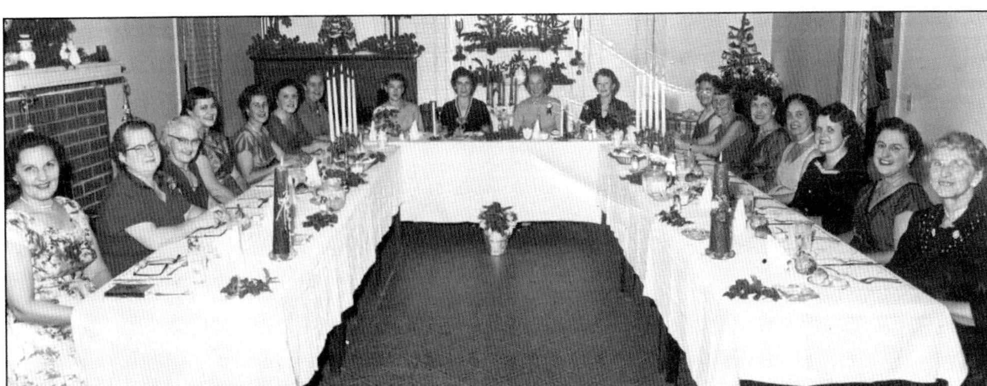

The local social group known as the Poodlers Club held their meetings at the Lafayette Hotel, now Donny's Inn, and are pictured during a holiday season event. From left to right are Thelma Taylor, Eva Minnon, Anna Barrett, Virginia Ingersoll, Leila Cope, Betty McCallum, Verna Luderitz, Edith Turpin, Jo Smith Lott, Edna Myers, Mickie Drayton, Mildred Kenny, Dot Kovar, Elsie Layton, Almeda Dawson, Peggy Costigan, Alberta Birch, and Mary McGeary

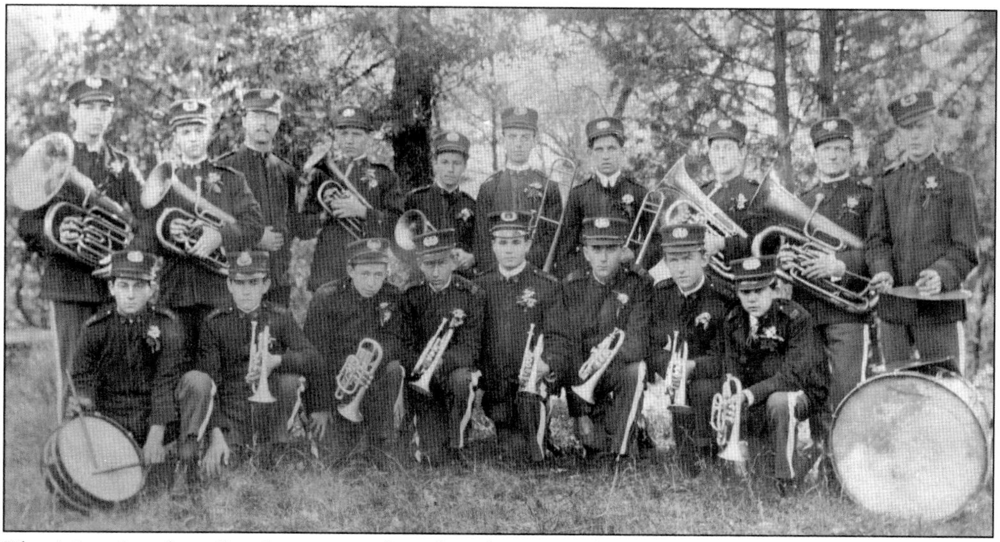

The Mays Landing Band poses in their handsome uniforms in 1910. From left to right are the following: (front row) Walt Heffner, James S. Turp, Irving Barrett, Herbert English, Robert Turp, Maurice Taylor, Harry Lee, and Fred Trumpy; (back row) Fred Luderitz, Joseph Wigglesworth, Frank Tarlicki, W. Orile, Ted Trumpy, Thomas Barrett, Sam Harris, Mark Harris, Frank Harris, and George Henry.

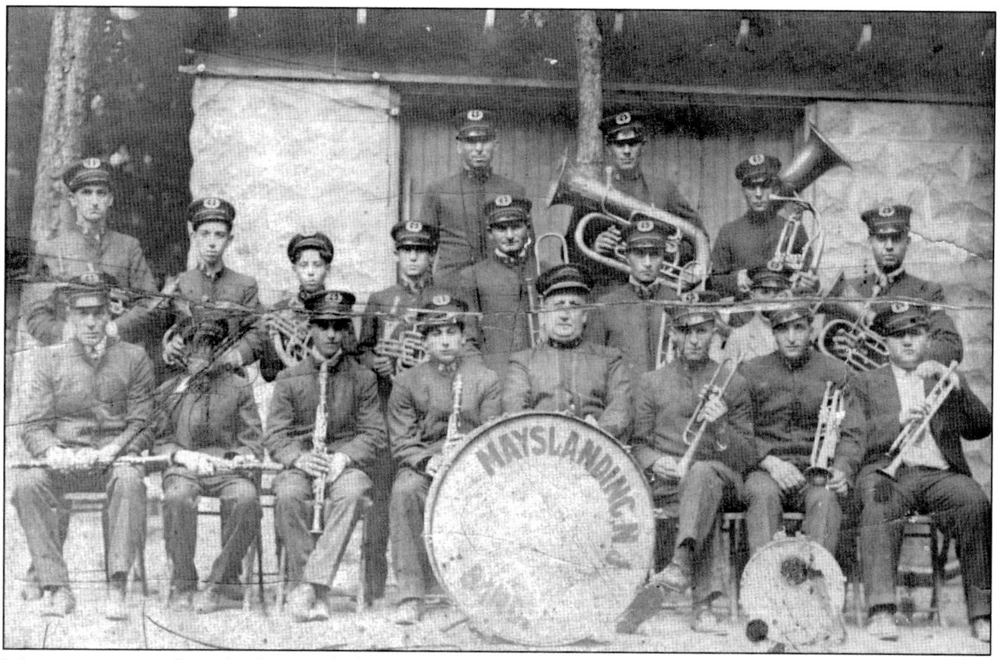

Many new members had joined the Mays Landing Band when this c. 1920 photograph was taken. From left to right are the following: (front row) Joe Cristinzio, unidentified, unidentified, Anthony Cirigliano, band leader Sam Traunto, unidentified, Joe Chaivese, and unidentified; (middle row) Jose Messina, unidentified, Anthony Giambattista, unidentified, Salvatore Spera, Tony Ferrante, unidentified, and Sam Yanniello; (back row) Sam Giambattista, Alex Barile, and Michael Cammorata.

The Mays Landing Athletic Association is composed of two appointed representatives from each of five local groups interested in civic welfare: the American Legion, Veterans of Foreign Wars, Chamber of Commerce, Rotary Club, and the governing body of the Township of Hamilton. In addition, others who are actively interested in the continuation of the local sporting program may be elected to membership in this association. For many years, the association sponsored a minstrel show as a fundraiser.

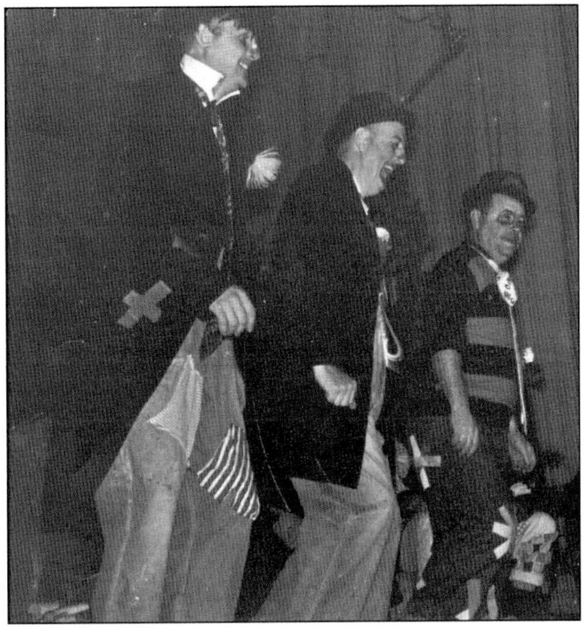

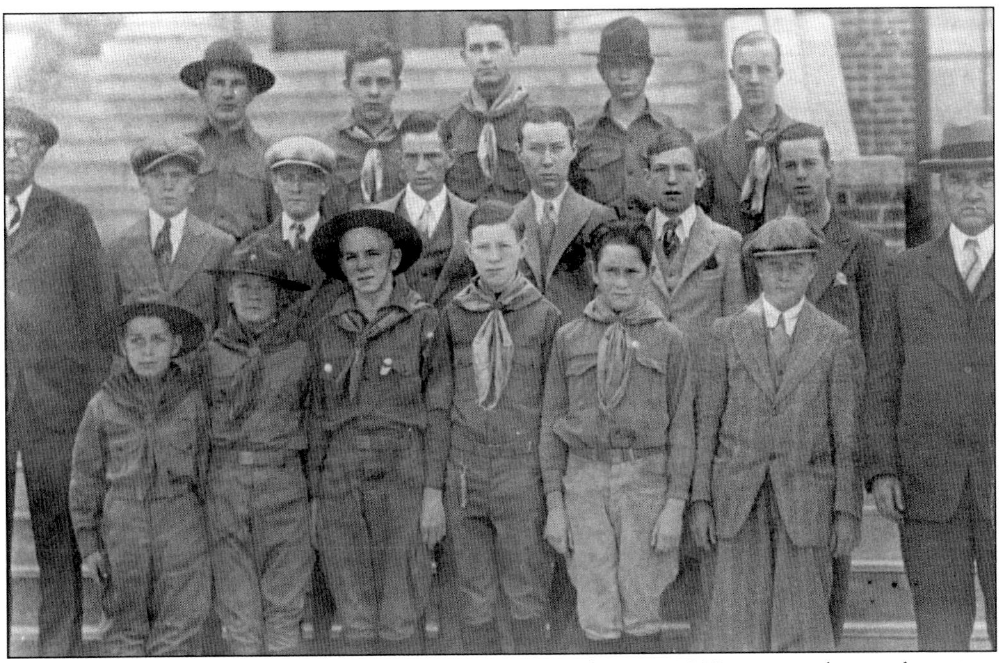

Most of the Mays Landing Boy Scout Troop 44 turned out *c.* 1928 to attend special services in the Presbyterian church. Shown, from left to right, are the following: (front row) Elwood "Buster" Gillespie, Paul Machner, Edward Duberson, John McGeary, Charlie Harris, Carl Smithouser, and Elvey Bailey; (middle row) George Myers, Ernie Henry, Irving "Beef" Taylor, Charles Russell Imlay, Charles McGeary, Dick Tillet, and Harold Duberson; (back row) Alexander Macauley, Roger Smith, Wilson Harris, Johnnie Leach, and Ed Bridgehouse. Roger Smith played with the New York Symphony Orchestra. George Myers was head of the brickyard and father of Newton Myers. Elvey Bailey was the eighth-grade teacher and scoutmaster of Troop 44.

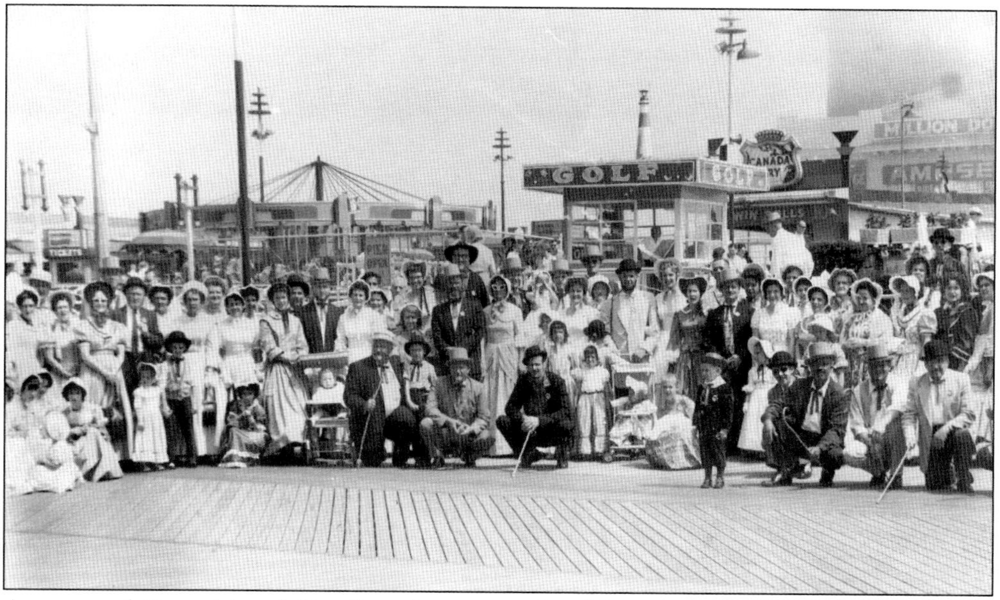

A group of Township of Hamilton bicentennial celebrants enjoys this 1960 outing on the boardwalk.

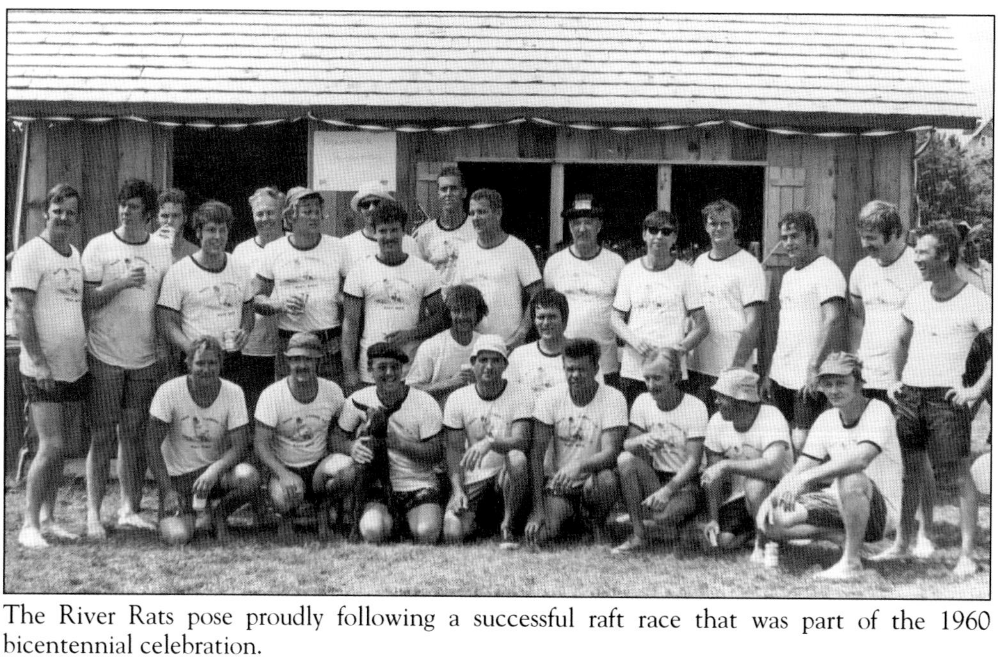

The River Rats pose proudly following a successful raft race that was part of the 1960 bicentennial celebration.

Eight

Hall of Fame

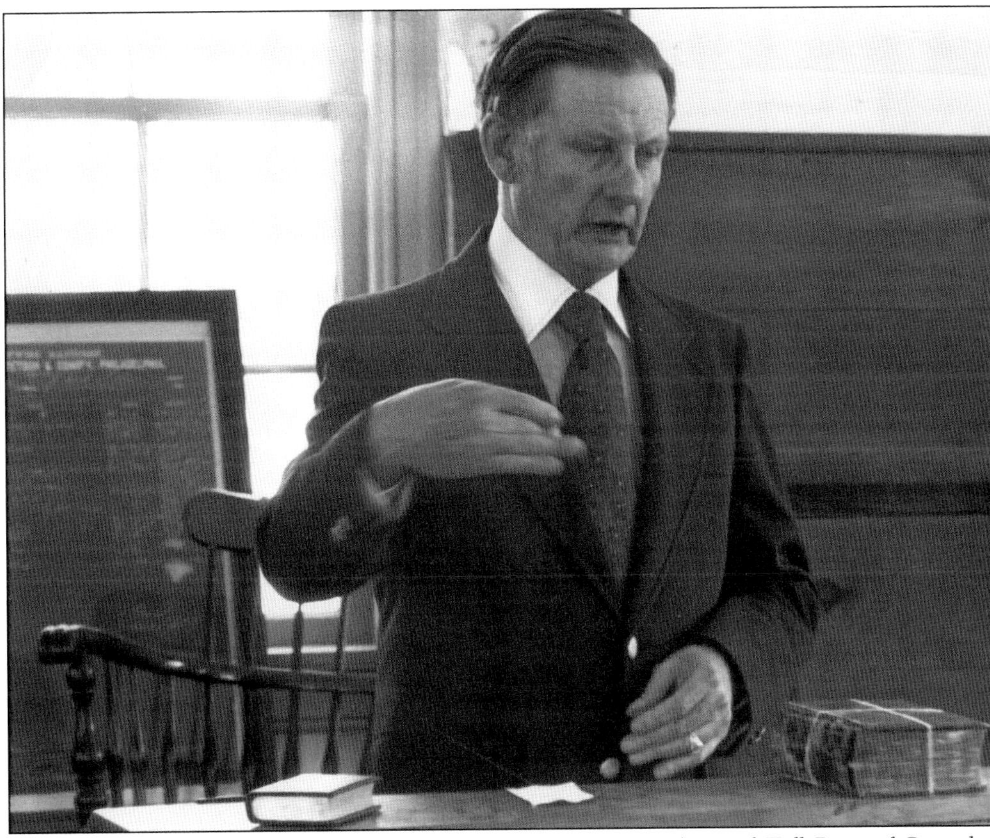

Kenneth N. Scull and his uncle, Clark S. Barrett, were coauthors of *Tall Pines of Catawba*, a book rich in the history of the area. In addition, Scull collected, researched, and lectured on local history. Due to his untiring efforts, many of the township's artifacts and papers have been preserved.

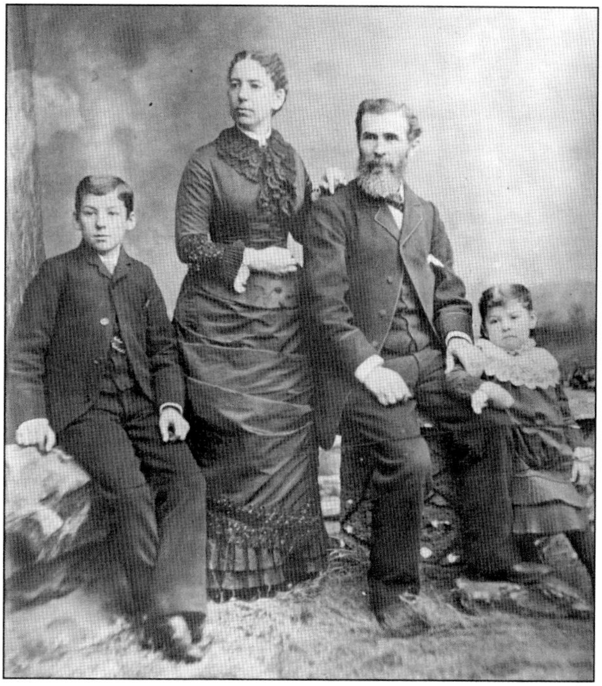

Dr. Denman Bevis Ingersoll, a self-educated teacher, later graduated from the University of Pennsylvania School of Medicine. He practiced in Mays Landing from 1865 until his death in 1890. He married Mary Hanthorn and was the father of Rachel, a teacher, and Robert, an attorney who served as vice chancellor of New Jersey courts.

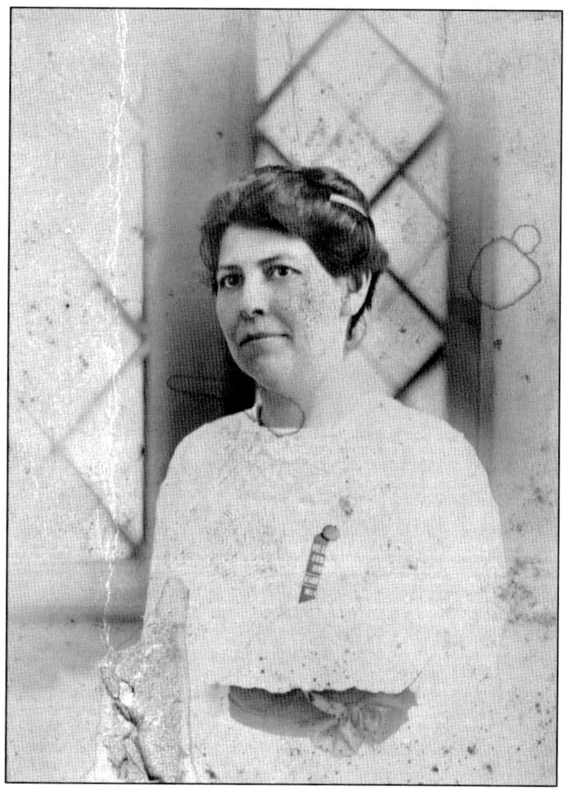

Rachel Ingersoll taught many of the Township of Hamilton's children until her retirement in 1931.

John W. Underhill was a public benefactor who came to Mays Landing during the first decade of the 20th century. For many years, he was its only African American resident. He established a small store that catered mostly to children, whom he loved.

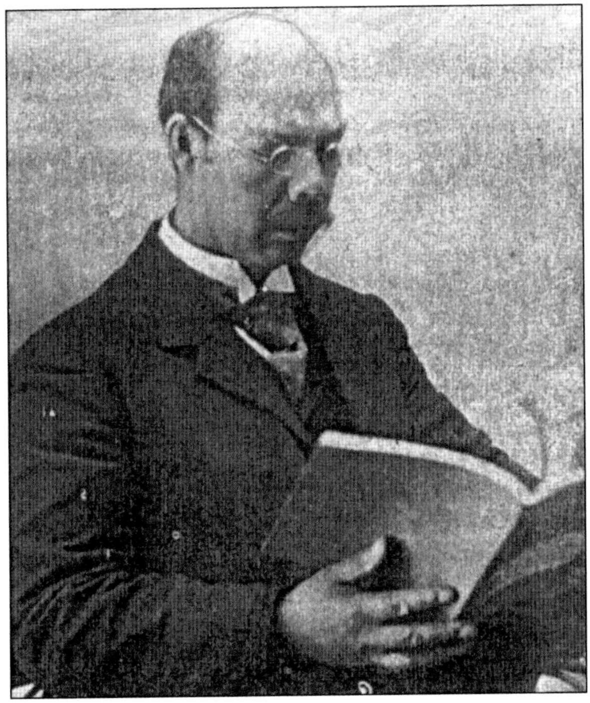

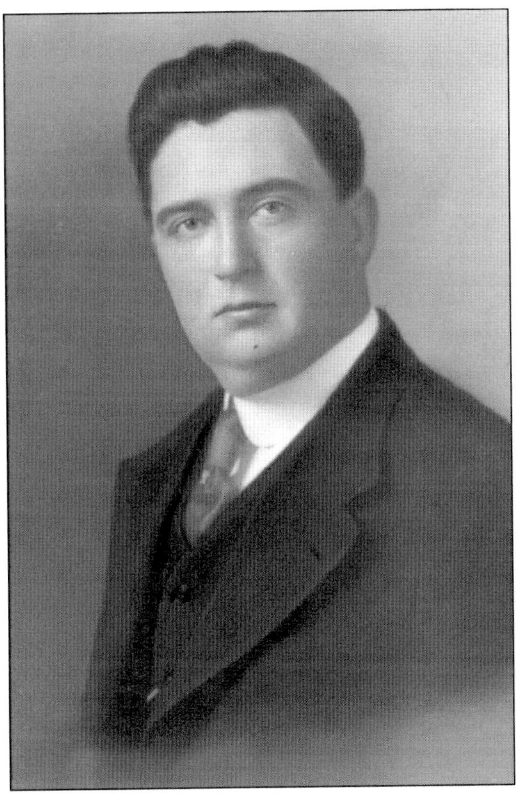

Joseph C. Shaner Sr. was born in 1892, the son of Emanuel C. and Lucinda Shaner. He was known for his community service, friendly disposition, beautiful baritone voice, and the fine example he set for others. He served as secretary of Unity Lodge No. 96 of the Free and Accepted Masons and, for many years, was superintendent of the Mays Landing Water Works. He was killed in an automobile accident while on a school errand. A new school erected in 1957 was named in his memory, a fitting tribute.

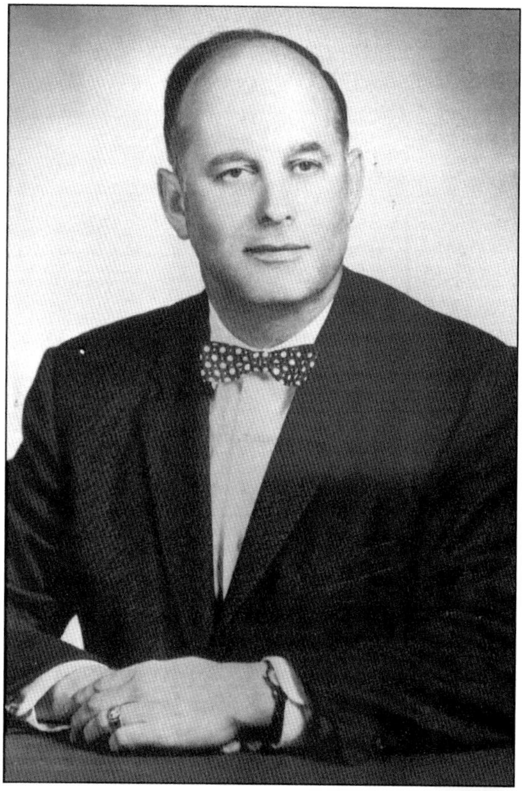

J. Harold Duberson was an active member of many school organizations and civic and service clubs. He was named Outstanding Citizen of the Year in 1965 by the Mays Landing Chamber of Commerce. The former Mays Landing High School was renamed the J. Harold Duberson School in 1972.

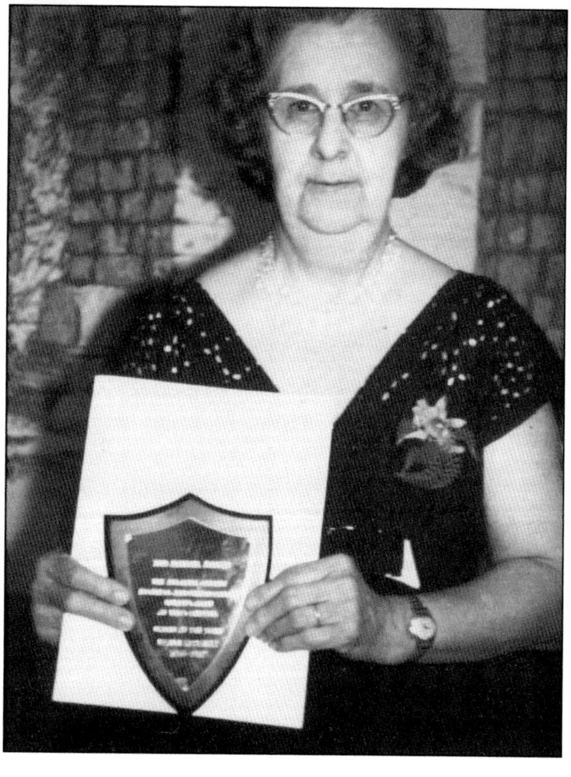

Verna Vannaman Luderitz of Mays Landing was named Woman of the Year in 1966 by the Mays Landing Chapter of Business and Professional Women in Atlantic County.

John S. Scheeler was a world champion wildlife wood carver. Self-taught, he began his career in the early 1970s. He was considered the most honored wood carver in America, having won numerous national awards. For seven consecutive years, he won the prestigious Ward Foundation Wildlife Woodcarving competition. He carved his birds in the workshop in his Mays Landing home.

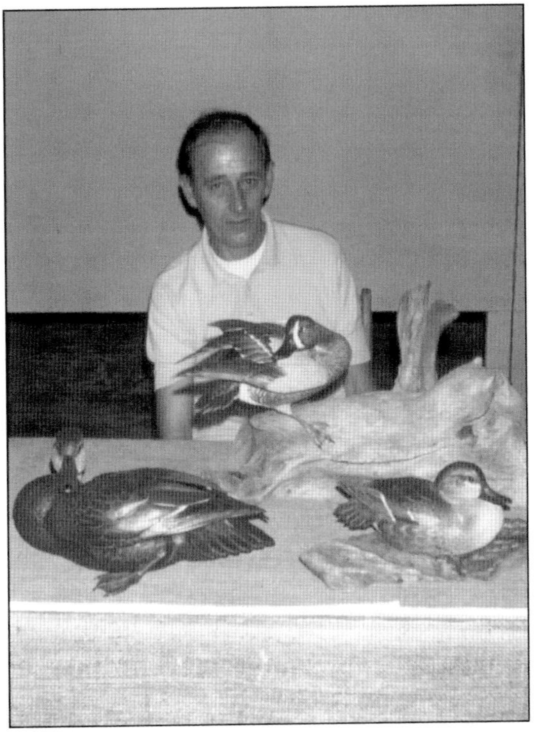

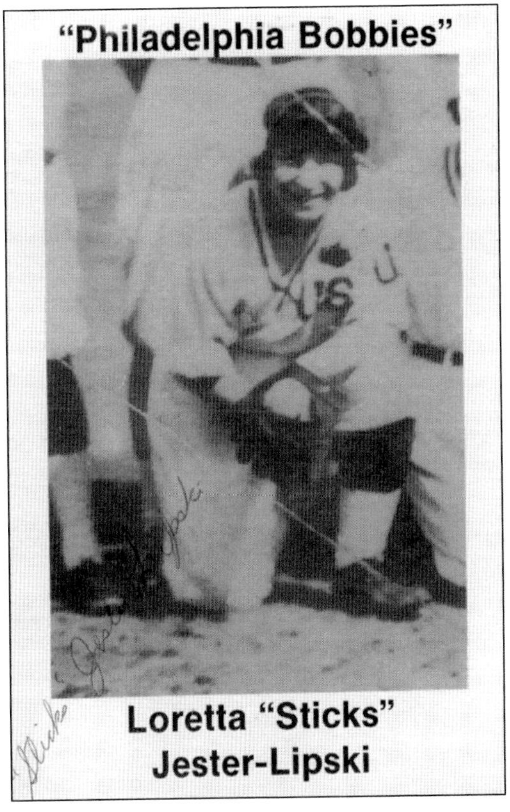

At age 16, Loretta "Sticks" Jester-Lipski was one of the charter members of the world's first all-woman professional baseball team. She played for the Philadelphia Bobbies from 1924 to 1927. A power hitter who played right field, she was known as one of their "Four Horsemen." She traveled with the team across the United States. After the Bobbies won the Women's National Championship in 1925, the team was invited by the Japanese government to tour their country. Jester-Lipski played exhibition games in several Japanese cities. She currently resides in the Township of Hamilton. At age 80, she was inducted into the Baseball Hall of Fame.

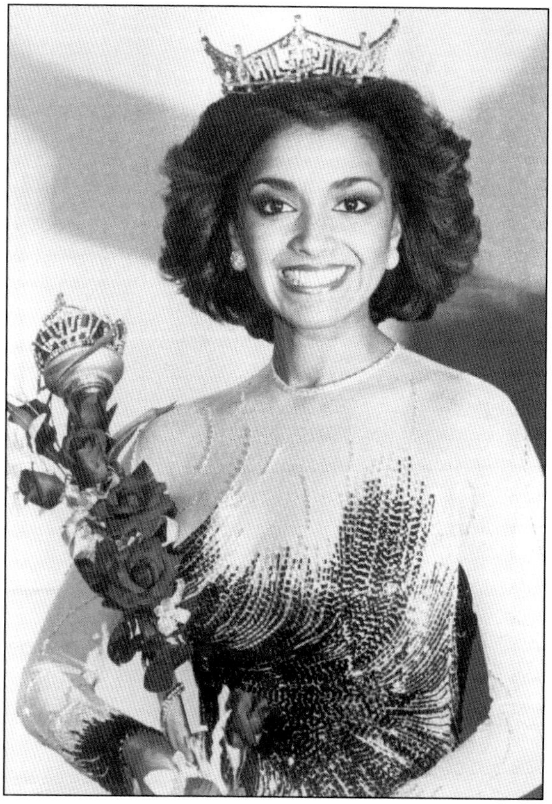

Suzette Charles, daughter of Charles and Suzette DeGaetano and a native of Mays Landing, was first runner-up to Miss America in 1984. She became Miss America in July 1984 when her predecessor relinquished the crown. Following Suzette's reign, she enjoyed a successful career in the entertainment industry.

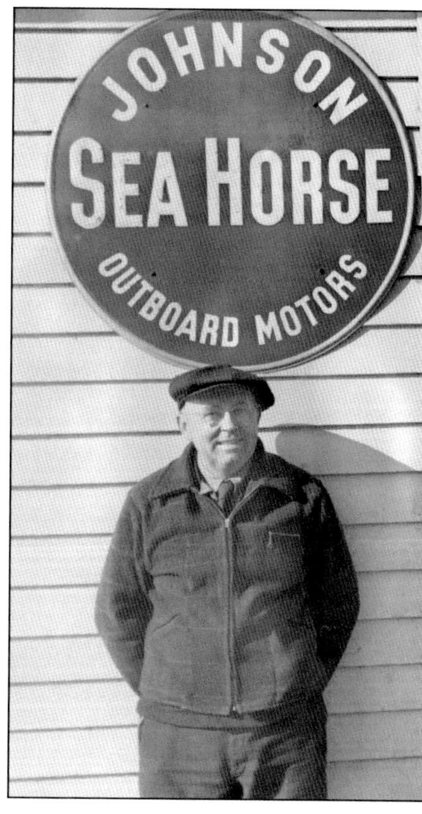

Harry Collins Sr., a local merchant and dealer in Johnson outboard motors and hunting, fishing, and marine supplies, also found time to be active in community affairs.

Cmdr. Robert Aumack of the U.S. Navy, a Mays Landing native, was a naval aviator and jet instructor. He flew with the Blue Angels as a flight leader and officer-in-charge of the unit.

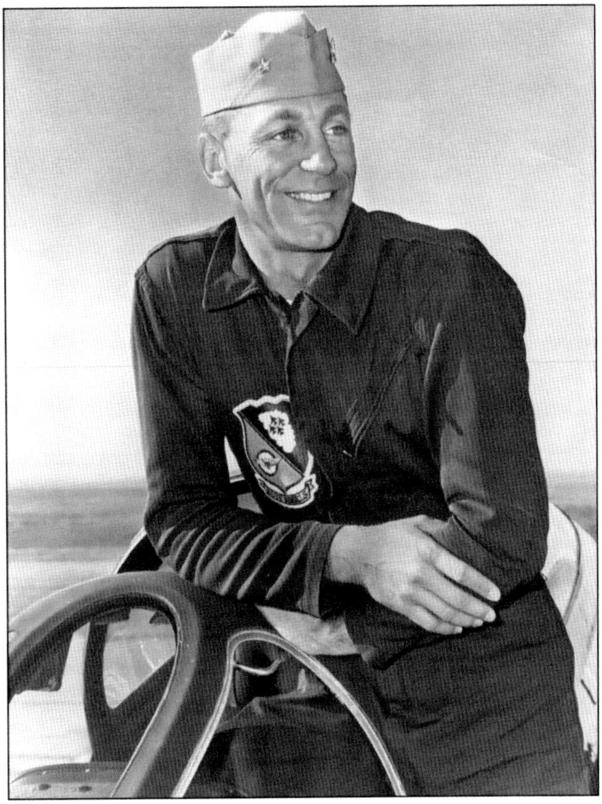

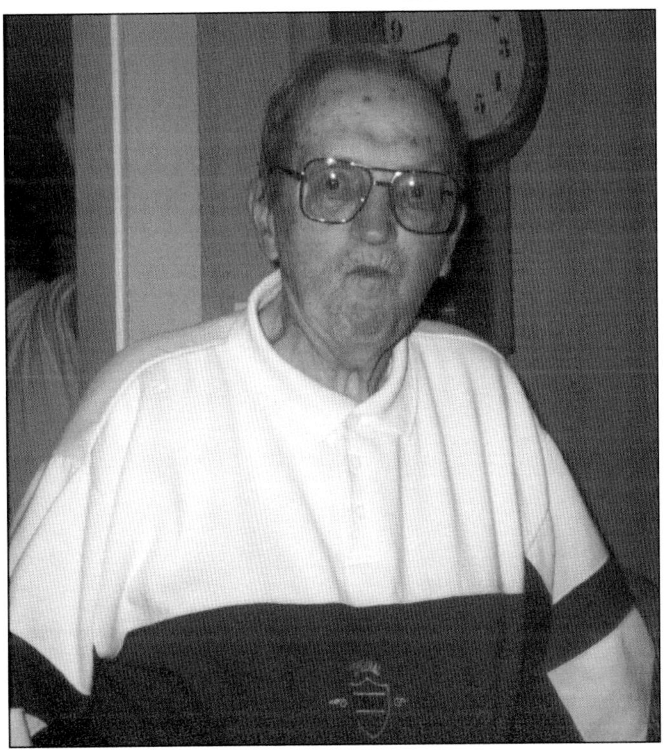

Charles Russell Imlay of Mays Landing was the recipient of an award presented by RCA for his participation in the Apollo space program and his contribution to the project to put an American on the moon.

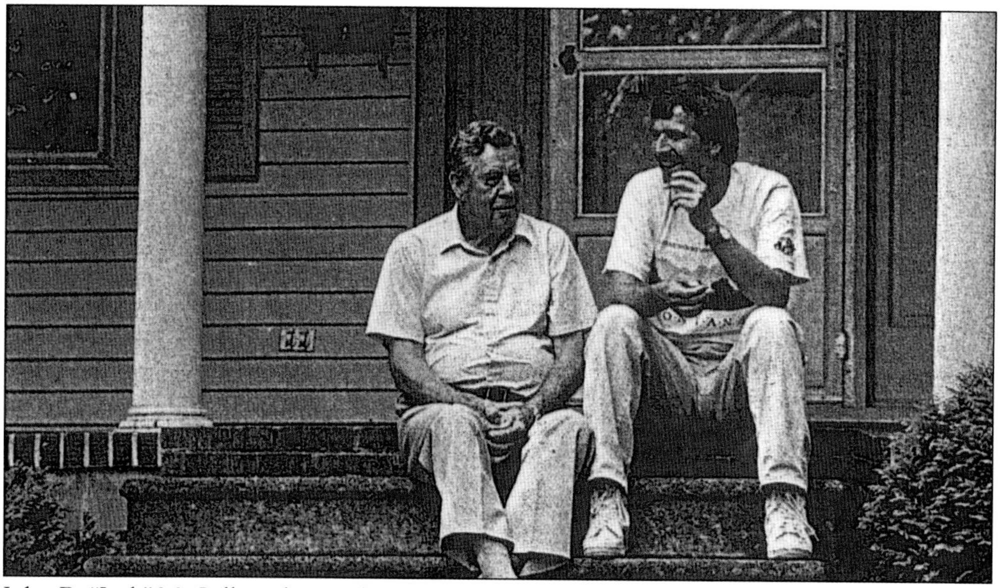

John D. "Jack" McCallum shares a happy moment with his son Jack, a writer for *Sports Illustrated* magazine. One of his articles recalls his favorite memories of a summer spent in Mays Landing. The article mentions local Oakcrest High School pitchers Bob Fink and Joe Cirigliano Jr. He noted that Cirigliano had received the 1989 Robert J. Gasko Memorial Award, which is presented in memory of a former Oakcrest outfielder "with a good eye and a sweet swing."

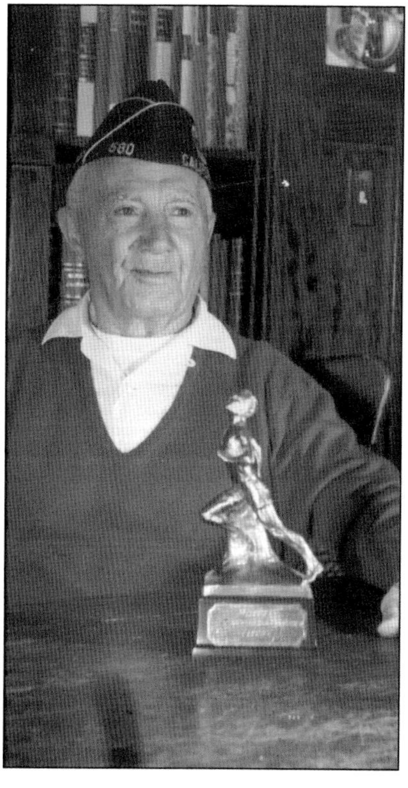

Abraham Lincoln Monteverde served the country in World War I. In later years, past his 60th birthday, he broke the world's record for hiking from New York to San Francisco.

Henry W. Denmead (1896–1976) served the Township of Hamilton as mayor, committeeman, and tax collector. He was one of the founders of American Legion Post No. 254 in Mays Landing and was also Mays Landing's first Boy Scout leader. Many will remember Denmead as the man who handed them their diplomas at school graduations, since he served as president of the school board for Oakcrest High School.

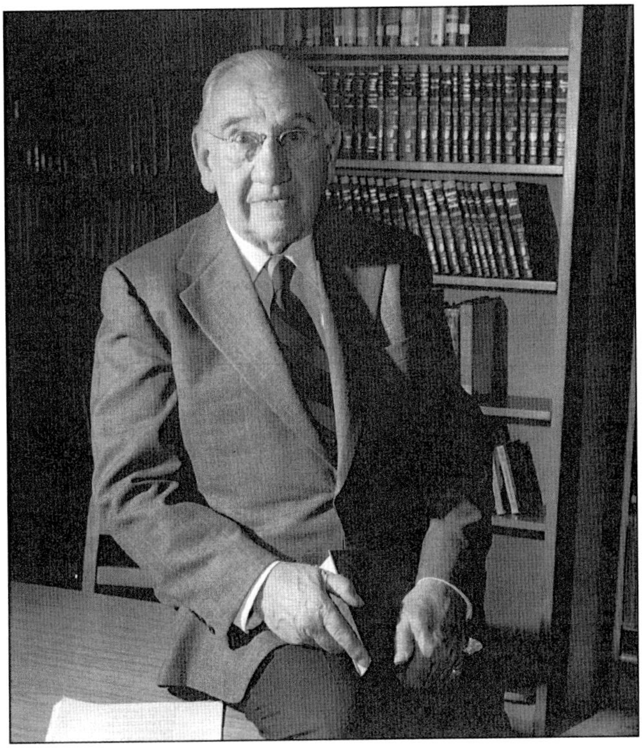

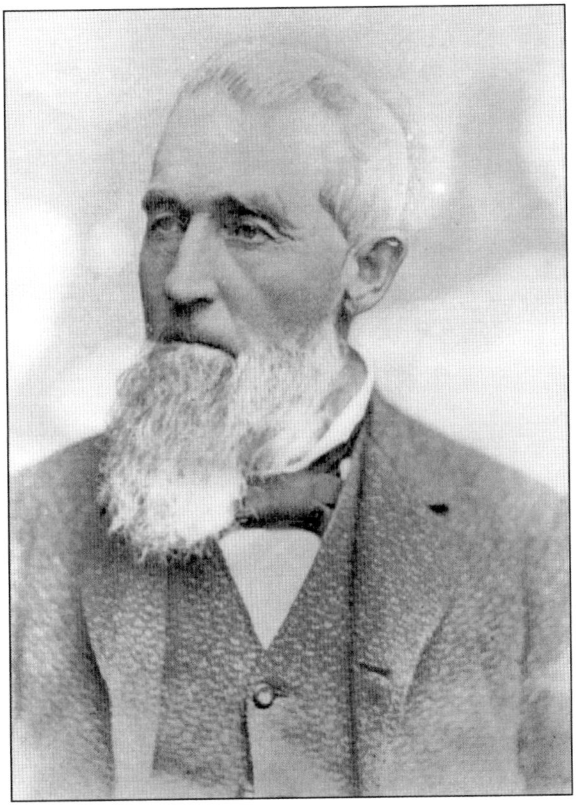

Capt. Shepheard S. Hudson came to Mays Landing at the age of six, went to sea with his father at the age of 11 as a cook, and became commander and owner of the *Jennie Sweeney*, which he built in 1876. He became a New Jersey assemblyman in 1889. Hudson sailed until within a year of his death. The *Jennie Sweeney* sank off the Bahamas on June 7, 1906, the same day Hudson was buried in Union Cemetery in Mays Landing.

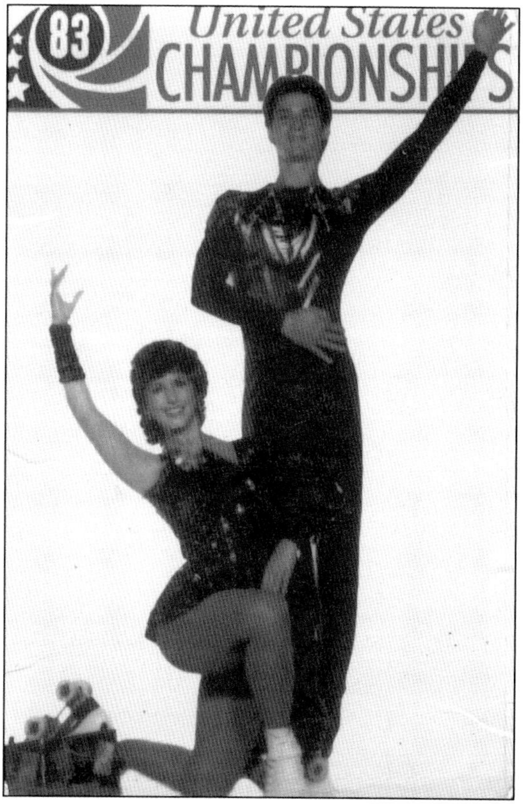

Bob Campbell Jr. and Tina Morris were victorious in the 1983 U.S. Roller Skating Championships. Campbell was raised in Mays Landing and is currently an attorney, practicing in his hometown.

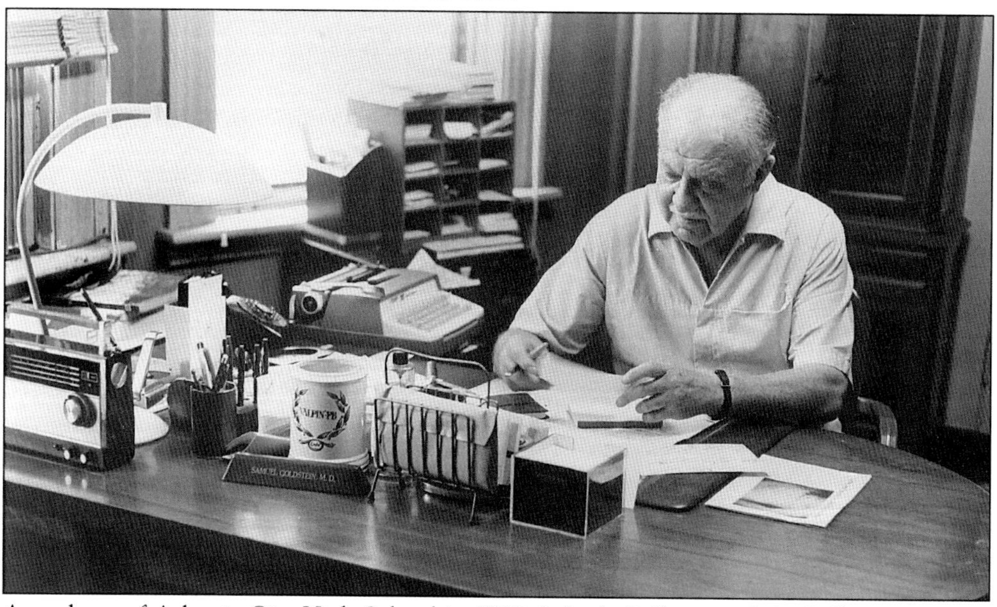

A graduate of Atlantic City High School in 1922, Lehigh College, and the Jefferson Medical College, Dr. Samuel Goldstein practiced medicine in Mays Landing for 50 years. He served as a captain with the 5th Army in Africa and Italy during World War II and was credited with being the first medical officer to set foot on the mainland of Europe in the invasion of Italy. He received the Mays Landing Outstanding Citizen Award in 1970.

New Jersey Sen. William Gormley (Republican, Atlantic County) was born and raised in Mays Landing, son of Sheriff Gerard Gormley. The senator is a well-known practicing attorney whose local office is located in the Hamilton Mall.

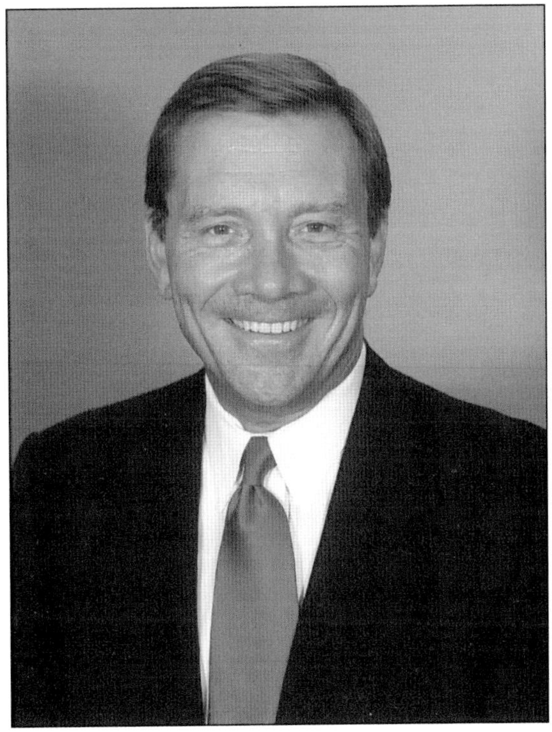

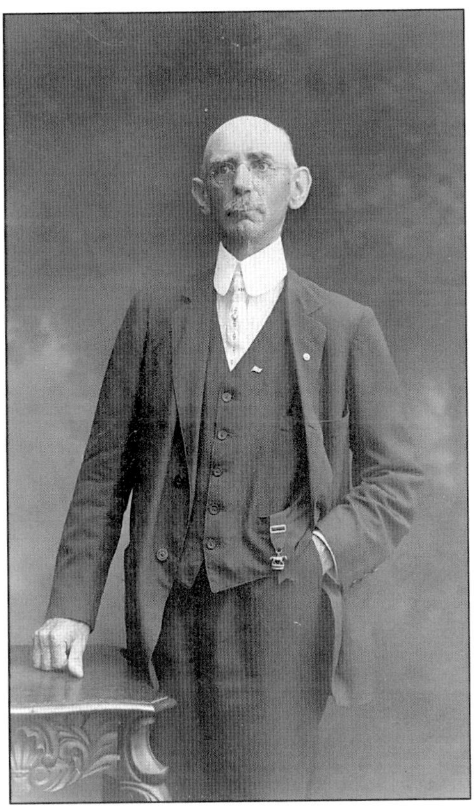

Simon Hanthorn (1818–1876) served as judge of the Inferior Court of Common Pleas in 1870. He moved from Salem County to Mays Landing in the early 1850s. He built a store, which still stands on the corner of Main and Hanthorn Streets.

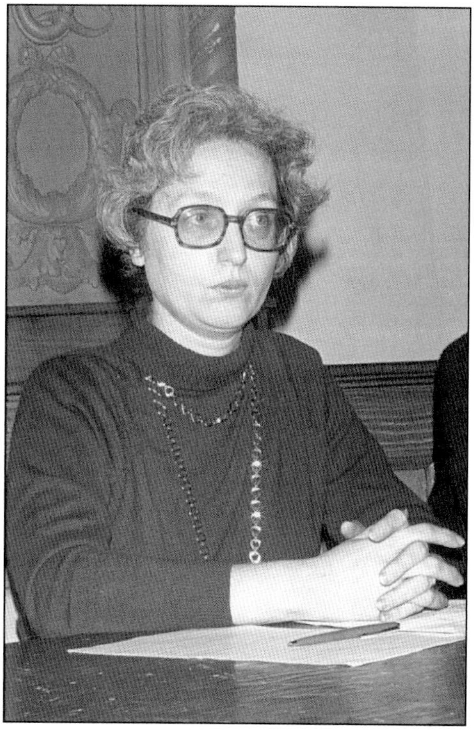

In 1974, Loretta Newman was the first woman elected to serve on the township committee.

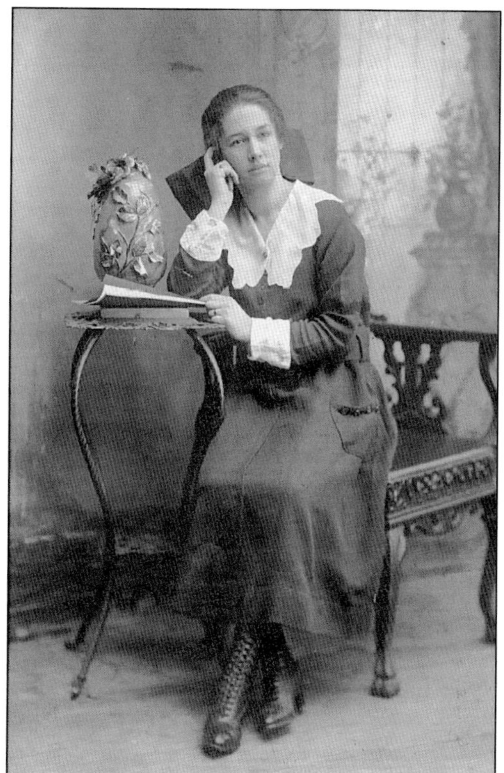

Sarah Ripley was the first telephone operator in Mays Landing.

Nine

MEMORIES

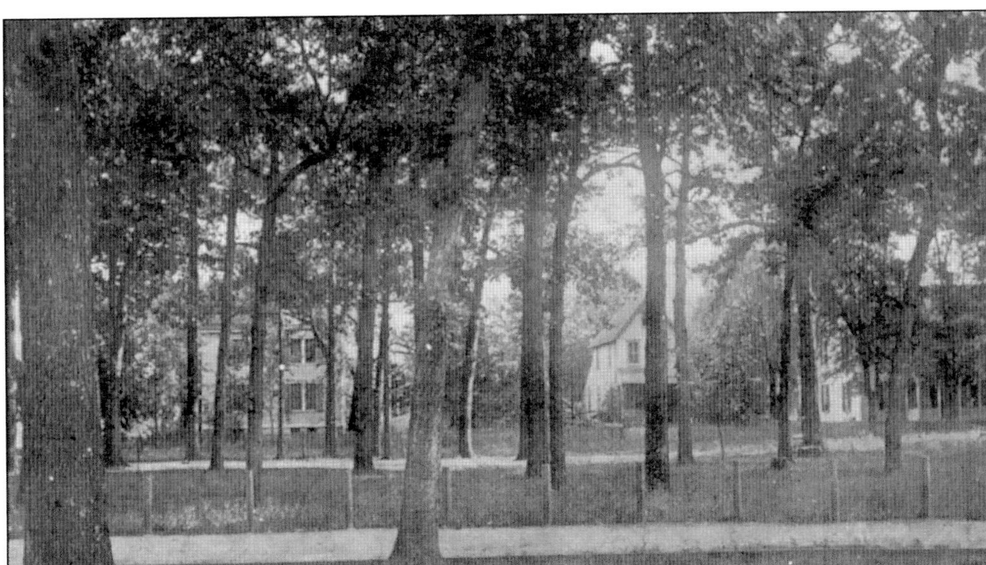

This is a view of Capitol Park at the corner of Main Street and Cape May Avenue in Mays Landing, now known as Memorial Park. The three structures beyond the trees, from left to right, are the Presbyterian Parsonage, the home of Laura Barrett, and the Methodist Parsonage.

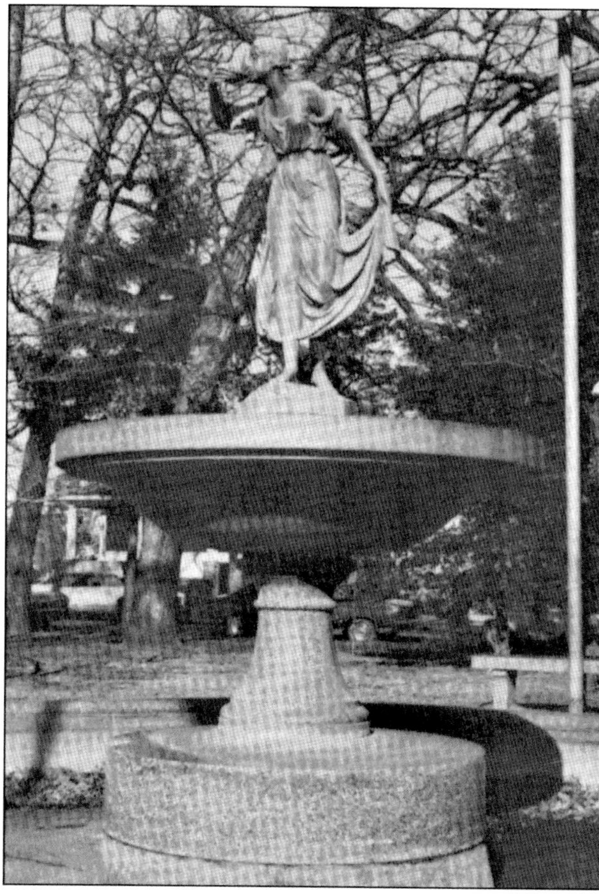

In his will, John W. Underhill left two thirds of his estate to the Township of Hamilton to be used for the Industrial Park, as it was then known. He stipulated that a public fountain and benches be placed in the park; this photograph offers proof that his wishes were carried out. The park is now known as Memorial Park and is located in the center of Mays Landing, adjacent to the court complex.

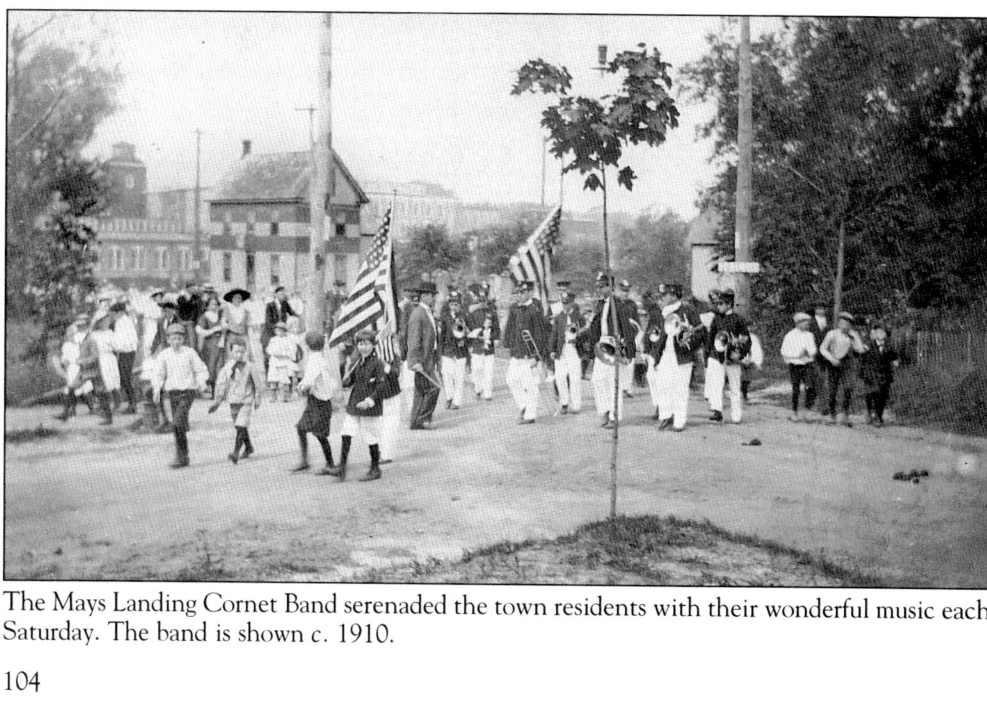

The Mays Landing Cornet Band serenaded the town residents with their wonderful music each Saturday. The band is shown *c.* 1910.

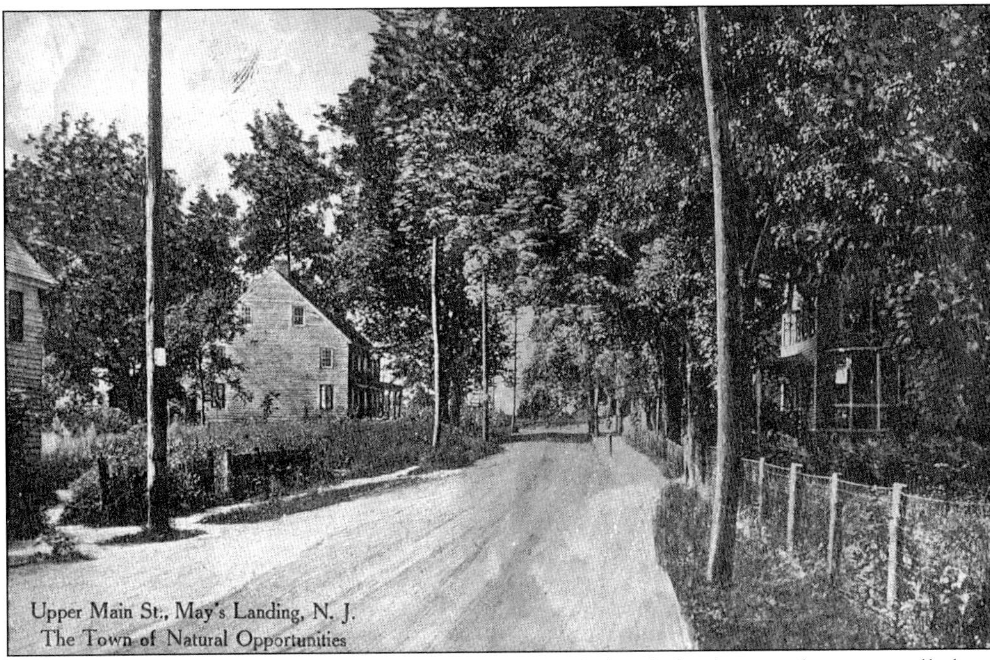

Upper Main Street in Mays Landing offered a tree-shaded path for those wishing to stroll about the town.

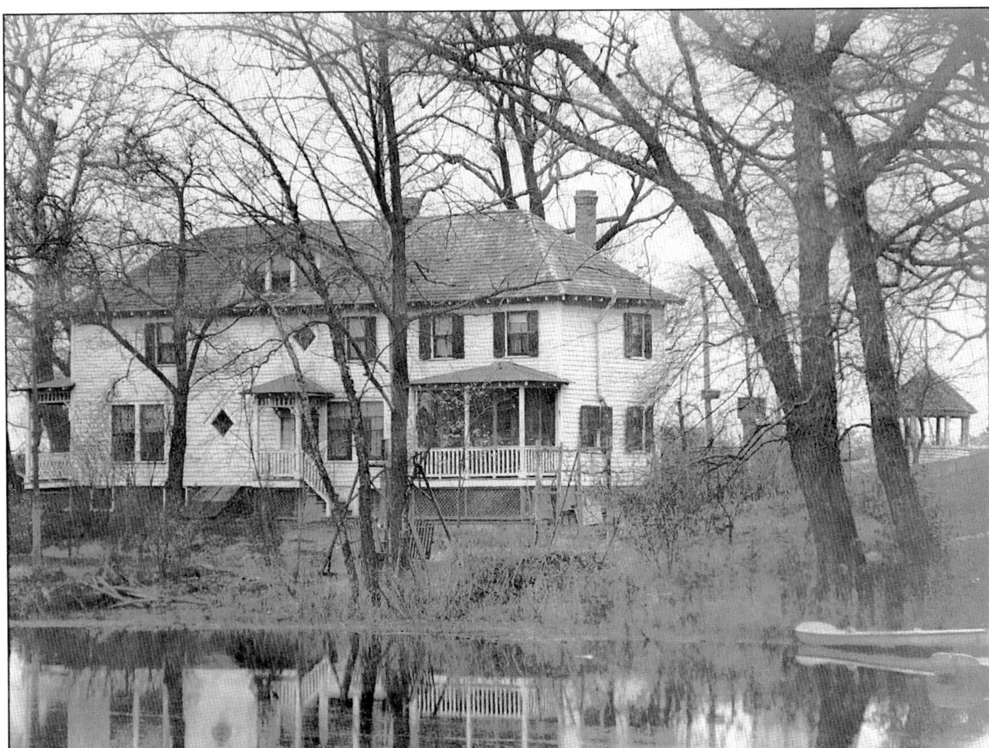

This building, located on Main Street in Mays Landing, was the home of J. Frank Davis.

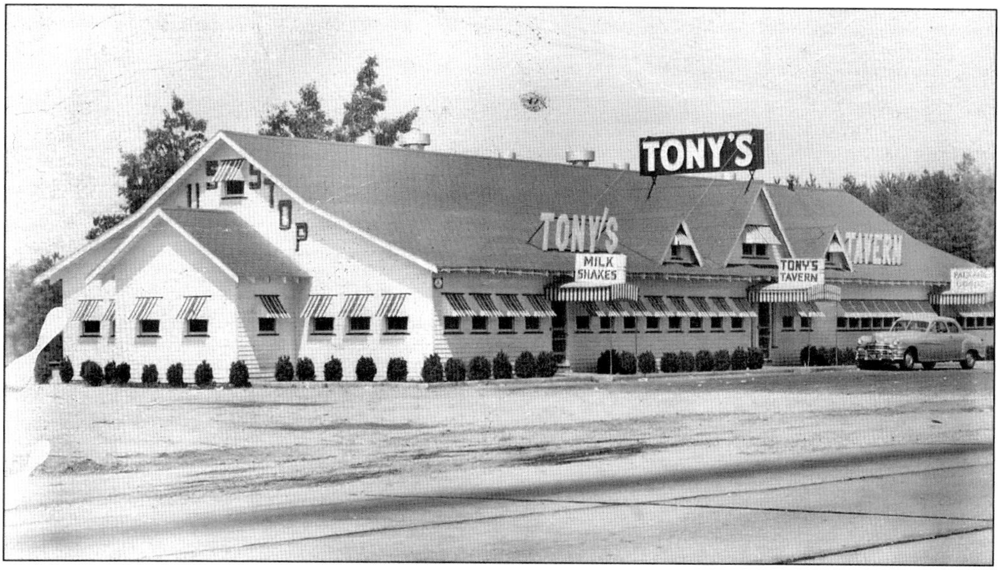

The tavern and motel owned by Tony Platanella was located in the Cloverleaf area of Mays Landing near the intersection of Routes 50 and 322 (Black Horse Pike). The tavern later burned, but the motel continued operating on this site.

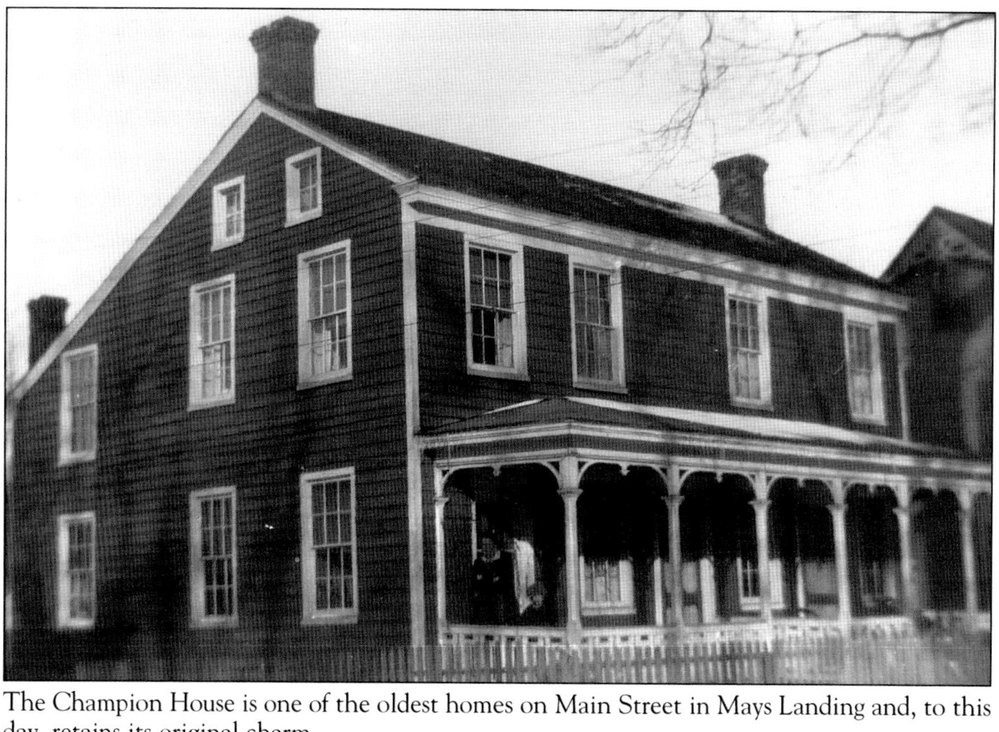

The Champion House is one of the oldest homes on Main Street in Mays Landing and, to this day, retains its original charm.

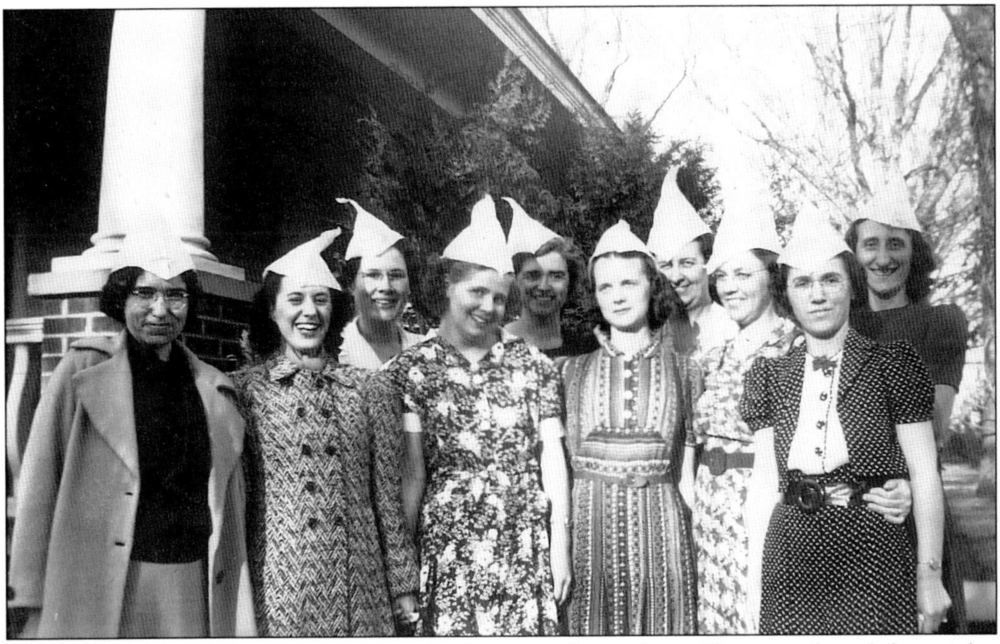

A community group poses for an occasion known only to them. They are, from left to right, Virginia Way, Alberta Birch, Ora Walling, Dorothy May, Olga Yetter, Millicent Barry, Verna Luderitz, Bertha Smithouser, Rose Barrett, and Reba Wittkamp. The photograph was taken *c.* the 1930s in front of Ora Walling's home, located on Seventh Street in Mays Landing.

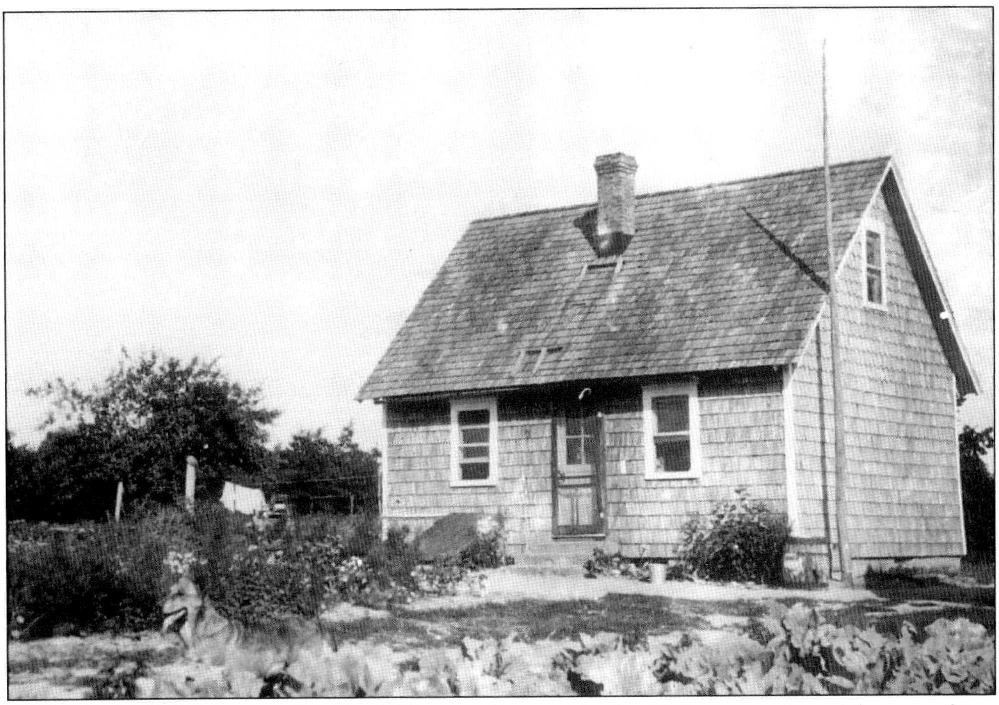

This old cottage, known as the Hagel House, is located in the Cologne section of the township.

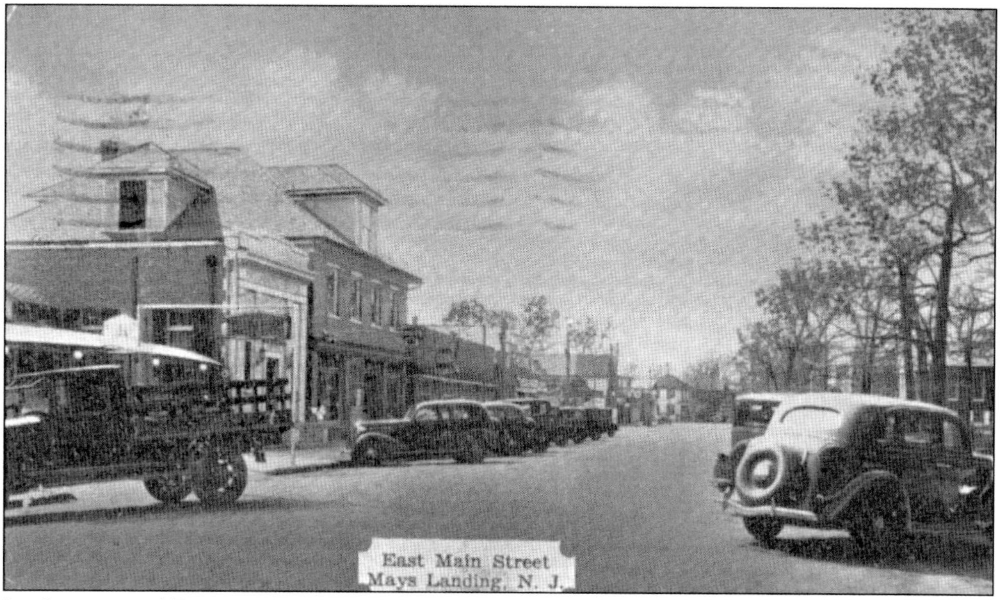

In this view of East Main Street in Mays Landing, the Court Diner and the Mays Landing Building and Loan Building (now Inland Insurance Agency) can be seen.

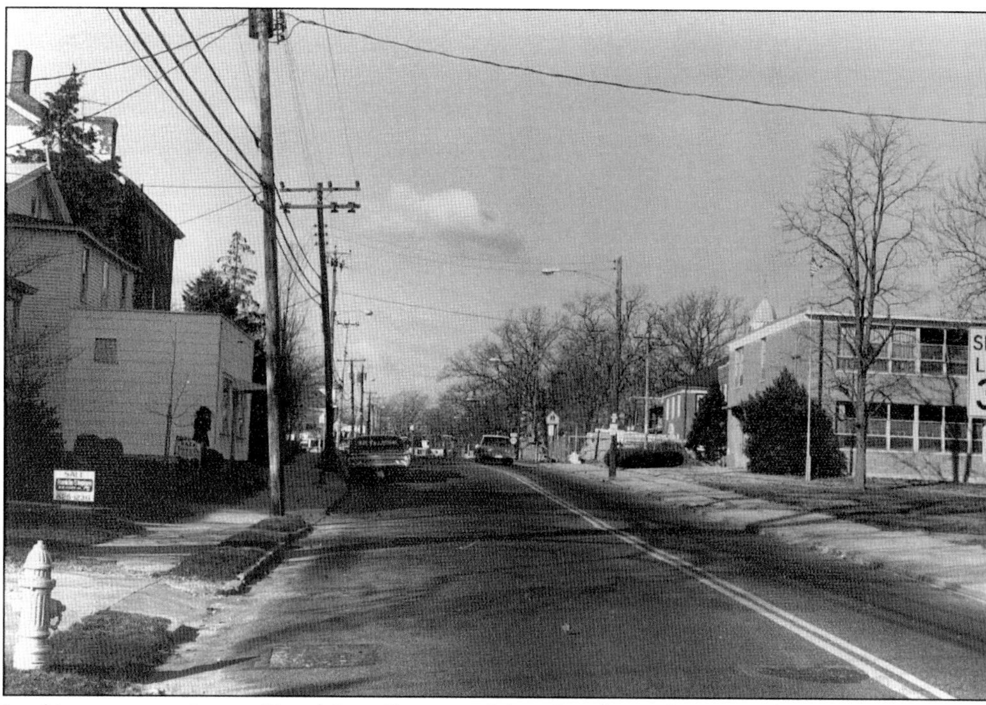

Looking west on Lower East Main Street in Mays Landing, this view shows a former news agency (left) and St. Vincent De Paul School (right).

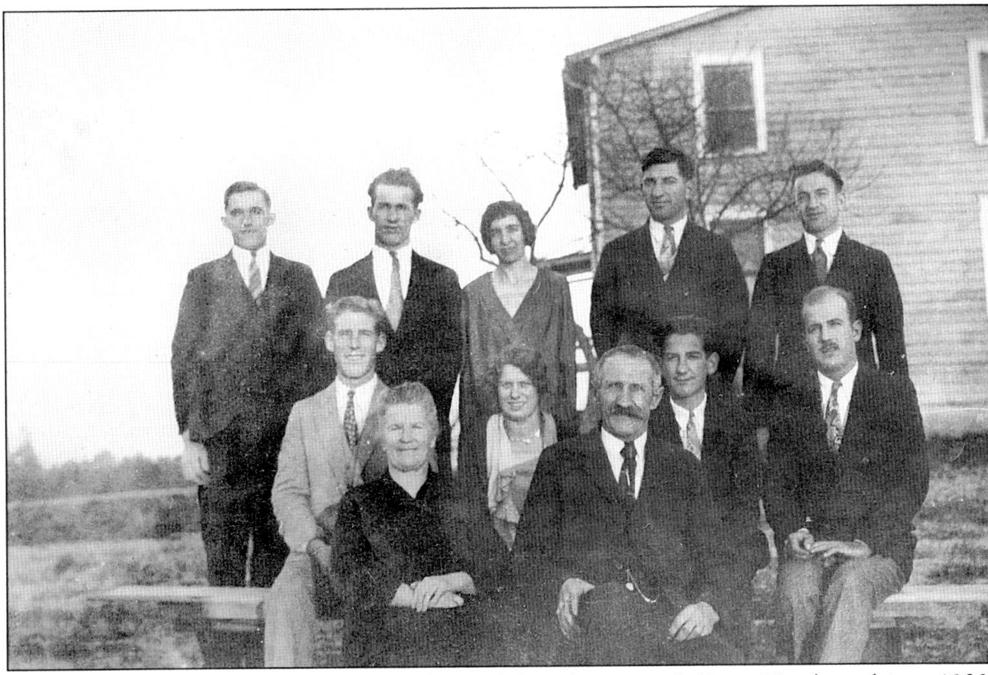

Members of the Mattle family pose in front of their homestead, Bears Head, in this *c.* 1930s photograph. From left to right are the following: (front row) Katherine and Jacob Mattle; (middle row) Frank, Anna, John, and Joseph Mattle; (back row) Jacob, Karl, Rose, August, and Anthony Mattle.

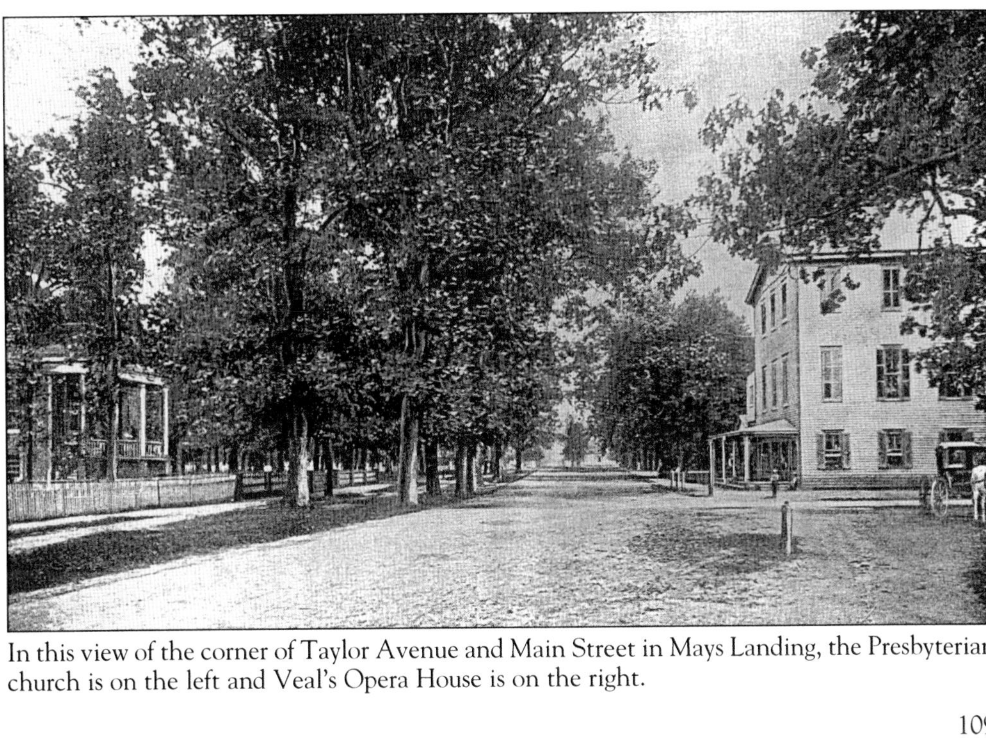

In this view of the corner of Taylor Avenue and Main Street in Mays Landing, the Presbyterian church is on the left and Veal's Opera House is on the right.

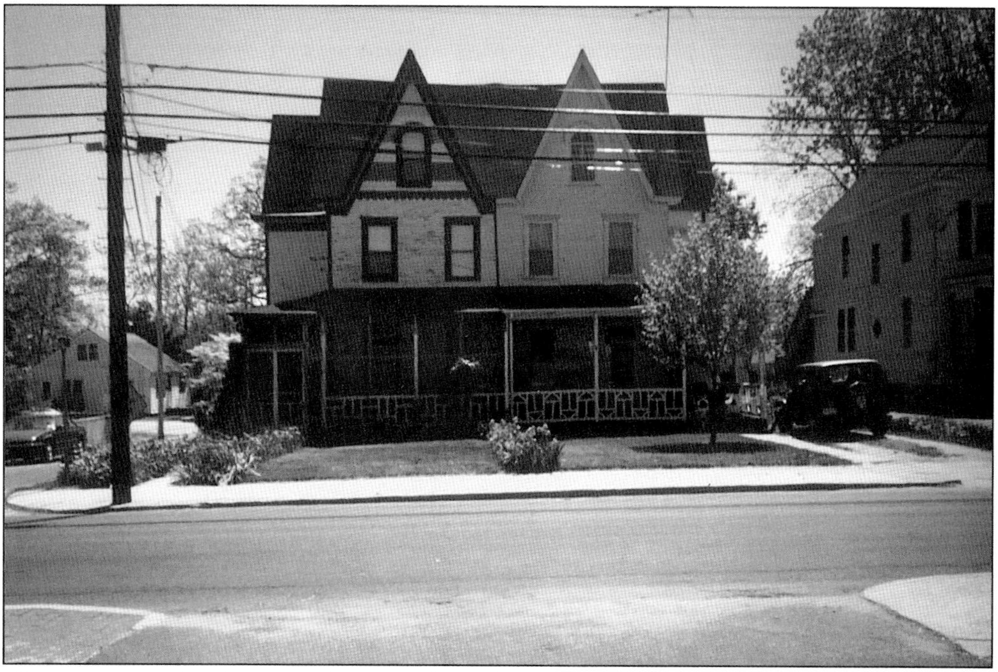

This is an example of a duplex home, *c.* 1891, located on Main Street in Mays Landing.

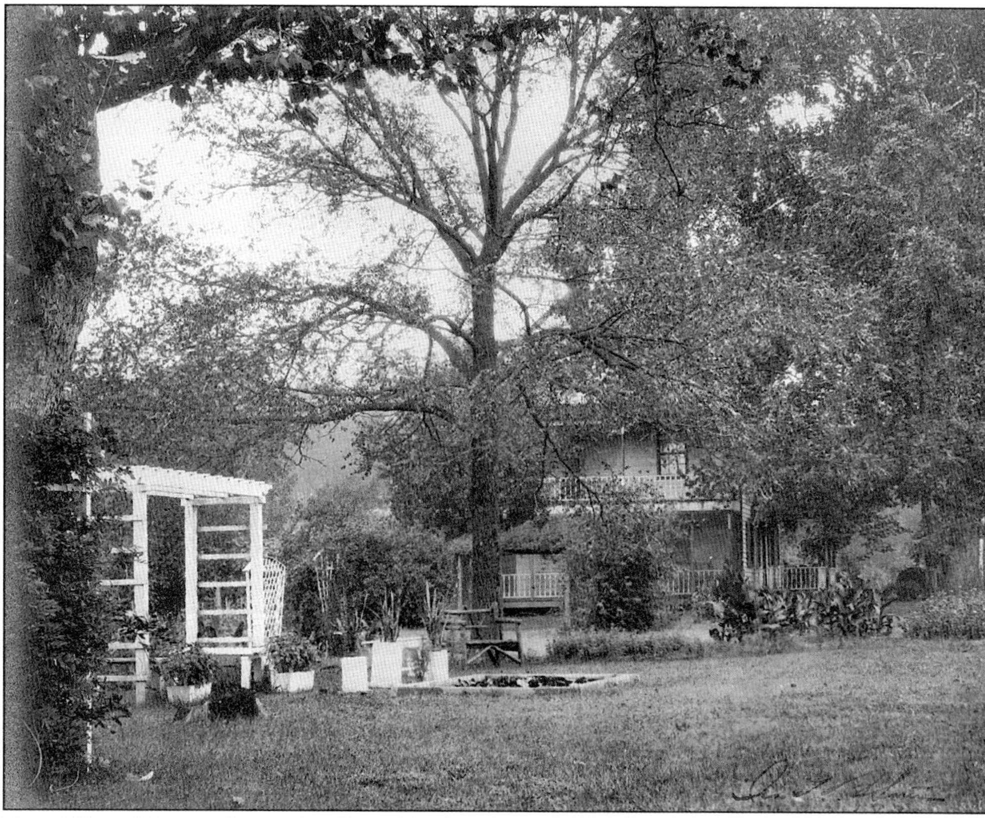

The Abbott Home is located at Gravelly Run in Mays Landing.

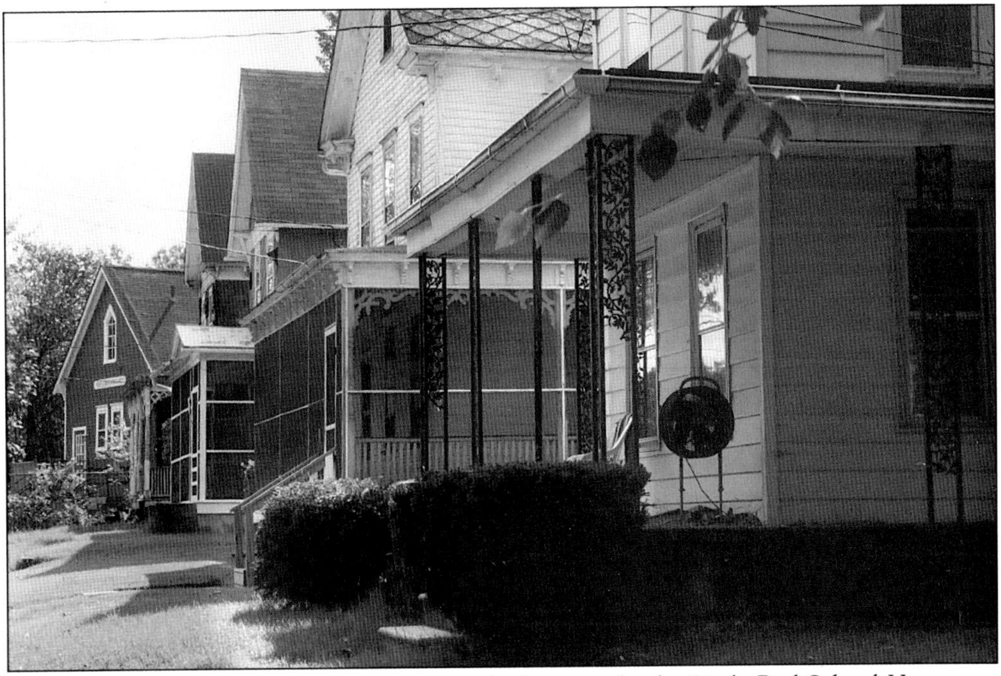

In this view of Mill Street in Mays Landing, looking south, the Little Red School House can be seen in the far background.

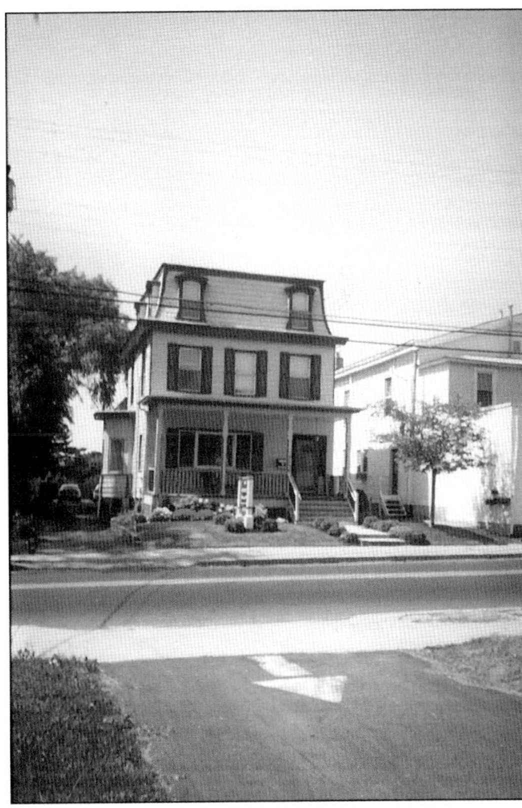

This building is located at 5734 Main Street in Mays Landing. It was built c. 1870 and features a concave mansard roof of the Second Empire style with fish scale shingles. It was the home of Capt. Lardner Clark and now serves as a law office.

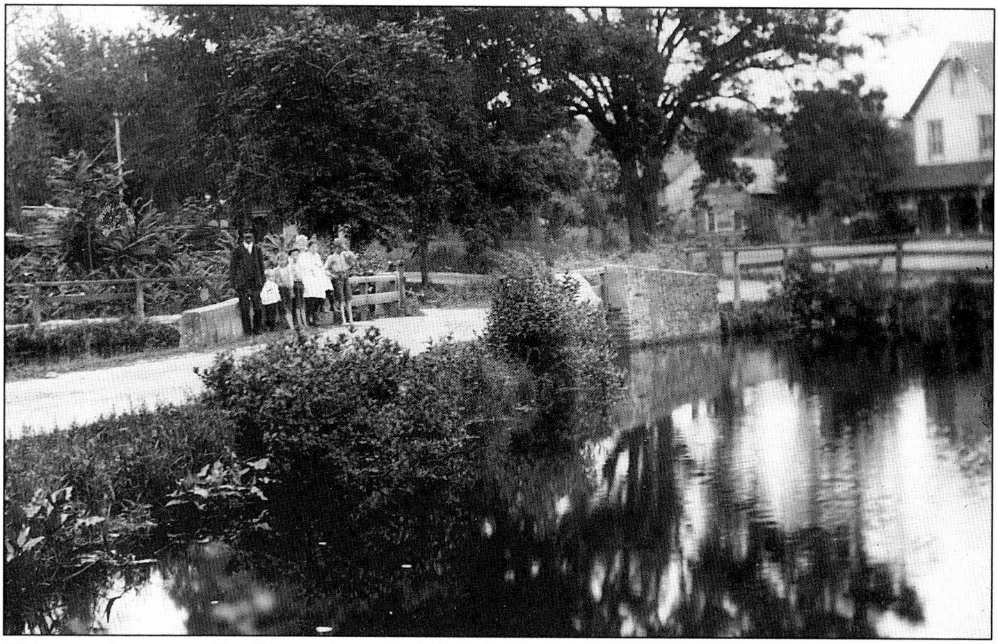

This area, known as Dry Run, where Park Road joins Lenape Avenue in Mays Landing, was and remains a gathering place for teenagers.

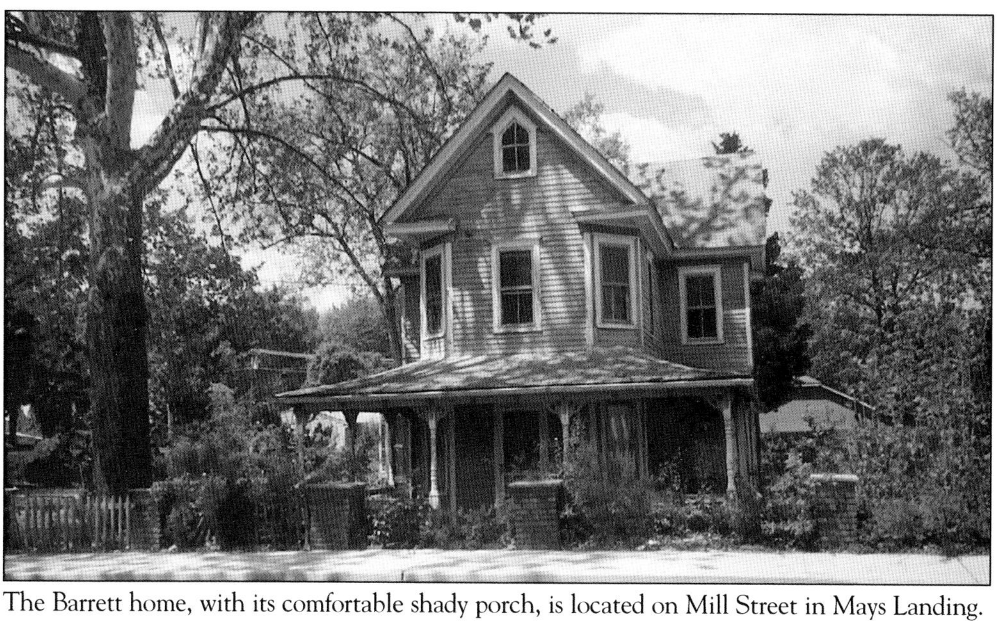

The Barrett home, with its comfortable shady porch, is located on Mill Street in Mays Landing.

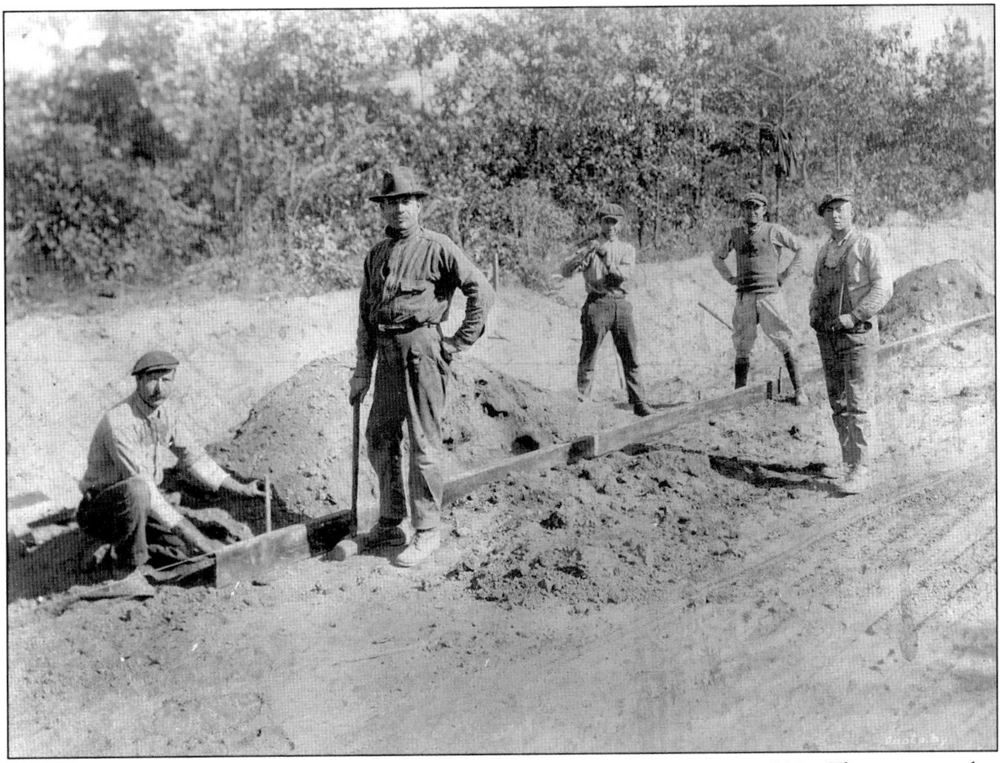

Workmen install forms on Route 40 prior to pouring concrete *c.* 1920. This route, also known as Harding Highway, was named after Pres. Warren G. Harding. Shown, from left to right, are Vincent Massey, Samuel Yanniello, Salvatore Bertolini (age 15), and two men from Landisville.

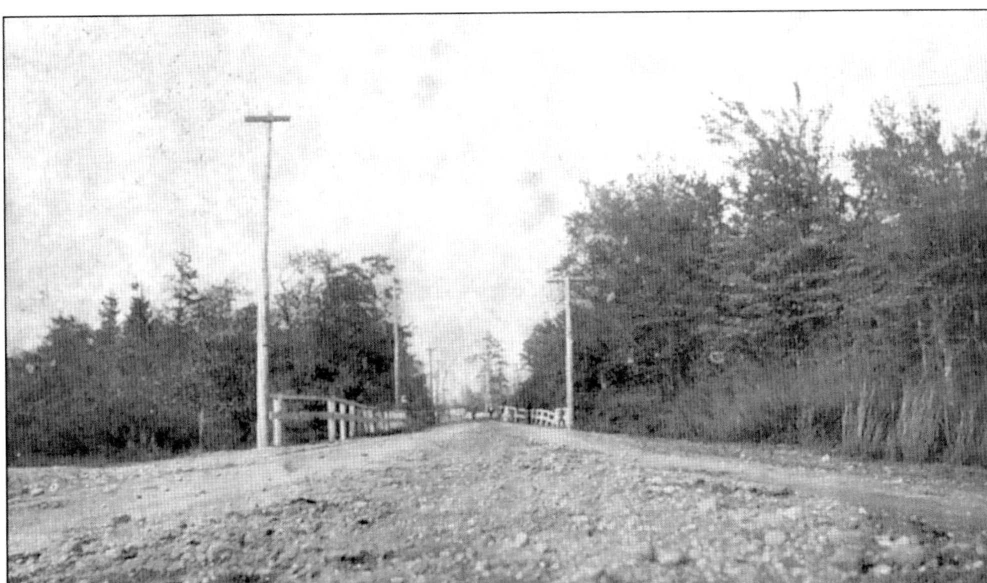

Known as the Watering Place, this area was a stopping point for watering horses on the road to Egg Harbor(Route 50) just before the Black Horse Pike.

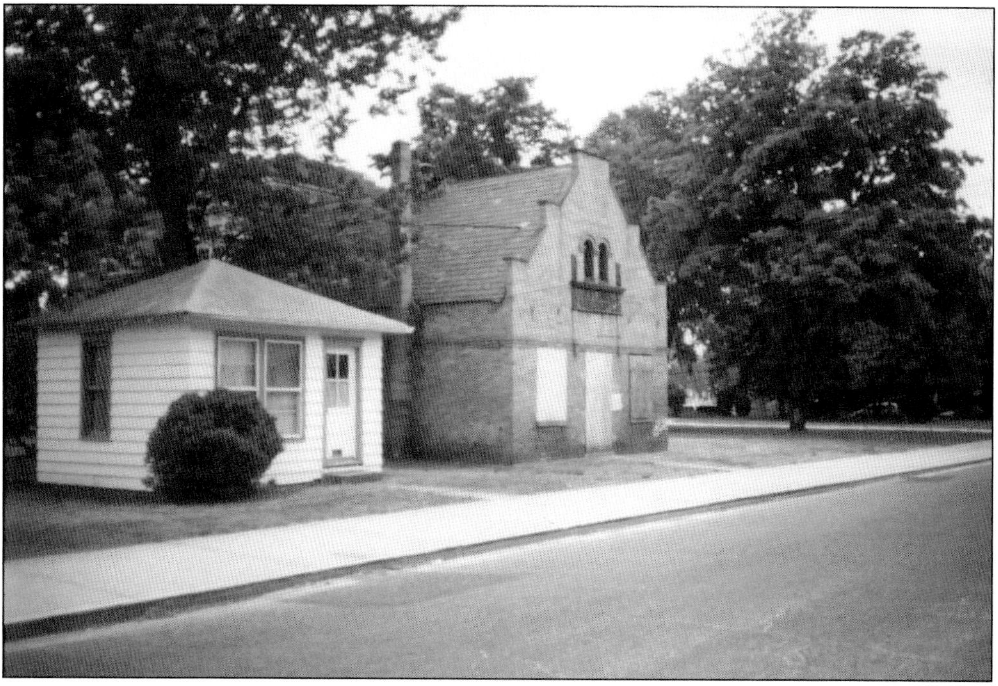

In this view of Farragut Avenue in Mays Landing, the first building on the left is the original Township of Hamilton branch of the Atlantic County Library. It was previously located directly across the street and housed the local candy store, where children rushed to spend their pennies. The second building is the waterworks.

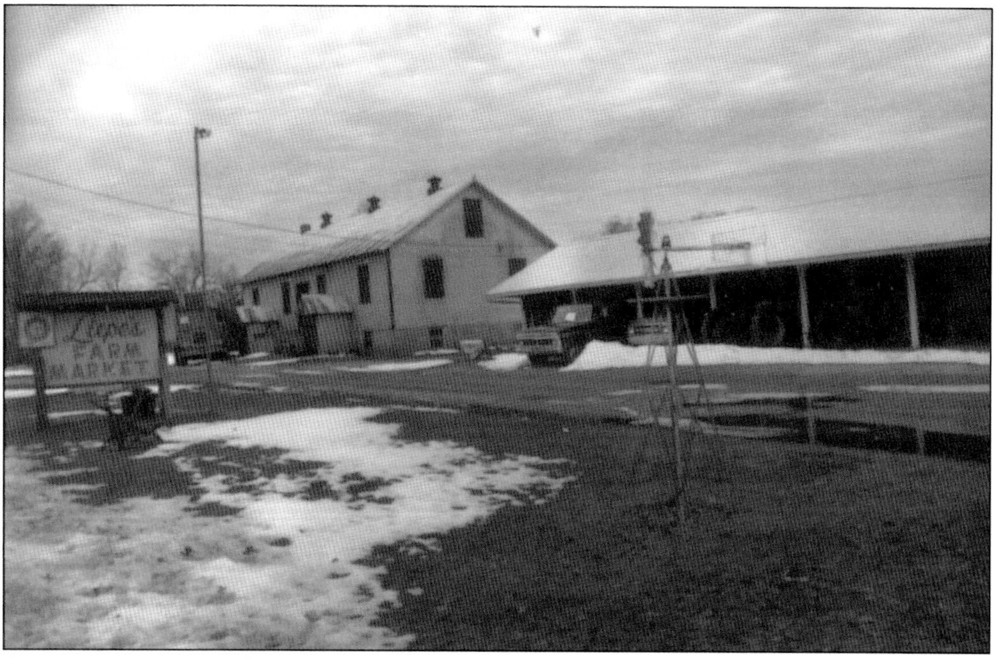

George Henry Liepe, who was born in a log house in Cologne in 1875, was raised on this farm, where his family was involved in trucking and fruit farming. In 1904, he began to develop the Black Diamond blackberry, which has become famous throughout New Jersey.

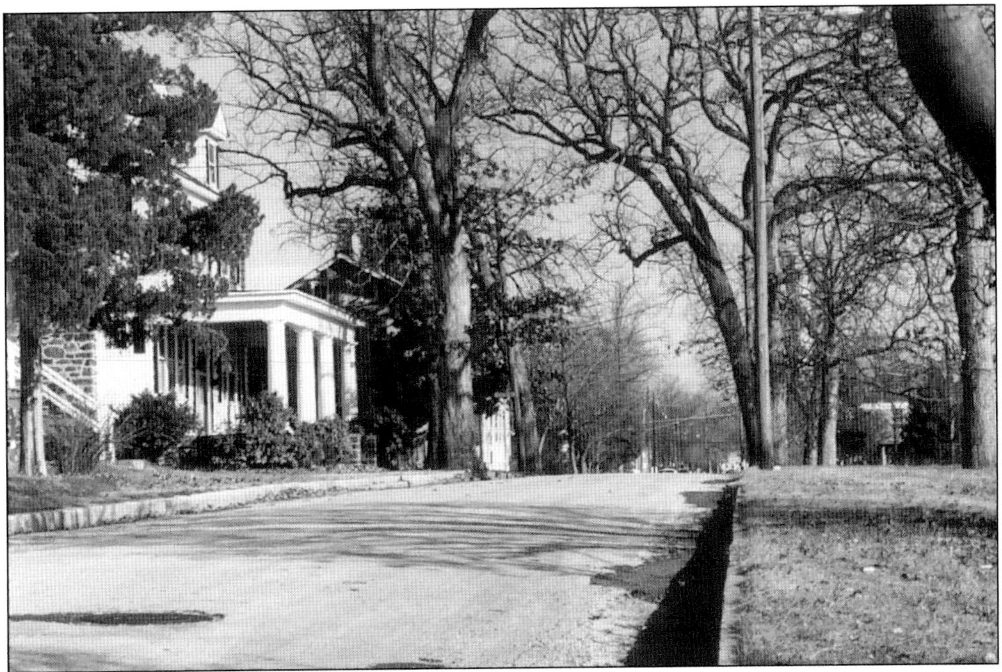

This view shows the Burton Gaskill home on South Farragut Avenue in Mays Landing, which overlooks Gaskill Park and the Great Egg Harbor River. Gaskill was a lawyer and also served as head of the Independent Order of Odd Fellows.

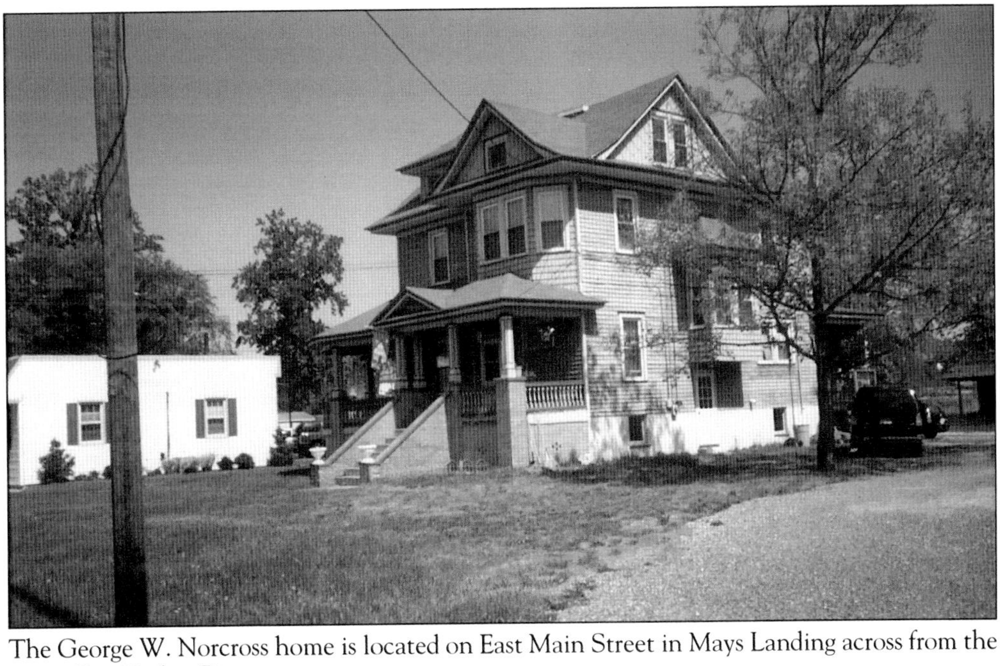

The George W. Norcross home is located on East Main Street in Mays Landing across from the Great Egg Harbor River.

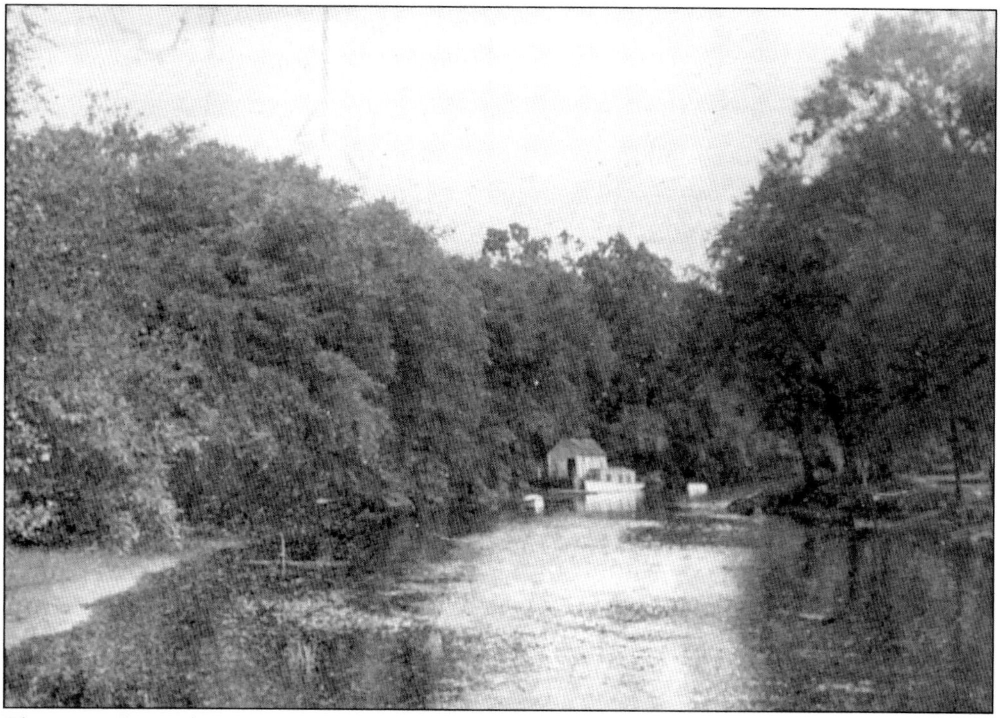

This view shows the Great Egg Harbor River from the Mill Street bridge in Mays Landing.

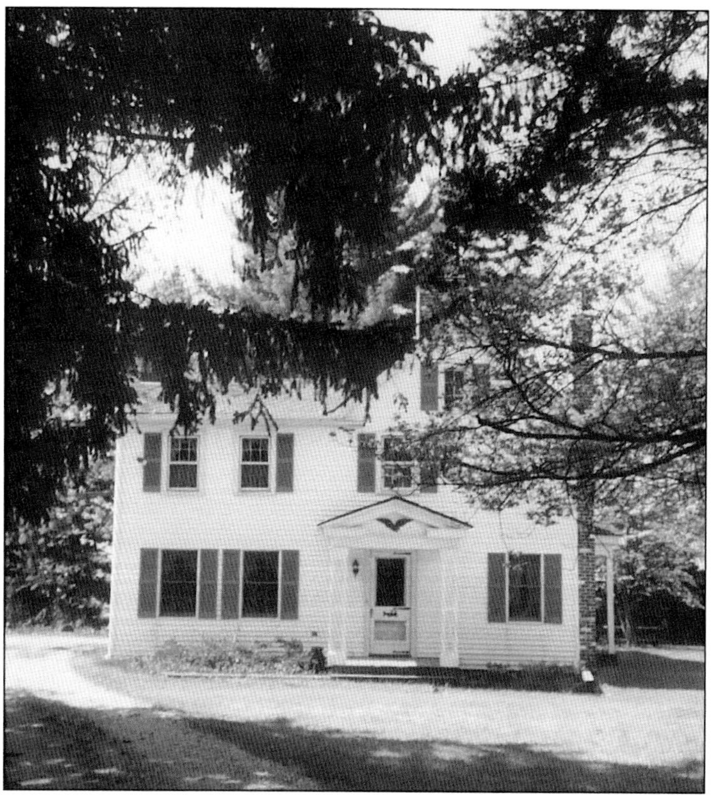

The John Newcomb home on River Road in Mays Landing is one of the oldest homes in the area.

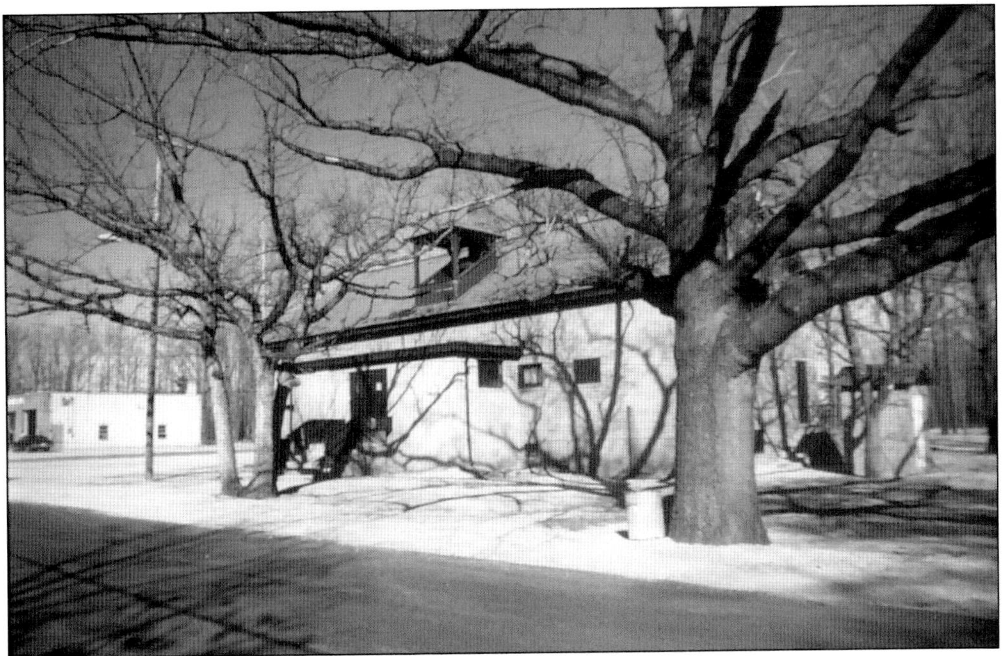

This two-room schoolhouse served the children from the Mizpah section of the township. The tree sheltering it still stands today.

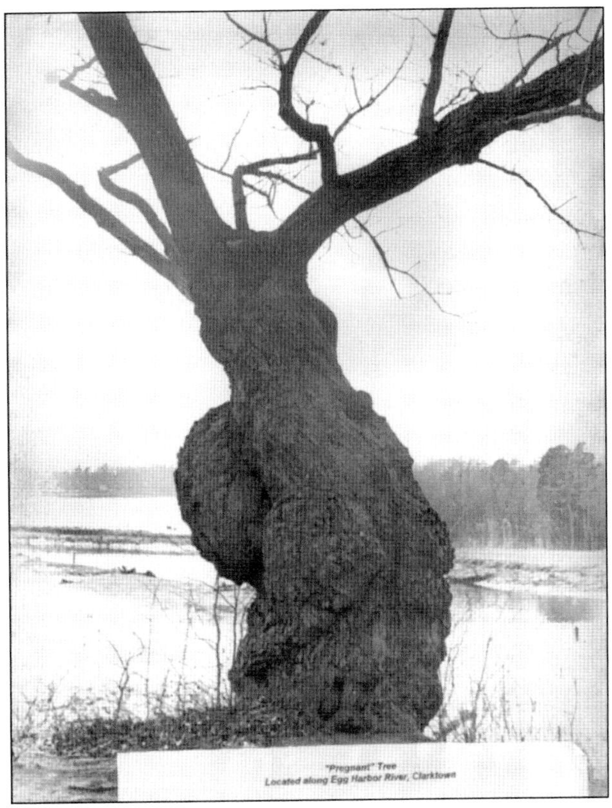

This curious old oak stands on the riverbank in the Clarktown section of the township. Known locally as the Pregnant Tree, it has a hollow trunk, which several generations of children have used as a favorite hiding place.

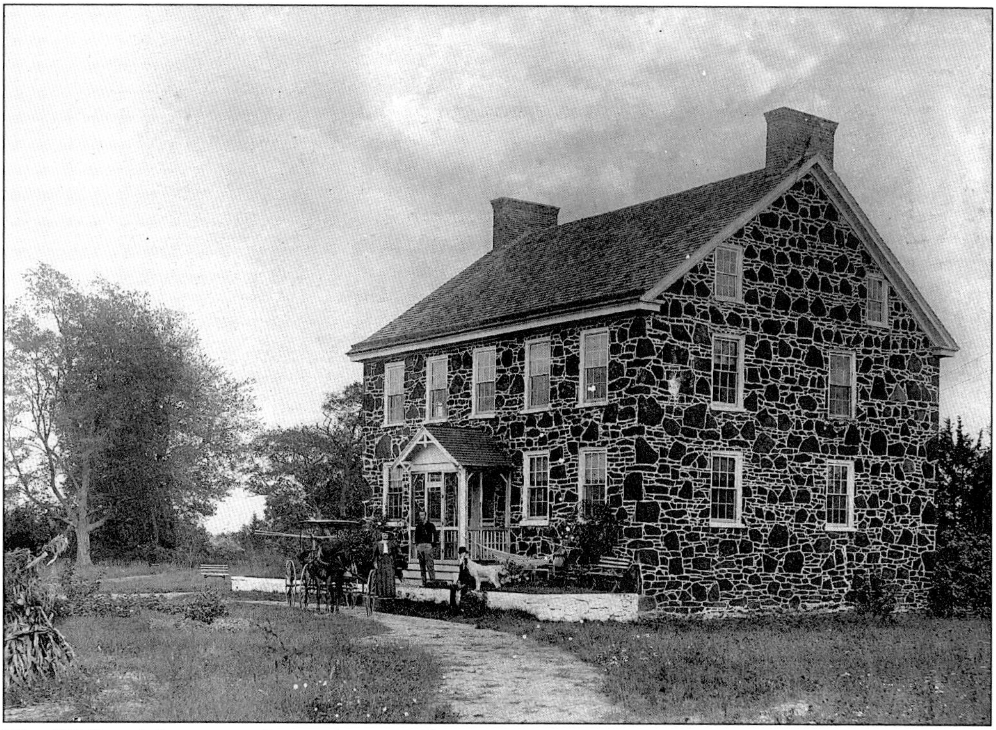

The Walker Mansion is located on Walkers Forge Road. It was formerly in the Township of Hamilton but is now in Weymouth Township.

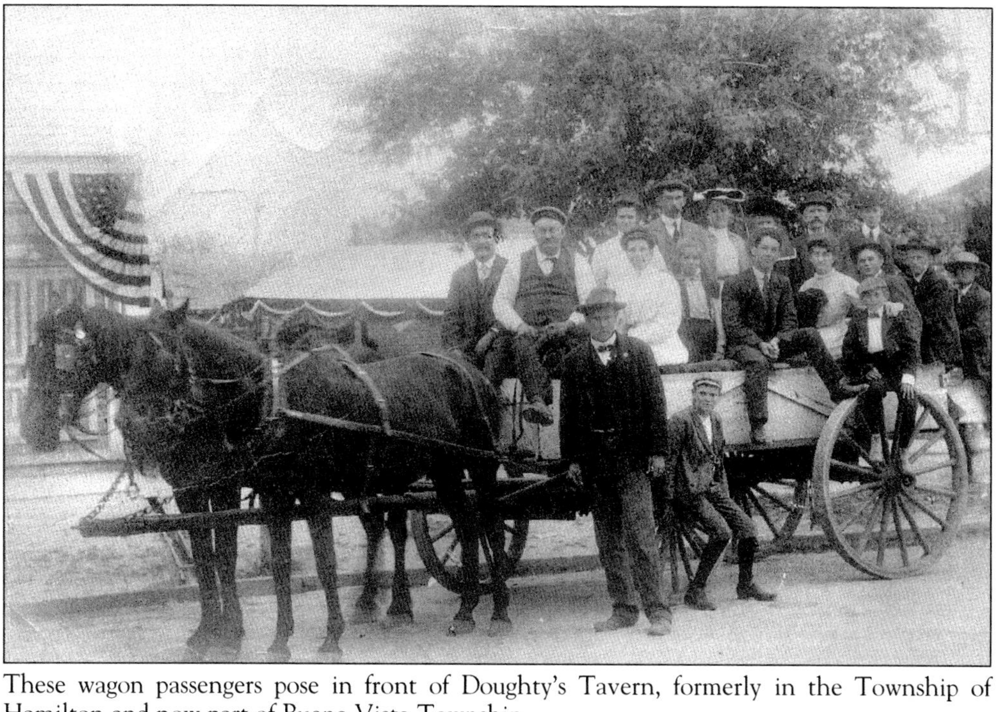

These wagon passengers pose in front of Doughty's Tavern, formerly in the Township of Hamilton and now part of Buena Vista Township.

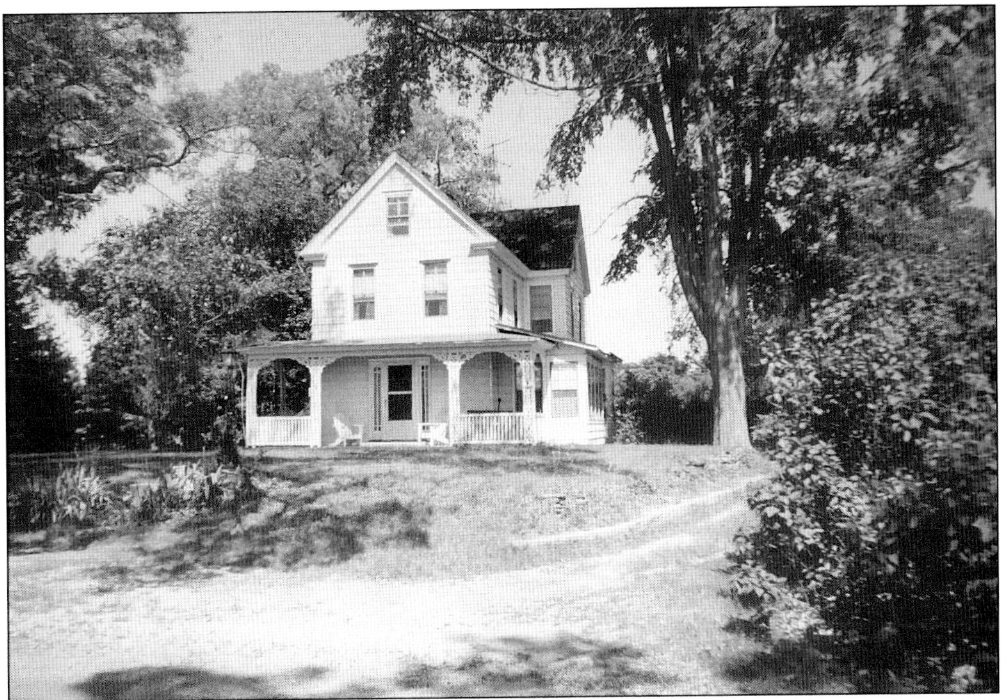

This home on the Great Egg Harbor River in Clarktown was built by James Clark c. 1843. Clark and his brother John were 19th-century shipbuilders on the same site where Christopher Rape built ships in the 1700s.

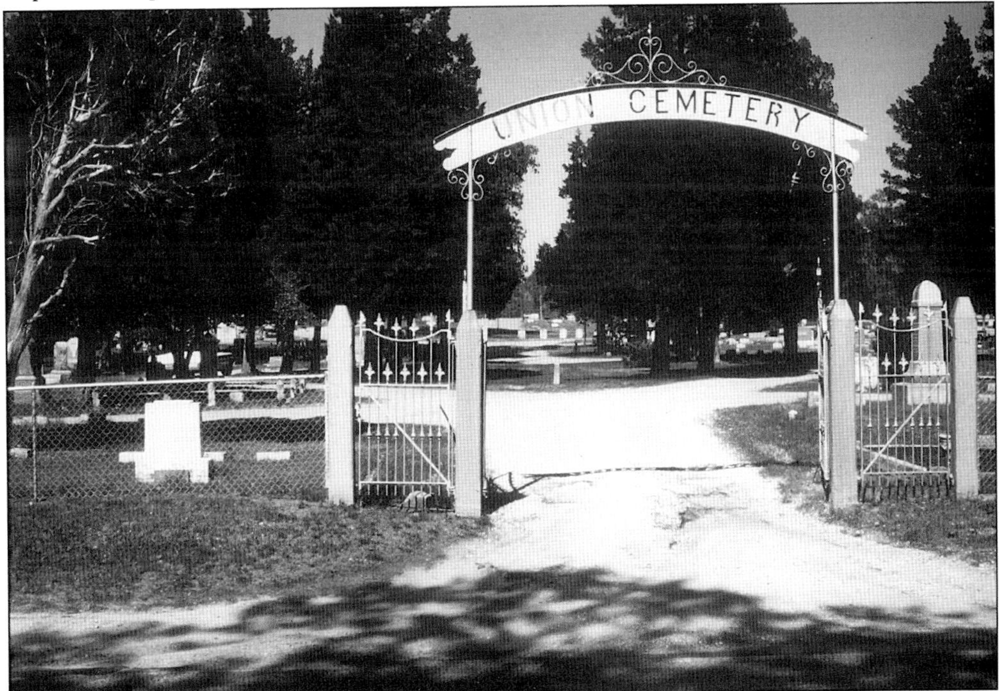

This arch graces the entrance to Union Cemetery, located on Route 559 in Gravelly Run. Many ancestors of our current residents are at rest here.

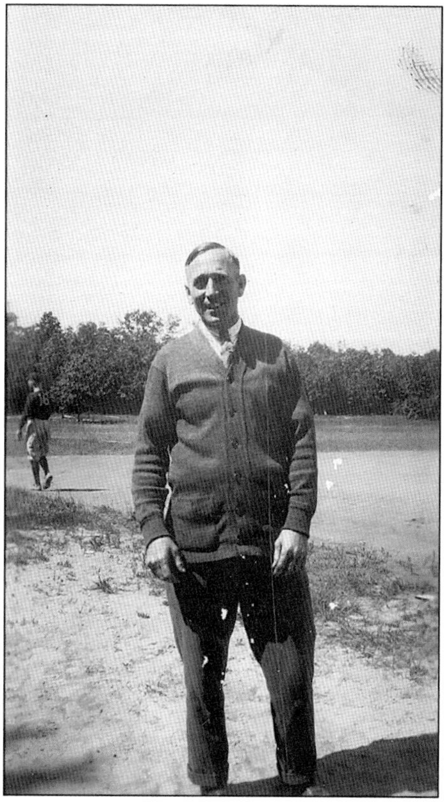

Samuel Keating was Mays Landing's first ambulance driver. He drove an old converted station wagon. Ted Gallo often assisted him. Between runs, he transported people to and from doctors' offices.

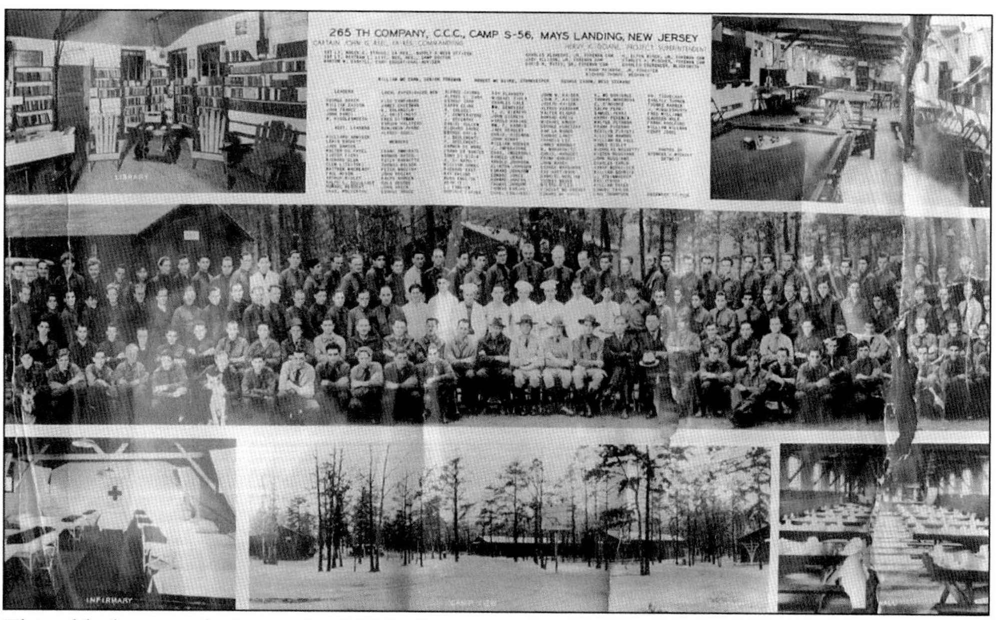

This old photograph shows the 265th Company Civilian Conservation Corps Camp 5-56 in Mays Landing.

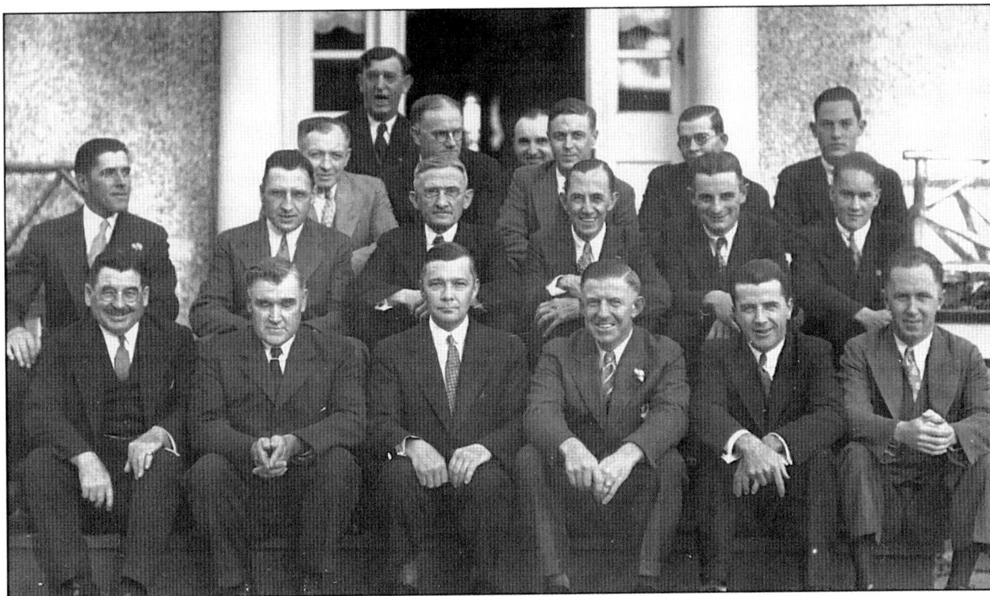

Gathered at a High School Alumni meeting in Mays Landing are, from left to right, the following: (front row) Robert H. Ingersoll (vice chancellor), Elvey S. Bailey, Elmer A. Hummell, Alfred Hensel, Expedit McGeary, and Otis Luderitz; (middle row) Archie H. Smith, Alex P. Denmead, S.G. Huber, Melvin M. Ripley, Charles Duberson, and Paul Taylor; (back row) B. Lehr Scull, Burton A. Gaskill, Charles C. Stewart, Stephen Bartha, Joseph Wigglesworth, Roy Hazelton, and Henry Loper.

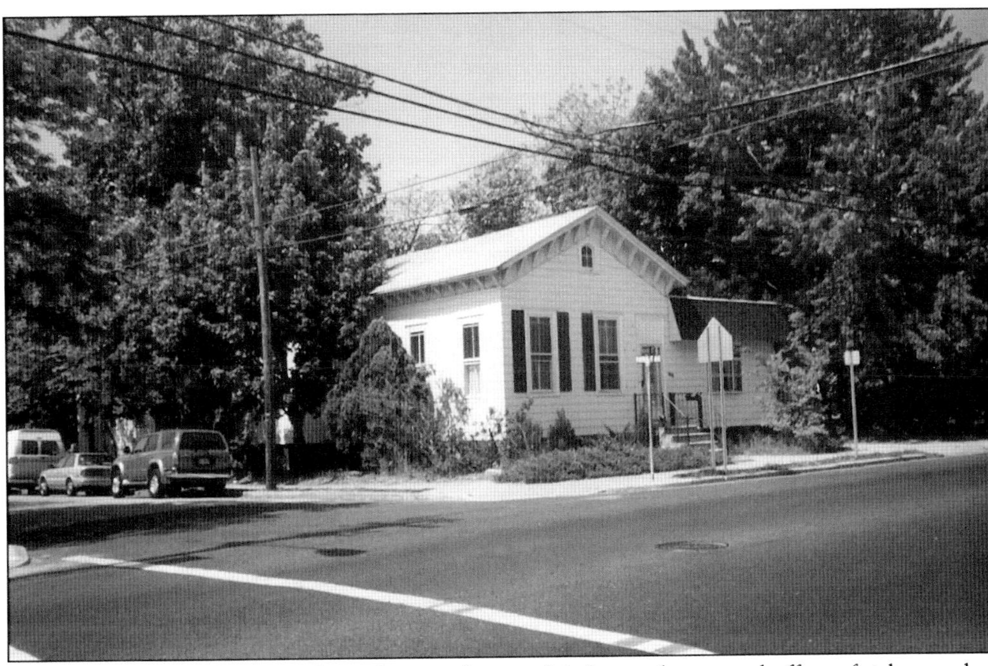

Located conveniently across from the courthouse, this former home and office of title searcher A. Esther Sauder is on the corner of Farragut Avenue and Main Street in Mays Landing. The addition on the right is about 40 years old.

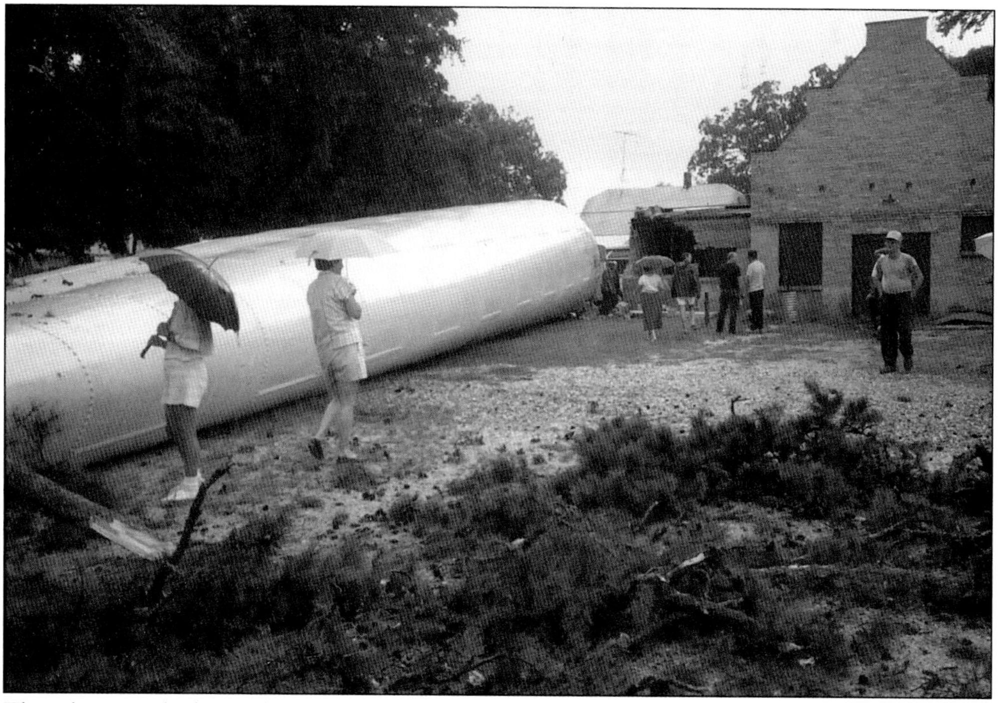

This photograph shows the demolition of the Mays Landing Water Works standpipe in 1989. Today, the brick building of the waterworks is a historic site.

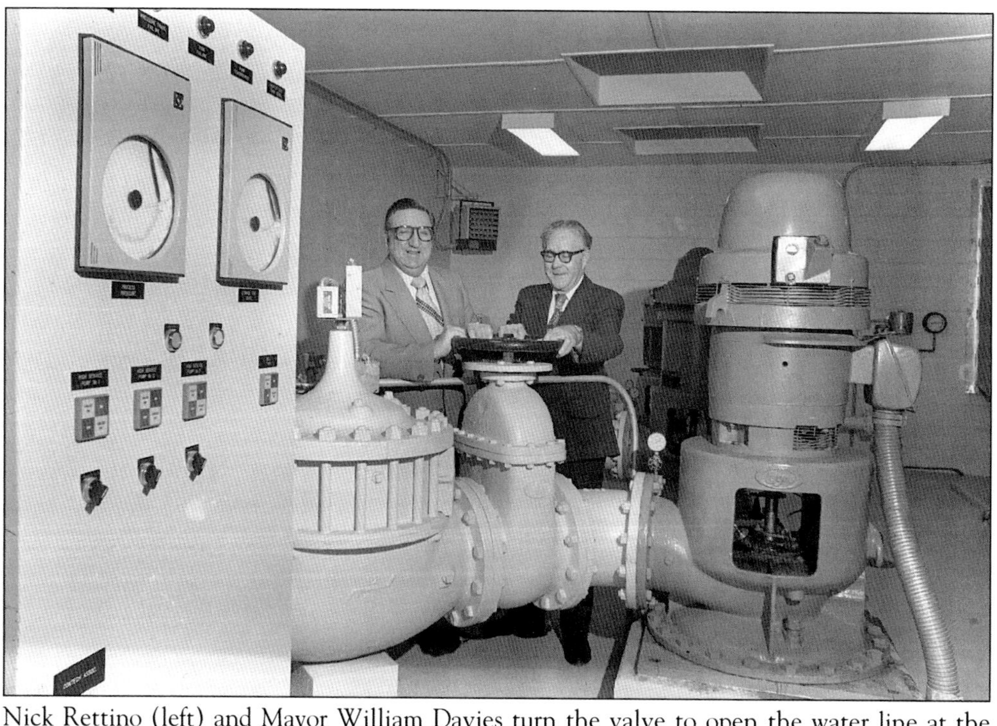

Nick Rettino (left) and Mayor William Davies turn the valve to open the water line at the Municipal Utilities Authority of the Township of Hamilton.

Capt. Daniel Vaughn was commander of several well-known vessels whose career won him local fame. Upon retirement from the sea, he became custodian of county buildings, until his death in 1930.

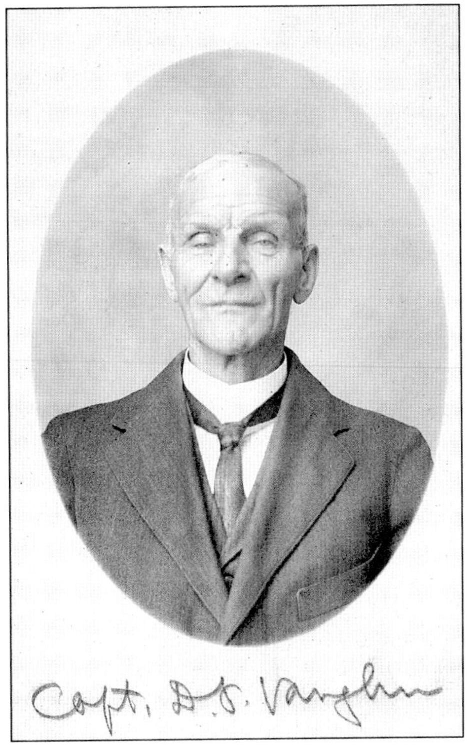

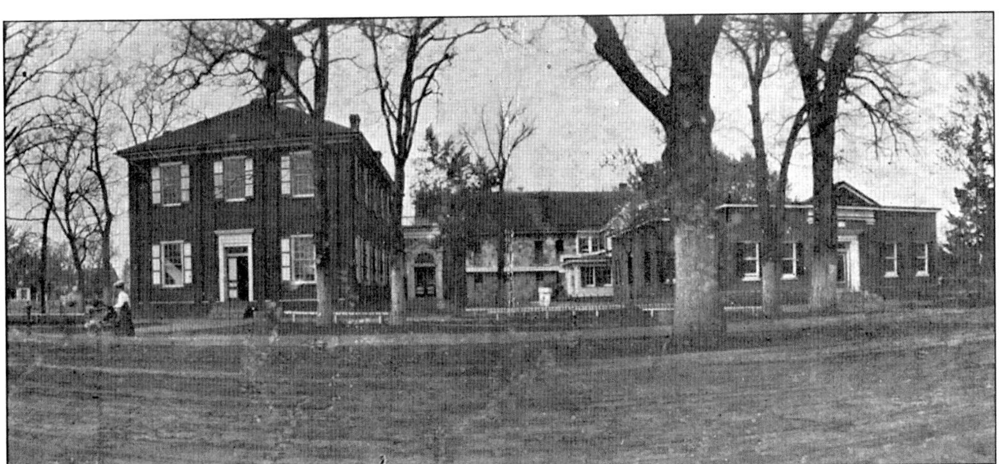

This view of the Atlantic County Courthouse in Mays Landing shows the old jail (center) and the clerk's office (right).

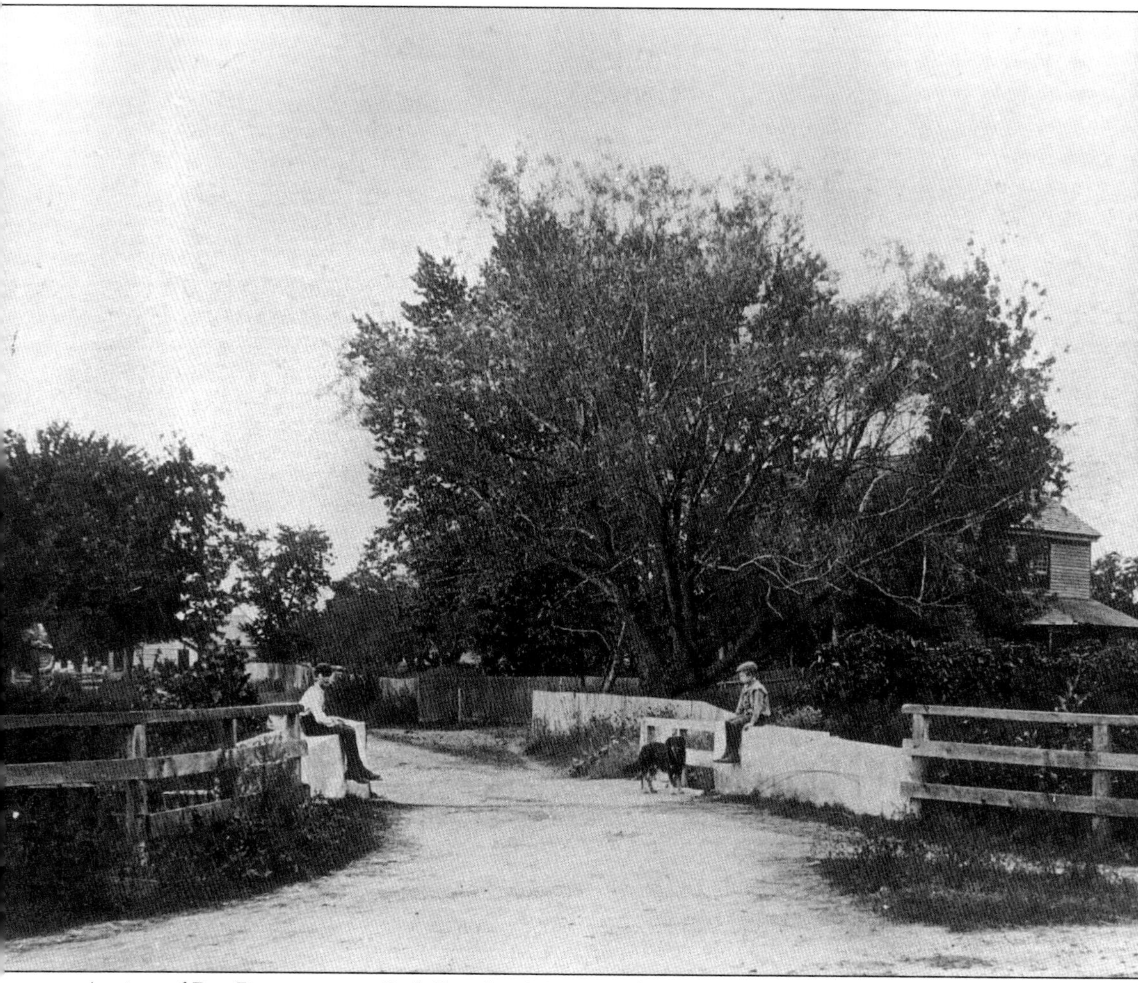

A view of Dry Run entering Park Road in Mays Landing on the way to the skating rink seems to be an ideal spot to rest.

The Mattle homestead, located in the Bears Head section of our township, is shown in this *c.* 1930s photograph. The home was later taken down and, in the 1940s, was replaced by a smaller house.

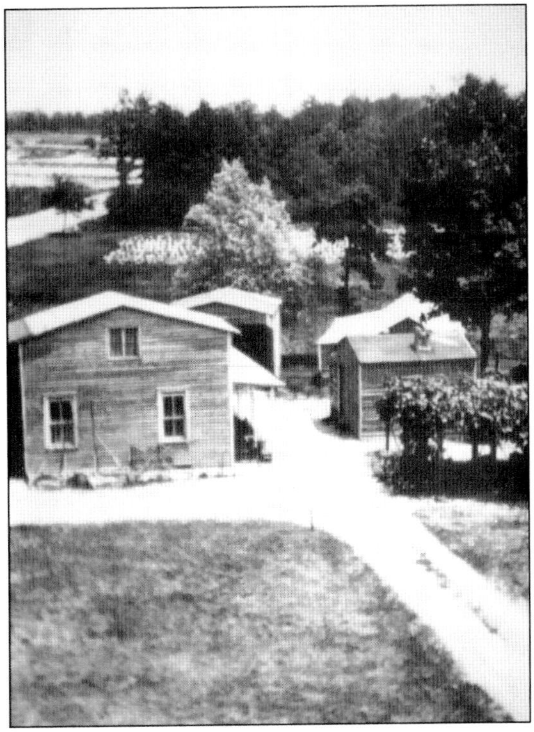

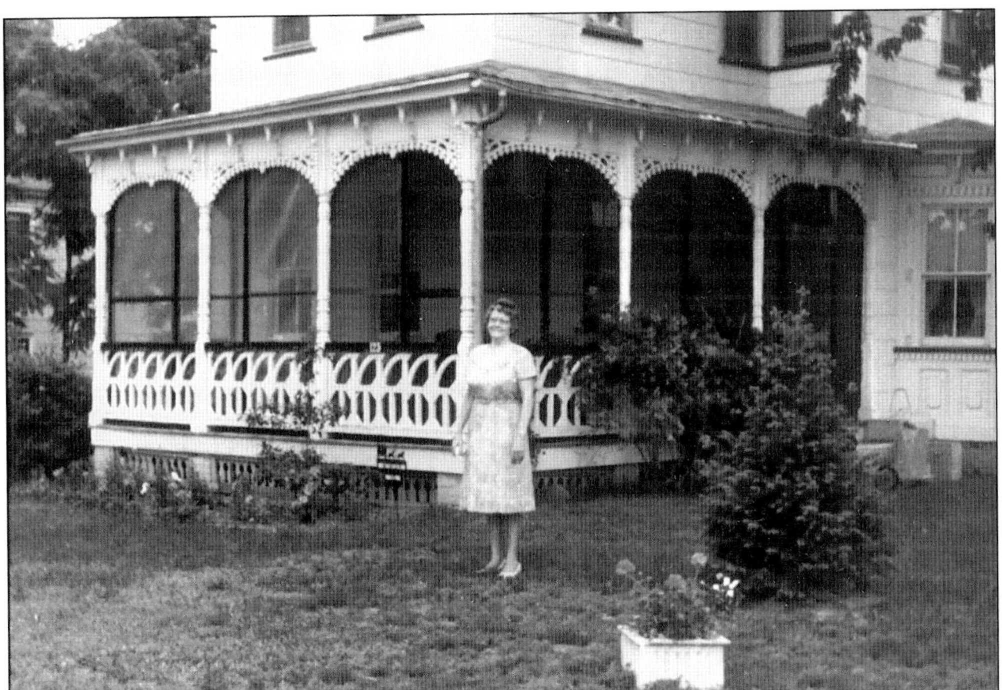

A lovely representation of beautiful gingerbread demonstrates the artistry of the carpenter. This vintage photograph shows the pride of the owner, Mary (Davies) Taylor. The home is located on Oak Street, now named Ken Scull Drive, in Mays Landing.

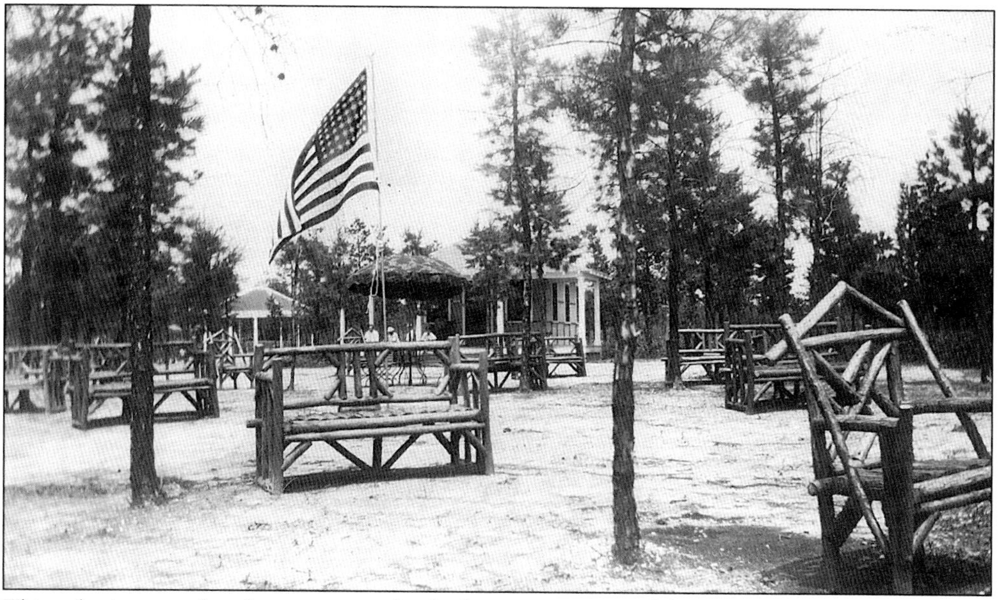

This relaxing area for observation and refreshment was part of the Mays Landing Golf Course.

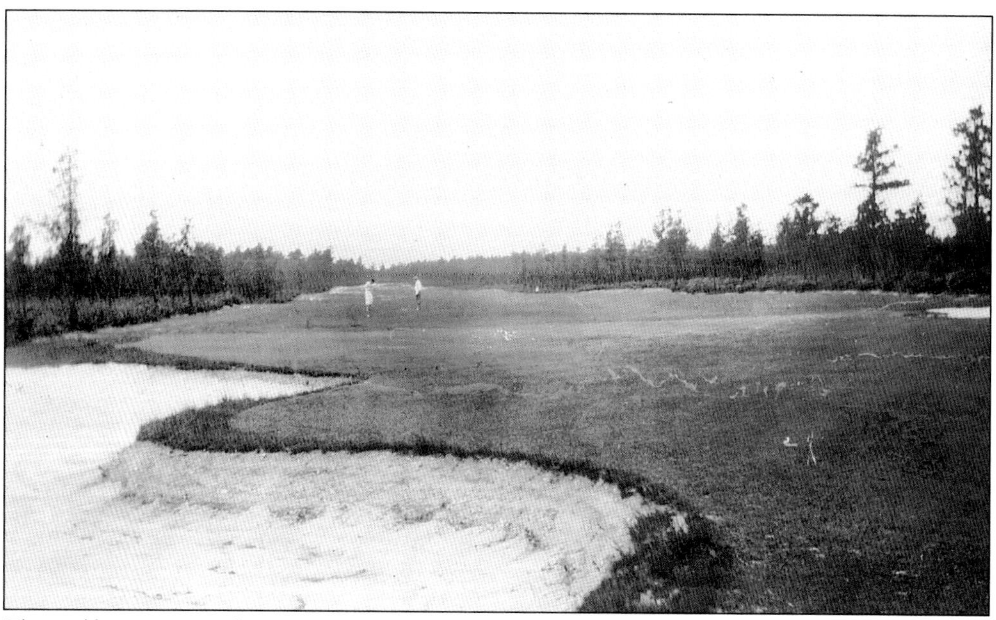

The golf course was located on the site of the present Atlantic City Racetrack near the Hamilton Mall.

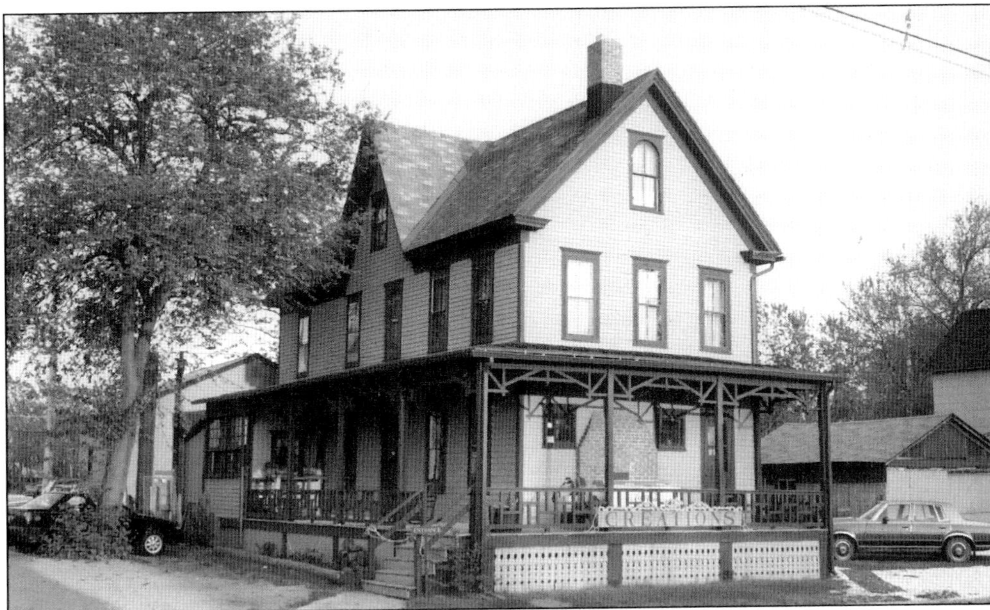

Original owners of this home at the corner of Route 50 near Main Street included Dorie Hoover and Angelo Marconi; the latter had his shoemaker shop in the front. It is now the site of a co-op craft shop.

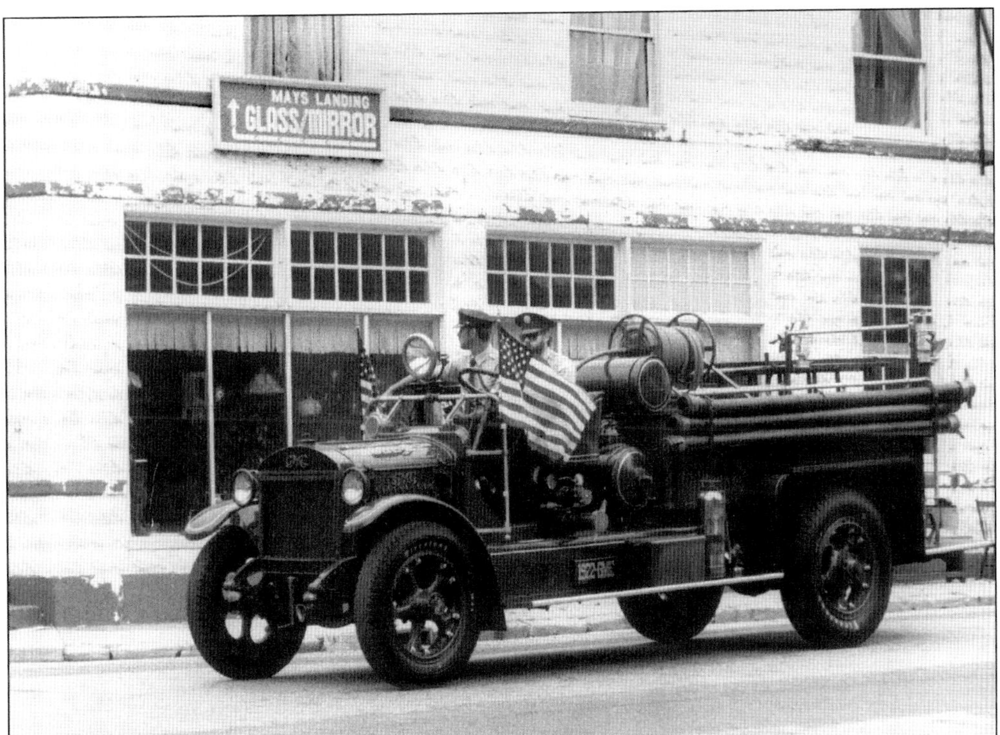

In 1922, this GMC-Hale Pumper was the pride of the Reliance Hose Company—Mays Landing's Volunteer Fire Department. Pictured are Sonny Russell (left) and Martin Ripley.

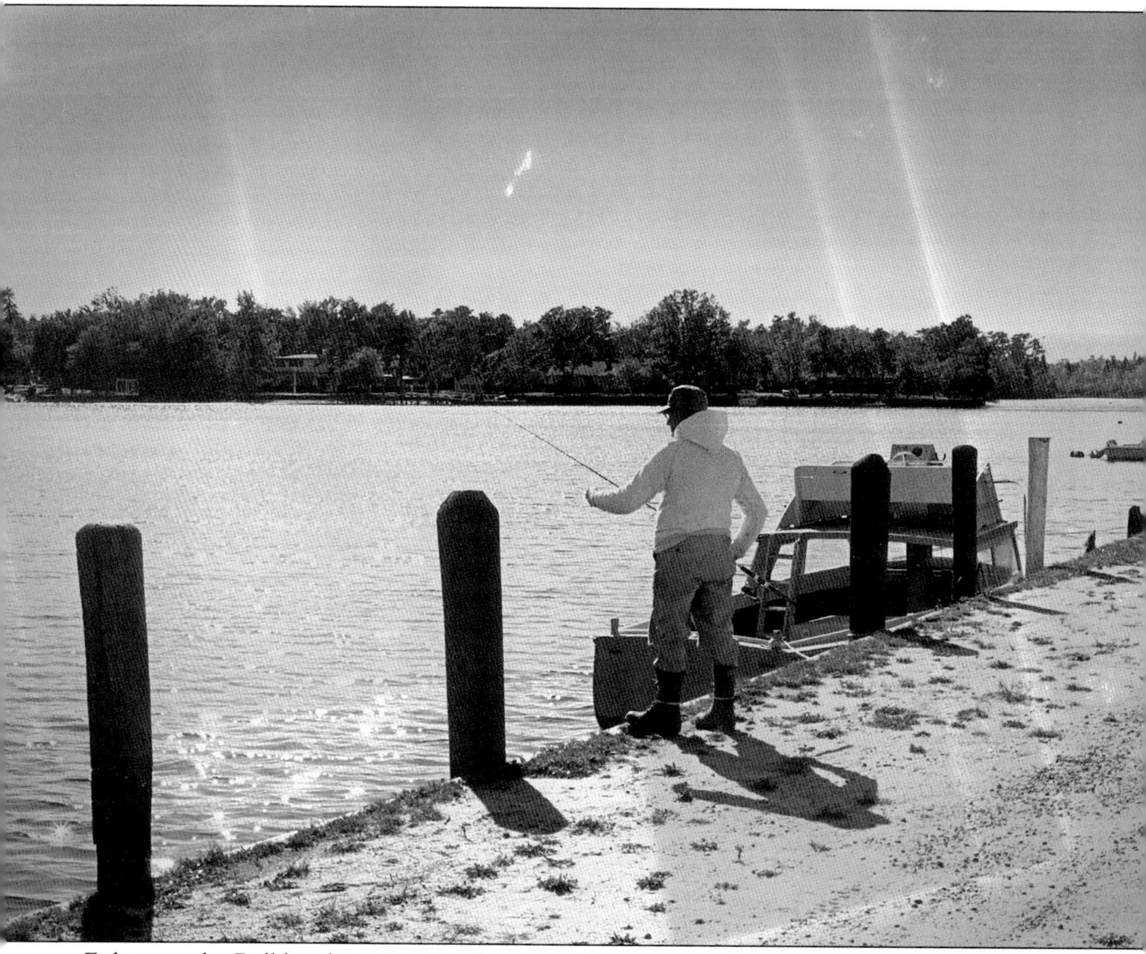
Fishing at the Bulkhead in Mays Landing is good no matter what season it is.